SARTRE

His Philosophy and Psychoanalysis

SARTRE

His Philosophy and Psychoanalysis

By

ALFRED STERN

Associate Professor of Languages and Philosophy
California Institute of Technology

1953

THE LIBERAL ARTS PRESS

NEW YORK

TO THE MEMORY OF MY BELOVED PARENTS
ROSE AND JULIUS STERN

ACKNOWLEDGMENTS

The author wishes to express his thanks to the following publishers and authors for their permission to reproduce the material quoted in this book:

The American-Scandinavian Foundation and Princeton University Press for Excerpts from *Concluding Unscientific Postscript* (1941), by S. Kierkegaard, translated by F. Swenson, completed by Walter Lowrie.

Harcourt, Brace and Company, Inc., New York, for excerpts from *The Republic of Silence* (1947), by J. P. Sartre, edited by A. T. Liebling; and *The Practice and Theory of Individual Psychology* (1929), by Alfred Adler.

Henry Holt and Company, Inc., New York, for excerpts from *Creative Evolution* (1911), by H. Bergson.

International University Press, Inc., New York, for excerpts from *Symbolic Realization* (1951), by M. Sechehaye.

Alfred A. Knopf, Inc., New York, for excerpts from *The Reprieve* (1947), by J. P. Sartre, translated by Eric Sutton.

Little, Brown and Company, Boston, for excerpts from "We Are Looking at You, Agnes," in *We Are The Living* (1933), by Erskine Caldwell.

W. W. Norton & Company, Inc., New York, for excerpts from *An Outline of Psychoanalysis* (1949), by S. Freud.

Philosophical Library, Inc., New York, for excerpts from *What Is Literature?* (1949), by J. P. Sartre, translated by B. Frechtman.

Random House, Inc. (The Modern Library), New York, for excerpts from *Light in August* (1950), by William Faulkner.

Schocken Books Inc., New York, for excerpts from *Anti-Semite and Jew* (1948), by J. P. Sartre.

William Sloane Associates, Inc., Publishers, New York, for excerpts from *Joan of Lorraine* (1946), by Maxwell Anderson.

The University of Buffalo Publications in Philosophy, Buffalo, New York, for excerpts from *Philosophic Thought in France and The United States* (1950), edited by Marvin Farber.

Excerpts from other works in French, German, Spanish, and other languages have been translated by the author.

Thanks and appreciation are extended to Professor George R. MacMinn and Professor Beach Langston, California Institute of Technology, Pasadena (Department of English), for their kind revision of the text of this volume and their valuable suggestions; and to Mrs. Matilde H. Nestor and Miss Mary T. Stockly for their competent clerical assistance.

ALFRED STERN

CONTENTS

PART I

SARTRE'S EXISTENTIALIST PHILOSOPHY

PART II

SARTRE'S EXISTENTIALIST PSYCHOANALYSIS

x CONTENTS

INTRODUCTION

The strongest influence brought to bear upon world literature during the first half of the twentieth century did not come from a writer, but from a psychiatrist—from Sigmund Freud and his psychoanalysis. Literature now repays its obligation by creating a psychoanalysis of its own—Sartre's so-called Existentialist psychoanalysis. We shall see whether this new enterprise, which emerged after the Second World War, will be able to influence psychiatry.

It is perhaps premature to ask whether this new psychoanalysis belongs to science or to literature. Sartre, however, is no ordinary man of letters. Not only a dramatist of great talent, a remarkable novelist and brilliant essayist, he is also a disciplined professional philosopher. We may even say that Sartre is basically a philosopher whose novels and plays are essentially different ways of exemplifying a certain type of philosophy: Existentialism. Created a century ago by the Danish Protestant theologian Sören Kierkegaard, Existentialism was systematized between the two world wars by the German philosopher Martin Heidegger. After World War II Sartre transformed Existentialism in a *grande mode*, giving it a kind of philosophical "new look."

Sartre's Existentialist psychoanalysis is an outgrowth of his philosophy and its most original contribution. Up to now, however, little attention has been paid to it by the commentators on modern Existentialism. It is the purpose of the present book to explore, to explain, and to appraise critically not only Sartre's philosophy but also his psychoanalysis, and to interpret his artistic work in the light of these disciplines.

Jean-Paul Sartre was born on June 21, 1905, into a Parisian middle-class family. His father, a graduate of the *Ecole Polytechnique*, was a marine engineer who died of tropical fever in Cochin China when Jean-Paul was still comparatively young. His maternal grandfather, a language teacher named Schweitzer, was a Protestant, while the rest of Sartre's family were Catholic. Like André Gide, Sartre is a religious hybrid and, like Gide, he is an atheist.

At the age of six Jean-Paul began to write; not the ABC's, like other children, but little comedies and poems—so at least maintains one of Sartre's enthusiastic biographers.[1] Be that as it may, the young boy was an intelligent pupil, whom teachers, however, tried vainly to cure of a deep dislike for mathematics. Educated after the First World War, when most traditional values were collapsing throughout Europe, Sartre belonged to what Drieu-la-Rochelle called the generation with the "empty bag." The young student was able to fill that empty bag only with difficulty. Although admitted to the famous *Ecole Normale Supérieure*, he failed in his first attempt to pass the *agrégation*. But the following year he passed brilliantly this very difficult competitive examination as the best among all candidates.

Following his graduation and up to the beginning of World War II, Sartre was professor of philosophy at the *lycée* in Le Havre, the French port which he was later to describe in one of his novels under the name of Bouville. He also studied for a year in Germany, at the University of Freiburg, stronghold of Husserl's Phenomenology and Heidegger's Existentialism. In 1938 Sartre published his first novel *La Nausée* ("Nausea"), in which are developed some of the basic elements of his philosophy in terms of an Existentialist's reactions toward the world. One year later appeared Sartre's *Esquisse d'une Théorie des Emotions*.[2] Together with a number of articles, these two books brought the young author to the attention of the younger artists and intellectuals, who began to look upon him as a possible leader of the *avant-garde*. But by the eve of World War II,

[1] Marc Beigbeder, *L'Homme Sartre; Essai de Dévoilement pré-existentiel* (Paris: Bordas, 1947).

[2] Amer. ed., *The Emotions*, tr. by Bernard Frechtman (New York: Philosophical Library, 1948).

his reputation was little more than local, limited to the Quartier Latin and Montparnasse.

Sartre was mobilized at the beginning of the Second World War, but because of a weak constitution was assigned to limited duty as a male nurse. (This experience resembles that of Nietzsche in the Franco-German War of 1870-1871. Sartre's philosophy, incidentally, has much in common with Nietzsche's, although he rarely quotes him.) Taken prisoner upon the surrender of the French Army, Sartre was released in 1941 and returned to Paris. In spite of the German occupation, he was able to write and to teach. A professor at the *Ecole Normale Supérieure* and at Charles Dullin's School of Dramatic Art, he also published his major philosophical treatise *L'Etre et le Néant* ("Being and Nothingness"); and two of his plays were produced on the Parisian stage, *Les Mouches* ("The Flies") and *Huis Clos* ("No Exit"). In the latter play, incidentally, the part of Garcin was played by Sartre's close friend, Albert Camus, with whom he later broke. Although Camus has a basically Existentialist attitude toward the universe, he is not a partisan of Existentialist *philosophy*, and his political credo is less radical than Sartre's.[3]

The question of Sartre's relationship with the occupation authorities is difficult to answer. Why was he permitted to publish his books and articles, and to produce his plays, when the German censors were so suspicious of French intellectuals? One can only assume that the strong impact of Heidegger on Sartre's work gave the Nazi authorities the impression that the young French philosopher was on their side. For example in *L'Etre et le Néant* German quotations in Heidegger's original barbaric language are strewn throughout the 722 pages. Yet the Nazis could hardly have been more mistaken in their man. For if Sartre is very strongly influenced philosophically by German ideas, politically he is not. And the same man who, under the watchful eye of the Gestapo, wrote irreproachable essays on non-political subjects in the best Parisian periodicals also wrote anonymous "subversive" articles in the clandestine press

[3] See below, footnote 7, p. 31.

and belonged to the underground resistance movement. No greater tribute has been given to the glory of the resistance than Sartre's play *Morts sans Sépulture* ("The Unburied Dead," entitled *The Victors* when produced in New York), for here is a drama which sometimes reaches the grandeur of an ancient Greek tragedy.

Although Sartre is obviously no Fascist, many of his critics call him a nihilist—an accusation the profounder significance of which must be deferred for examination until later. Superficially the designation is accurate. For example, Father Troisfontaines, one of his most severe critics, sees Sartre as an individual uprooted from the traditional values of religion, family, home, and the like. By way of summary, he calls Sartre *"l'homme au café"*—the café intellectual.[4]

Now, as a matter of fact, Sartre does spend a great deal of his time and originally wrote much of his work surrounded by the odor of cigarettes and coffee, the sound of clinking china and glassware, the comings and goings of a Parisian café. Here gather his friends and students, who solve with him basic problems of existence over *apéritifs* and demitasses. What the Academy was for Plato, the Lyceum for the Peripatetics, the Café de Flore is for Existentialism. This little café in Saint-Germain-des-Prés will perhaps one day enter the history of philosophy. Yet history is always in suspense or, as Sartre himself says, "on reprieve"; and this Mecca of Existentialism seems already to have been supplanted, since Sartre has become prosperous, by the more fashionable bar of the Hôtel Pont-Royal.

So deeply is the café atmosphere rooted in Sartre's mind that he even draws upon it in demonstrating metaphysical theories in his most erudite work *L'Etre et le Néant*. For instance, in explaining the two basic concepts of being and nothingness, he writes:

When I enter the café in order to look for Pierre, there takes place a synthetic organization of all the objects of the café, so that they

4 R. Troisfontaines, *Le Choix de J.-P. Sartre* (Paris: Aubier, 1945), pp. 51-52.

become the background against which Pierre is given as that which
is supposed to appear. And this organization of the café into a background is the first "naughtization." [5]

Sartre had previously shown that "this café itself, with its
customers, its tables, its benches, its mirrors, its lights, its
atmosphere of smoke and noise of voices, of clashing saucers
and footsteps, is a wholeness of being." Pierre, however, is not
here; he "is absent from the *whole* of the café. Thus his
absence congeals the café," and Pierre becomes "the nothingness on the background of the naughtization of the café." [6]

From this café example Sartre deduces his dubious metaphysical principle, in which he agrees with Heidegger, that "non-
being does not come to things by the judgment of negation,
but, on the contrary, the judgment of negation is conditioned
and upheld by non-being." [7]

Similarly, when Sartre attempts to establish his thesis that
classical logic with its principle of identity is invalid for the
human personality, "which is what it is not and is not what it
is," he demonstrates it in terms of the *garçon de café*, who
only "plays at being a café waiter." [8]

Finally, in his novel *Le Sursis* ("The Reprieve"), Sartre
describes his young protagonist, Boris, a philosophy student at
the Sorbonne, who reflects in the following "profoundly"
philosophical fashion upon the possibility that he will be called
in the draft of World War II:

The number of times that I will go to a café after today can be cal-
culated: Suppose that I go twice a day, and that I am called up in
a year: that makes 730 times. 730 times! That's not very often.
. . . People who could look forward to 10,000, to 15,000 evenings at
cafés! [9]

[5] *L'Etre et le Néant* (Paris: Gallimard, 1943), p. 44.
[6] *Ibid.*, pp. 44, 45.
[7] *Ibid.*, p. 46.
[8] *Ibid.*, pp. 97-99.
[9] *Le Sursis* (Paris: Gallimard, 1945), p. 215; Amer. ed. *The Reprieve* (New
York: Knopf, 1947), p. 272.

So we see that Sartre even measures a human lifetime by the number of visits to cafés! A modern Protagoras, he likes to consider the café the measure of all things.

We shall see later that to Freud's Oedipus complex, to Adler's inferiority complex, and to Bachelard's Prometheus complex,[10] Sartre adds his own Actaeon and Jonah complexes. There may exist even another complex, from which Sartre himself is suffering, and which may be called the "Pascal complex." With this name we do not refer to France's great philosopher and mathematician, but to the Armenian trader Pascal, who, in 1672, opened the first Parisian café near Saint-Germain-des-Prés.

Sartre's café complex does not, however, prevent him from being a very gifted writer and philosopher. His intellectual power may thereby even be stimulated. Michelet describes the very strong coffee that Diderot and Rousseau used to drink at the Café Procope, similarly situated further up the Boulevard Saint-Germain—coffee that "nourished the strong age of the Encyclopedia . . . added its heat to that of the ardent souls and its light to the penetrating insight of the prophets," for "coffee . . . is powerfully cerebral . . . increases the distinctness and lucidity . . . and causes the flash of truth to break forth." [11] This remarkable effect might well be that of coffee served in Parisian cafés, described by Montesquieu as a beverage prepared "in such a way as to make those who drink it exceedingly witty. At any rate," Montesquieu continues sarcastically, "when they depart, all of them believe themselves to be at least four times as intelligent as when they arrived." [12] Thus it is perhaps that Parisian Existentialists persuade themselves, when leaving the Café de Flore, the Deux Magots, or the

[10] Gaston Bachelard, professor at the Sorbonne, is the author of *La Psychanalyse du Feu, L'Eau et les Rêves, L'Air et les Songes, L'Expérience de l'Espace dans la Physique contemporaine, La Dialectique de la Durée, Lautréamont, Le Pluralisme cohérent de la Chimie moderne,* and other works.

[11] J. Michelet, *Histoire de France,* Vol. XIV: *La Régence* (Paris: Flammarion, 1874), pp. 162-164.

[12] *Oeuvres de Montesquieu,* Vol. VI: *Lettres persanes* (Paris: Lequien, 1829), Letter XXXVI, p. 75.

Pont-Royal, of having made revolutionary philosophical discoveries of many things that others, less exalted, consider self-evident.

Nevertheless, Sartre's philosophical and literary work is not only a fashion of left-bank cafés and night clubs. Animated by a deeply earnest, passionate search for philosophical truth, Sartre's writings reveal some basic problems of human existence, which the forthcoming pages will try to interpret.

SELECTED BIBLIOGRAPHY

SARTRE'S WORKS

L'Imagination (Paris: Alcan, 1937).

La Nausée (Paris: Gallimard, 1938); Amer. ed., *Nausea* (New York: New Directions, 1949).

Esquisse d'une Théorie des Emotions (Paris: Hermann and Cie, 1939); Amer. ed., *The Emotions* (New York, Philosophical Library, 1948).

Le Mur (Paris: Gallimard, 1939); Amer. ed., *Intimacy* (Copyright by New Directions, 1948; published, Norfolk, Conn., 1952).

L'Imaginaire (Paris: Gallimard, 1940); Amer. ed., *The Psychology of Imagination* (New York: Philosophical Library, 1948).

Les Mouches (Paris: Gallimard, 1943); Amer. ed., *No Exit and The Flies* (New York: Knopf, 1937).

L'Etre et le Néant (Paris: Gallimard, 1943).

Huis clos (Paris: Gallimard, 1944); Amer. ed., *No Exit and The Flies* (New York: Knopf, 1947).

Les Chemins de la Liberté (Paris: Gallimard):
  I. *L'Age de Raison* (1945); Amer. ed., *The Age of Reason* (New York: Knopf, 1947).
  II. *Le Sursis* (1945); Amer. ed., *The Reprieve* (New York: Knopf, 1947).
  III. *La Mort dans l'Ame* (1949); Amer. ed., *Troubled Sleep* (New York: Knopf, 1951).

Morts sans Sépulture (Lausanne: Marguerat, 1946); Amer. ed., *The Victors*, included in *Three Plays* by Jean-Paul Sartre (New York: Knopf, 1949).

L'Existentialisme est un Humanisme (Paris: Nagel, 1946); Amer ed., *Existentialism* (New York: Philosophical Library, 1947).

La Putain respectueuse (Paris: Nagel, 1946); Amer. ed., *The Respectful Prostitute*, included in *Three Plays* by Jean-Paul Sartre (New York: Knopf, 1949).

Réflexions sur la Question juive (Paris: Morihien, 1946); Amer. ed., *Antisemite and Jew* (New York: Schocken, 1948).

Les Jeux sont faits (Paris: Nagel, 1947); Amer. ed., *The Chips Are Down* (New York: Lear, 1948).

Baudelaire (Paris: Gallimard, 1947); Amer. ed., *Baudelaire* (Norfolk, Conn.: New Directions, 1950).

Situations I (Paris: Gallimard, 1947).

Situations II (Paris: Gallimard, 1948); Amer. ed., *What Is Literature?* (New York: Philosophical Library, 1949).

Les Mains sales (Paris: Gallimard, 1948); Amer. ed., *Dirty Hands*, included in *Three Plays* by Jean-Paul Sartre (New York: Knopf, 1949).

Situations III (Paris: Gallimard, 1949).

Le Diable et le bon Dieu (Paris: Gallimard, 1951).

Saint-Genet, Comédien et Martyr (Paris: Gallimard, 1952).

Most of Sartre's articles have been published in the magazine *Les Temps Modernes*, Paris, which he has been directing since 1946, and many have been reproduced in the three volumes of *Situations*. Besides, see especially, "La République du Silence," *Eternelle Revue I* (Paris, 1945); Amer. ed., *The Republic of Silence*, ed. A. T. Liebling (Harcourt-Brace: New York, 1947).

COLLATERAL READING

Adler, A., *Study of Organ Inferiority and Its Psychical Compensation* (New York, 1917).

———— *The Practice and Theory of Individual Psychology* (New York, 1929).

Bachelard, G., *La Psychanalyse du Feu* (Paris, 1938).

———— *L'Eau et les Rêves* (Paris, 1942).

Beauvoir, S. de, *Pyrrhus et Cinéas* (Paris, 1945).

———— *Pour une Morale de l'Ambiguité* (Paris, 1946); Amer. ed. *The Ethics of Ambiguity* (New York, 1949).

———— *Le Sang des Autres* (Paris, 1947).

Beigbeder, M., *L'Homme Sartre, Essai de Dévoilement pré-existentiel* (Paris, 1947).

Berger, G., *Existentialism and Literature in Action* (Buffalo, 1948).

Benda, J., *Trois Idoles romantiques: le Dynamisme, l'Existentialisme, la Dialectique matérialiste* (Geneva, 1948).

Bobbio, N., *La Filosofia del Decadentismo* (Torino, 1944); Engl. ed., *The Philosophy of Decadentism* (Oxford, 1948).

Blackham, H. J., *Six Existentialist Thinkers* (New York, 1952).

Boutang, P., *Sartre est-il un Possédé?* (Paris, 1946).

Campbell, R., *Jean-Paul Sartre ou Une Littérature philosophique* (Paris, 1947).

Camus, A., *L'Etranger* (Paris, 1942).

———— *Le Malentendu* (Paris, 1942), Amer. ed., see below.

———— *Caligula* (Paris, 1943); Amer. ed., *Caligula and Cross-purpose* (Norfolk, Conn., 1947).

———— *Le Mythe de Sisyphe* (Paris, 1943).

———— *La Peste* (Paris, 1947); Amer. ed., *The Plague* (New York, 1948).

———— *L'Homme révolté* (Paris, 1951).

Collins, J. D., *The Existentialists* (Chicago, 1952).

Dempsey, P. J., *The Psychology of Sartre* (Westminster, 1950).

Freud, S., *The Basic Writings of Sigmund Freud* (New York, 1938); in *Gesammelte Werke* (London, 1942).

———— *The Problem of Anxiety* (New York, 1936).

———— *An Outline of Psychoanalysis* (New York, 1949).

Foulquié, P., *L'Existentialisme* (Paris, 1947); Engl. ed., *Existentialism* (London, 1948).

Gilson, E., *L'Essence et l'Existence* (Paris, 1948).

Grene, M., *Dreadful Freedom* (Chicago, 1948).

Hegel, G. F. W., *The Logic of Hegel* (Oxford, 1874).

———— *Phänomenologie des Geistes* (Leipzig, 1907).

Harper, R., *Existentialism, A Theory of Man* (Cambridge, 1948).

Heidegger, M., *Sein und Zeit* (Halle, 1927, 1935).

———— *Was ist Metaphysik?* (Bonn, 1929); Amer. ed., *Existence and Being* (Chicago, 1951).

———— *Vom Wesen des Grundes* (Halle, 1929).

———— *Platons Lehre von der Wahrheit, mit einem Brief über den Humanismus* (Bern, 1947).

———— *Vom Wesen der Wahrheit* (Frankfurt, 1949).

———— *Holzwege* (Frankfurt, 1950).

Husserl, E., *Gesammelte Werke* (Hague, 1950).

Jaspers, K., *Tragedy Is Not Enough* (Boston, The Beacon Press, 1952).

Jolivet, R., *Les Doctrines existentialistes de Kierkegaard à J.-P. Sartre* (Paris, 1948).

Juin, H., *Jean-Paul Sartre ou La Condition Humaine* (Brussels, 1946).

Kierkegaard, S., *Gesammelte Werke* (Jena, 1911-1922).

Kuhn, H., *Encounter with Northingness* (Chicago, 1949).

Lefebure, H., *L'Existentialism* (Paris, 1946).

Lefèvre, L. J., *L'Existentialiste est-il un Philosophe?* (Paris, 1946).

Lévinas, E., *De l'Existence à l'Existant* (Paris, 1947).

Lukacs, G., *Existentialisme ou Marxisme?* (Paris, 1948).

Maritain, J., *Court Traité de l'Existence et de l'Existant* (Paris, 1947) ; Amer. ed., *Existence and the Existent* (New York, 1948).

Marcel, G., *The Philosophy of Existence* (New York, 1949).

Merleau-Ponty, M., *La Phénoménologie de la Perception* (Paris, 1946).

Mounier, E., *Introduction aux Existentialismes* (Paris, 1947) ; Amer. ed., *Existentialist Philosophies, An Introduction* (New York, 1949).

Pontalis, G. B., *et al.*, *Pour et contre l'Existentialisme* (Paris, 1948).

Natanson, M., *A Critique of Jean-Paul Sartre's Ontology* (Lincoln, 1951).

Nicol, E., *Historicismo y Existencialismo, La Temporalidad del Ser y la Razón* (Mexico, 1950).

Ruggiero, G. de, *Existentialism, Disintegration of Man's Soul* (New York, 1948).

Troisfontaines, R., *Le Choix de J.-P. Sartre* (Paris, 1945).

Truc, G., *De J.-P. Sartre à L. Lavelle, ou Désagrégation et Réintégration* (Paris, 1946).

Varet, G., *L'Ontologie de Sartre* (Paris, 1948).

Wahl, J., *Etudes Kierkegaardiennes* (Paris, 1938).

——— *Petite Histoire de l'Existentialisme* (Paris, 1946) ; Amer. ed., *A Short History of Existentialism* (New York, 1949).

Wolff, W., *Values and Personality, An Existential Psychology of Crisis* (New York, 1950).

For articles see:

Douglas, K., *A Critical Bibliography of Existentialism* (*The Paris School*), *Listing, with brief Comments, Books and Articles in English and French by and about Jean-Paul Sartre, Simone de Beauvoir, Maurice Merleau-Ponty* (New Haven, 1950).

Gilson, E., "Limites existentielles de la Philosophie," in *L'Existence* (Paris, 1945), pp. 69-87.

PART ONE

SARTRE'S EXISTENTIALIST PHILOSOPHY

Didst Thou forget that man prefers peace, and even death to freedom of choice in the knowledge of good and evil?—

FEODOR M. DOSTOEVSKI,
The Brothers Karamazov

CHAPTER ONE

EXISTENCE OR BEING?

Is it not odd that philosophy should try to explain the nature of existence to man? Is it not like trying to explain the meaning of swimming to fish or of flying to birds? Existence is even more natural to man than flying is to birds, for birds do not fly all the time, but man always exists, as long as he is alive, even when he sleeps. How should he not know what existence is? Why should he need to have philosophy explain it to him? Even the most uneducated man knows existence by virtue of his permanent, most intimate, inward and outward experiences.

However, as soon as man tries to conceptualize his existence, he runs into difficulties. Will philosophy and especially a philosophy of existence help him to overcome these difficulties? That is what we shall try to find out.

Although existence is as old as mankind, a philosophy of existence, or Existentialism, is a rather young branch of human knowledge. Traditional classical philosophy dealt only with "being" (εἶναι, esse, être, Sein, essere, ser, etc.), sometimes replacing this term with the word "existence" (existentia, Dasein), but using them interchangeably without any conceptual difference. In the medieval Scholastic distinction between essentia and existentia the latter term was used as a synonym for "being," at least from the fifteenth or sixteenth century on.

During the last two centuries the philosophical concept of being has become more and more abstract and, consequently, more and more empty. In vain Leibnitz tried to remind philosophers that we could not possibly "have the idea of being if we were not beings ourselves and thus would find being in ourselves." [1] It was German idealism which, forgetting this reminder

---

[1] G. W. von Leibnitz, *Nouveaux Essais sur l'Entendement humain*, I (1765), p. 23.

from Leibnitz, evaporated being into such cloudy altitudes of speculation that it lost almost all connection with our individual being here and now, our human "existence." In Kant's philosophy being is no longer "a real predicate, that is, a concept of something which could be added to the concept of a thing. It is only the positing of a thing or of certain determinations in themselves."[2]

But it was Hegel who reached the climax in this process of the dehumanization of being when, in his *Logic,* he declared:

Being, pure being without any further determination . . . is pure indeterminateness and vacuity. . . . Nothing, pure nothing . . . is complete emptiness, without determination or content. Nothing . . . is the same lack of determination as pure being. . . . Pure being and pure nothing are, then, the same.[3]

Foreseeing that this unusual equation would arouse serious psychological objections, Hegel wrote:

If being and nothing are identical, say the objectors, it follows that it makes no difference whether my home, the air I breathe, this city, the sun, the law, mind, God, are or are not. Now in some of these cases the objectors foist in special and private aims or the utility a thing may have for a particular person, and then ask whether it be all the same to that person if the thing exist and if it do not. As to that, indeed, we may note that the teaching of philosophy is precisely what frees man from the endless crowd of finite aims and intentions by making him so indifferent to them that their existence or non-existence is to him a matter of no moment.[4]

One can easily see that this haughty attitude of Hegel's idealistic philosophy toward individual existence, with all its pain, anxiety, sorrow, and uncertainty, would provoke a kind of anti-idealistic revolution. It came from a man of dynamic temperament, endowed with a sharp analytical mind, a caustic eloquence, and an extraordinary capacity for moral suffering—Sören Kierkegaard, the Danish Protestant thinker who had deeply experi-

---

[2] I. Kant, *Kritik der reinen Vernunft,* III. Hauptstück, p. 472.
[3] G. W. F. Hegel, *Wissenschaft der Logik,* ed. G. Lasson, I, pp. 66-67.
[4] *The Logic of Hegel* (Oxford, 1874), p. 140.

enced Moses Mendelssohn's dictum: "If we start from ourselves . . . existence is a common word for acting and suffering." [5]

Kierkegaard's writings are a violent protest against all idealistic evasions of real issues into impersonal, objective, timeless schemes and eternal truths. He not only defended subjective truth but affirmed that " truth *is* subjectivity." Having gone through all the tragic antinomies and grim oppositions of individual existence with the terrifying "either-or" decisions it imposes, Kierkegaard rejected Hegel's solvent "mediation" of these oppositions by means of an automatic dialectical process which deals with timeless ideas and hollow generalities. Throwing the acid of his irony against Hegel's system, Kierkegaard wrote:

Can the principle of mediation also help the existing individual while still remaining in existence himself to become the mediating principle, which is *sub specie aeternitatis*, whereas the poor existing individual is confined to the strait-jacket of existence? Surely it cannot do any good to mock man, luring him on by dangling before his eyes the identity of subject and object, when his situation prevents him from making use of this identity, since he is in process of becoming, in consequence of being an existing individual. How can it help to explain to a man how the eternal truth is to be understood eternally, when the supposed user of the explanation is prevented from so understanding it through being an existing individual, and merely becomes fantastic when he imagines himself to be *sub specie aeternitatis*? What such a man needs instead is precisely an explanation of how the eternal truth is to be understood in determinations of time by one who, as existing, is himself in time, which even the worshipful Herr Professor concedes, if not always, at least once a quarter when he draws his salary.[6]

These bitter words were written in Copenhagen, in 1846, fifteen years after Hegel, professor at the University of Berlin, had died of cholera. His reputation was still bathed in glory, and Kierkegaard's protests found little echo. Nowadays Existentialists renew the same attacks with more success, when they reproach classical philosophy for having "de-existentialized being"

[5] *Morgenstunden* (Berlin, 1785), I, p. 81.
[6] S. Kierkegaard, *Concluding Unscientific Postscript* (published by Princeton University Press for The American-Scandinavian Foundation, 1941), pp. 171-172.

and thus emptied it of its "existential explosive." [7] These are the words of a prominent Catholic Existentialist, Etienne Gilson of the Collège de France.

All Existentialists, today as always, criticize the practice of traditional philosophy that determines being in a general way while remaining indifferent to the question of whether or not such being exists. Thus a classical philosopher seems to act like a geometrician who deals with the relations of geometrical forms or figures without being concerned with the problem of whether there actually exists in nature something which corresponds to these ideal constructions. But an individual is something other than a mutilated species, since the individual exists while the species does not.

Attacks of this type caused a sharpening of the antithesis between being and existence, so that today we may characterize them in the following manner:

Being is universal, abstract, timeless, and unlimited by space. *Existence* is individual, concrete, limited to a definite, very short time, and confined to a restricted spatial environment.

Being is "everywhere" and "always." *Existence* is only "here and now" (*hic et nunc*).

Being embraces everything and everyone. *Existence* is always one's own—my own, your own.

Being is unaware of itself. *Existence* is self-conscious and understands itself.

Being is objective, determined, and logically necessary; for whatever I think I have to think its being, at least as a possible thought. *Existence* is subjective, completely fortuitous, sheer fact, free, without any necessity.

Being is the synthesis and identity of the subject and the object; thus it represents fullness. *Existence* is the insurmountable separation of the subject from the object, the permanent non-coincidence and tension between subject and object, even when this object is the subject's own personality; *existence* is the unbridgeable abyss between knowing and being, between the lack provoking the subject's wishes and the objectives which would satisfy them. Thus *existence* is characterized by a "lack of being," a kind of emptiness.

---

[7] "Limites existentielles de la Philosophie," *L'Existence* (Paris, 1945), pp. 69-87.

This subjectivity of existence places it almost beyond the reach of philosophy. While being is always objective, existence is subjective in such an exclusive way that it can never become object—not even to itself. This is one of the stumbling blocks of Existentialism as a philosophy of existence; for by its very nature philosophy is conceptualization, and concepts necessarily are objective. Since existence is always subject and can never become object, it seems that there cannot be any philosophy of existence. As merely a subjective, emotional condition, existence is even beyond the reach of explanation, because explanation is made up of objective concepts. In trying to objectivize existence, concepts denature it, thus changing it into something else, namely, another variety of abstract being.

Existentialist philosophers, then, find themselves somehow in the situation of Saint Augustine who, when asked: "What is time?" answered: *"Si nemo ex me quaerat scio; si quaerenti explicare velim, nescio."* [8]

It was probably for this reason that Kierkegaard did not create any kind of systematic philosophy and did not want to create any. He only expressed subjective Existentialist feelings in a rather artistic form. Therefore some modern thinkers—like Nicolai Berdiayeff—consider Kierkegaard and the similarly unsystematic, subjectivistic, and artistic Nietzsche to be the only true Existentialists. "Only in subjectivity," Berdiayeff says, "can we know existence, and not in objectivity. In my opinion this central idea has disappeared in Heidegger's and Sartre's ontology." [9]

It is, indeed, very strange that Heidegger's most important work has the title *Sein und Zeit* ("Being and Time") and that Sartre's basic theoretical book is called *L'Etre et le Néant* ("Being and Nothingness"). Alternative titles like *Dasein und Zeit* ("Existence and Time") and *L'Existence et le Néant* ("Existence and Nothingness") would obviously have been more appropriate. The reason for the titles chosen is that both Sartre and

[8] "If nobody asks me, I know; but if I wished to explain it to one who should ask me, I do not know." *S. Augustini Confessionum* Liber XI, Cap. XIV.

[9] Quoted in J. Wahl, *Petite Histoire de l'Existentialisme* (Paris, 1947), p. 67.

Heidegger want to offer an "ontology," a theory of being. However, Berdiayeff is right in saying that "in an ontology, existence disappears . . . because it cannot be objectivized." We may also agree with Jean Wahl, professor of philosophy at the Sorbonne, when he writes: "We have to know whether existence is not something which has to be reserved to solitary meditation. . . . Perhaps we have to choose between Existentialism and existence?" [10]

Confronted with this choice, Sartre, Heidegger, Jaspers, Gabriel Marcel, and Jean Wahl have—evidently—chosen Existentialism, for otherwise they would be just as unknown as the millions who are confined to solitary meditation on existence. If thus these Existentialist philosophers have somehow become unfaithful to the true meaning of Existentialism, their sacrifice has not been in vain, since it has brought them fame, and, in the case of Sartre, even wealth. And this makes existence much more bearable, even to Existentialists.

[10] *Ibid.*, p. 61.

CHAPTER TWO

EXISTENCE AS BEING-IN-THE-WORLD

The readers of Heidegger's and Sartre's philosophical writings certainly have noticed the great number of hyphens linking as many as four to seven consecutive words. These hyphens are not just the expression of a typographical caprice but have a basic philosophical meaning in Existentialism. One may even designate Existentialism as "a philosophy of hyphens."

The most frequent of these expressions is "being-in-the-world" (Heidegger's *in-der-Welt-sein*), or "man-in-the-world" (Sartre's *l'homme-dans-le-monde*). What is the philosophical meaning of these words compounded by hyphens?

In order to understand, we must remember that, unlike being, which is timeless and unlimited by space, existence is *now* and *here*. Consequently, the existing man is always a man now and here; in short, a man in the world. To emphasize the essential necessity and indissoluble character of this association between man and his world, Heidegger links by hyphens the words designating man's existence and his world. "The compound expression 'being-in-the-world'," he writes, "shows already in its coinage that with it a unitary phenomenon is meant." [1]

From a common sense standpoint, this position looks like a truism; and yet, philosophically, it has important implications. In ethics, it means a defiance of the classical concept of man as such, independent of space and time and subject to one unitary type of moral requirements—the idea of man which is the basis of traditional humanism and humanitarianism. For gnosiology, it means a defiance of the classical concept of a subject which, being timeless and spaceless, is a subject without a world; and this

[1] M. Heidegger, *Sein und Zeit* (4th ed.), p. 53.

9

subject without a world has always been the starting point of idealism as well as of realism. Heidegger writes:

The clarification of the being-in-the-world showed that there is not at first a mere subject without a world, that it is never given. And thus it is finally neither at first an isolated ego given without the others.[2]

Since existence is being *now* and *here,* or "being-in-the-world," Heidegger concludes that the world of the existing man is always that which he shares with other men. This being-in-the-world means also "being-with-others" (*Mitsein* or *Mitsein-mit-Anderen*).

Thus with the basic position of being-in-the-world and being-with-others, Existentialism places itself beyond realism and idealism, both of which, starting from a subject without a world, need to have the world outside the subject demonstrated afterward. If this demonstration is considered possible, we speak of "realism"; if it is considered impossible, we speak of "idealism."

"The scandal of philosophy," Heidegger says, is not that this demonstration is still missing, but that it is being expected and tried again and again. "Existence, well understood, is opposed to such demonstrations, because it *is* already in its being all that which ulterior proofs think necessary to demonstrate."[3]

Only from this approach can we understand the French Existentialist Levinas when he describes Existentialism by saying:

The novelty Heidegger adds to our thousand-year-old knowledge . . . when stating "being-in-the-world" or "being-for-death" or "being-with-the-others" is that these prepositions "in," "for," "with" are the root of the verb . . . ; that they articulate the event Being. . . . We may say that Existentialism consists of feeling and thinking that the verb "to be" is transitive.[4]

Sartre adopts all these basic positions of Heidegger's Existentialism as a starting point. His teacher Laporte, late professor at the Sorbonne, warned him against the kind of abstraction by

---

[2] *Ibid.,* p. 116.
[3] *Ibid.,* p. 205.
[4] Quoted in Wahl, *Petite Histoire de l'Existentialisme,* pp. 85-86.

which we think of as isolated certain things which are not made to exist alone. Another of Sartre's teachers, Edmund Husserl, the famous creator of modern phenomenology, who died in 1938, taught him that, unlike the abstract, the concrete is a "whole" which can exist isolatedly, by itself. Sartre concludes:

The concrete is man-in-the-world with this specific union of man and the world which Heidegger, for example, calls "being-in-the-world." . . . It suffices to open the eyes and to question in all ingenuity this wholeness which is "man-in-the-world." [5]

Thus in Existentialism, Descartes' *Cogito ergo sum* ("I think, therefore I am") is reversed and replaced with a plain *sum* ("I am," in the sense of "I-am-in-the-world"), followed by cognition: *sum, ergo cogito.*

While Descartes' *cogito* places modern philosophy on the foundation of the primacy of cognition, Existentialism tries to place it on the foundation of the primacy of existence. For Heidegger, "cognition is nothing but a mode of existence as being-in-the-world." [6]

Although Sartre, as a Frenchman, refuses to take part in Heidegger's violent anti-Cartesian campaign and affects to remain faithful to Descartes' *cogito,* he modifies it, under the name *cogito préréflexif,* in such a way that he can deny Descartes' primacy of cognition and thus fall in line with Heidegger. For instance, he declares:

Consciousness is the knowing being as far as it *is* and not as far as it is *known.* This signifies that we have to abandon the primacy of cognition if we want to found this cognition itself. [7]

After having declared that Descartes' primacy of cognition is an "illusion," Sartre states that it is a non-reflective consciousness which makes reflection possible. "There is a pre-reflective *cogito* which is the condition of the Cartesian *cogito.*" [8]

[5] *L'Etre et le Néant* (Paris, 1943), p. 38.
[6] *Sein und Zeit,* p. 61.
[7] *L'Etre et le Néant,* p. 17.
[8] *Ibid.,* p. 20.

With the pre-reflective consciousness, existing by itself, Sartre believes himself to have found an "absolute." [9] Thus in spite of his rejection of Descartes' primacy of cognition and in spite of his own insistence on the primacy of existence, Sartre thinks that he has preserved the Cartesian subjectivity as a starting point of philosophy, and that he has taken a middle road between Heidegger and Descartes. As a matter of fact, he is much closer to Heidegger than to Descartes. As we shall see later, Sartre draws the most important ethical conclusions from his basic ontological position that our mind is only secondary to our existence, as a simple manifestation of the latter.

But, for the moment, let us go back to Sartre's affirmation (inspired by Husserl's phenomenology) that it suffices "to open the eyes and to question in all ingenuity" this concrete wholeness which is man-in-the-world. What is the answer to this question according to Sartre's philosophy?

"Being," he writes, "will be revealed to us by some immediate means of access, like nuisance, nausea, etc." [10] Where Heidegger's "existence" is revealed as "sorrow" (*Sorge, cura*), Sartre reveals existence as "nausea." Those who read his novels (where, according to Marcel Thiebaud, "kisses are given between diarrheas and declarations of love made between vomitings") will not be astonished to see the physiological state of nausea promoted to the rank of a metaphysical category.

9 *Ibid.,* p. 23.
10 *Ibid.,* p. 14.

CHAPTER THREE

THE REVELATION OF EXISTENCE: CONTINGENCY, ABSURDITY, ANXIETY

We spoke of the intrinsic difficulty of explaining existence in terms of objective concepts; because existence, being basically subjective, cannot be objectivized without being denatured. Heidegger, having at his command the objective, abstract concepts of the philosopher, was unable to unveil existence in its most immediate emotional character. His "sorrow" is a category, not a suffering.

Sartre, on the other hand, is not only a philosopher but an artist, endowed with imagination and intuition. Thus he can try to represent subjectively in novels and dramas things which the objective concepts of the philosopher cannot grasp. Consequently it is not astonishing that Sartre's most impressive characterization of existence is not to be found in his great theoretical treatise *L'Etre et le Néant* ("Being and Nothingness") but in his early novel *La Nausée* ("Nausea"). Let us translate from this novel a passage in which the hero, Roquentin, an historian, intuitively grasps the meaning of existence and describes it as follows:

It took my breath. Never, before these last days, had I felt the meaning of to "exist".... Ordinarily existence hides itself. It is there, around us, in us, it is we, one cannot say two words without speaking of it; and, finally, one does not touch it. . . . If somebody had asked me what existence is, I should have answered in good faith that it is nothing, just an empty form which came from outside to add itself to things, without changing their nature in any respect.[1]

And now, behold! at one blow it was there, it was as clear as day: Existence had revealed itself suddenly. It had lost its inoffensive aspect of an abstract category: it was the very dough of things. . . .

[1] This is obviously an allusion to Kant's definition of existence which we quoted previously.

The diversity of things, their individuality was nothing but an appearance, a varnish. This varnish had melted. What was left were monstrous soft masses in disorder, naked in frightening nudity. . . .

Existence is not something which can be thought from a distance: it must invade you bluntly, it must sit down on you, weigh heavily upon your heart like a big, motionless animal.[2]

This is *how* Sartre's hero experiences existence. But as *what* is it revealed to him? Three words describe it: *contingency, absurdity,* and *anxiety*. Roquentin suddenly feels that everything, including himself, is superfluous, gratuitous, supernumerary (*de trop*), because, logically, existence can no more be justified than can non-existence.

Nietzsche had already asked: "Is my existence as compared with my non-existence something which can be justified?"[3] Sartre, without referring to his great predecessor, bluntly retorts: No! Those who do not share his opinion, but try to justify their existence as necessary, are relegated by Sartre to a new philosophical category and denounced as *salauds* (filthy stinkers).

Here is another portion of Sartre's *La Nausée* where his hero, Roquentin, states these ideas more explicitly:

The essential is contingency; I mean that by definition existence is not necessary. To exist is simply to be there; the existing beings appear but can never be deduced. I believe there are people who have understood it. They tried to overcome their contingency, inventing a necessary Being which is the cause of itself. But no necessary Being can explain existence: contingency is not a false appearance which can be dissipated; it is the *absolute* and, consequently, the perfect gratuitousness. Everything is gratuitous—this garden, this town, I, myself. When we realize this, then it turns our hearts, everything begins to float . . . *that is nausea*; that is what *les salauds* . . . try to hide from themselves with their idea of *rights*. What a poor lie! *Nobody has rights!* These fellows are entirely gratuitous, just as other men. . . .[4]

The term *salaud* (filthy stinker) is not just an angry expression of Sartre's hero in a moment of overwhelming nausea, but a

---

[2] *La Nausée* (Paris, 1938), pp. 166-172. Amer. ed., *Nausea*, trans. by Lloyd Alexander (New York: New Directions, 1949).

[3] F. Nietzsche, *Gesammelte Werke* (Munich, 1925), XVI, p. 252.

[4] *Op. cit.,* p. 171.

category maintained by the philosopher in his theoretical works also. In *L'Existentialisme est un Humanisme,* for example, Sartre gives the following definition:

"Those who will try to show that their existence is necessary, although it is the very contingency of man's appearance on earth, I shall call them *salauds.*" [5] In *La Nausée* Roquentin concludes by saying: "Every existing being is born without reason, prolongs itself by weakness, and dies by fortuitousness." [6] Maurice Maeterlinck, the great Belgian poet, expresses a similar idea in *Pelléas et Mélisande* when he speaks in beautiful prose of his young heroine full of melancholy: "She was born . . . without any reason . . . in order to die; and she dies without any reason." We have here a poetical expression of that age-old truth which Heidegger voiced later when he said that without any reason man is cast into a world where his being is "essentially sorrow" and "being toward death." [7] Lord Byron, and others, wrote in similar vein.

Sartre concludes that our being-in-the-world and the being-of-the-world are absolute absurdity. He even goes as far as to establish an equation between the absolute and the absurd. Where Spinoza says, *Deus sive natura* ("God or nature"), Sartre says *l'absolu ou l'absurde* ("the absolute or the absurd"). [8]

The absurd is that which cannot be deduced logically. Thus Sartre has to include all nature in his absolute absurdity.

Sartre is an inhabitant of a large city and a café habitué. He has apparently no real relation to nature, no love for or understanding of nature. In none of his novels can any impressive description of nature be found. His only reaction toward nature is dread. His hero Roquentin, looking down from the heights above a city called Bouville ("Mudville" a fictional disguise for Le Havre), thinks that the townspeople are foolish to feel that they are protected from the nature which surrounds them.

5 *L'Existentialisme est un Humanisme* (Paris, 1946), pp. 84-85. Amer. ed., *Existentialism,* trans. by B. Frechtman (New York: Philosophical Library, 1947).

6 *Op. cit.,* p. 174.

7 *Sein und Zeit,* pp. 180, 266, *passim.*

8 *La Nausée,* p. 169.

"I see this nature, I see it," Roquentin says to himself. "I know that nature's submission of itself to us is laziness, I know that it has *no laws;* . . . It has nothing but habits, and tomorrow it may change some of them." [9]

Sartre-Roquentin imagines some consequences of such a possible change. For instance, a mother may suddenly see that her child's cheek has cracked and exposed a third eye which laughs; or some day we may discover that our clothes have changed into living beings; or somebody suddenly feels something scrape his mouth: "He will go to a mirror and open his mouth; and his tongue will have become an enormous live centipede . . . etc."

Here Sartre was obviously influenced by his venerated Franz Kafka who in *The Metamorphosis* describes how Gregor Samsa, a commercial traveler, awakes one morning in his room and finds himself changed in his bed to a monstrous, gigantic insect, with a little head and a big brown belly, divided by bowed corrugations; and how he tries in vain to regain contact with his family, which has remained human. Kafka philologists explain that this story illustrates man's complete isolation as a punishment for his hidden wish to escape his responsibilities toward human society. The symbolization of this idea, however, is so absurd that it explains why, twenty years after his death, Kafka has been promoted to the rank of an Existentialist. For Existentialists not only discover the absurd where it is, but also invent it where it is not. The absurd has apparently become their *raison d'être,* although Existentialism, by definition, denies any raison d'être.

Sartre's reaction toward the gratuitousness and absurdity of existence is nausea. Observing his fellow men, Roquentin cries out: "I should like to vomit!" [10]

Inasmuch as vomiting is the climax of nausea, we can understand why, in most of his novels, Sartre describes the vomiting of different persons. He is perhaps influenced here by William Faulkner, whose work Sartre greatly admires. Mme Simone de Beauvoir, disrespectfully called "la grande Sartreuse," devel-

[9] *Ibid.,* p. 204.
[10] *Ibid.,* p. 160.

ops a similar theme in her novel *Le Sang des Autres* ("The Blood of the Others"). Sartre himself describes with phenomenological accuracy these repugnant physiological processes and their results. Sometimes, in a paroxysm of perversion, the vomitings of Sartre's characters are linked to sexual desires, as in his story "Intimité," or his novel *L'Age de Raison,* where we can read the following description of a "love scene" between the professor of philosophy Mathieu Delarue and one of his drunken students, the young girl, Iwich: "A slightly bitter smell of vomit escaped from her mouth, so pure. Mathieu passionately inhaled that odor." [11]

It would be difficult to find elsewhere in literature a more perverse and repugnant description, but Sartre's novels abound with even worse examples.

Saleté poisseuse (sticky filth) is the name Roquentin gives existence,[12] and Sartre's other metaphors for the characterization of existence swarm with images similarly "viscous." Vomit also is viscous. The metaphysical meaning of viscosity in Sartre's philosophy will be revealed later by Existentialist psychoanalysis.

Existence is linked to a physiological body; consequently, our body is, for Sartre, a main object of nausea. Here is what he says about this in his treatise *L'Etre et le Néant:* "A discrete and insuperable nausea perpetually reveals my body to my consciousness." The reason is that our body, too, is sheer fact, without any logical necessity. "It can happen that we seek pleasure or physical pain in order to free ourselves from it, but as soon as pain or pleasure exist for consciousness, they . . . manifest its [the body's] facticity and contingency, and it is on the ground of nausea that they reveal themselves." [13]

Christian Existentialists consider this incarnation a paradoxical scandal. Sartre's Existentialism, which, like Heidegger's, never overcame its theological heritage, seems sometimes to emphasize

[11] *L'Age de Raison* (Paris, 1945), p. 255; Amer. ed. *The Age of Reason* (New York, Knopf, 1947).
[12] *La Nausée,* p. 176.
[13] *L'Etre et le Néant,* p. 404.

this scandal of incarnation by delving into the most repugnant details of carnal manifestations; but the accompanying morbid pleasure indicates that, Sartre, after all, is not averse to that "scandal."

It would be erroneous to believe that Sartre's nausea is the result of a specific physiological predisposition. To him nausea is something metaphysical. Sartre insists that we must not take "the term 'nausea' as a metaphor drawn from our physiological disgusts; on the contrary, it is on metaphysical grounds that all concrete and empirical nauseas begin and produce vomiting. (Nauseas produced by the sight of rotten meat, fresh blood, excrements, etc.)"

Nausea and anxiety are closely related. In his essay *Was ist Metaphysik?* Heidegger describes anxiety in a way which closely resembles Sartre's nausea. In anxiety, Heidegger says, we feel a kind of "floating" sensation (*Schweben*) because reality "slips away from us." Anxiety reveals nothingness [14] and, basically, the nothingness of death.[15]

When nauseated, Sartre's Roquentin has likewise the impression that "everything begins to float," and "nothing seems real." [16]

Heidegger insists that anxiety (dread, *Angst*) must not be confused with fear (*Furcht*). Following Kierkegaard, Freud clarified this difference when he wrote: "I think that anxiety is related to the subjective condition, abstracting from any object, while in fear the attention is precisely directed toward an object." [17]

Similarly Heidegger emphasizes that anxiety represents the essential impossibility of defining the "what" which causes it. Thus anxiety is endowed with a certain character of "indefinite-

[14] *Was ist Metaphysik?* (Bonn, 1929), p. 14; Amer. ed., *Existence and Being* (Chicago: H. Regnery Company, 1929).

[15] *Sein und Zeit*, p. 266.

[16] *La Nausée*, pp. 105, 171.

[17] S. Freud, *Vorlesungen zur Einführung in die Psychoanalyse* (Vienna, 1916), p. 417.

ness and objectlessness." [18] We shall see later how in Sartre's philosophy anxiety is linked to his basic concept of freedom.

The diffuse anxiety related to no definite object, but vaguely linked to man's feeling of forlornness and isolatedness as an individual confronted with the nothingness of death, predominates also in Roquentin's nausea.

"I ran along the docks . . . the houses, with their gloomy eyes, watched me fleeing. I repeated to myself anxiously: Where shall I go, where shall I go? Everything may happen!" [19]

But we cannot run away from ourselves, from the only certainty we have in this life: each of us will have to go alone through the somber door of death. "We shall die alone," as Pascal says.[20] And Camus reminds us that life is nothing but a terrifying apprenticeship to death.

[18] Freud, *The Problem of Anxiety* (Albany, New York, 1936), p. 147.
[19] *La Nausée*, p. 106.
[20] *Pensées*, III, 211.

CHAPTER FOUR

FIRST CRITICAL INTERMEZZO

Roquentin's nausea still was not philosophy, but only a subjective intuition and emotional interpretation of existence as sheer contingency, absurdity, and anxiety. However, our philosophies, as conceptual systems, greatly depend upon our subjective intuitions of existence—a fact which may explain, in part, the diversity of those systems.

The same nature can be interpreted emotionally in quite opposite ways, as a comparison between Sartre and Chateaubriand, for instance, will show. To Sartre, a tree's root is a "voracious claw rending the earth, extorting from it its nourishment," and defiantly, in order to play with the world's absurdity, his Roquentin kicks the root violently with his heel.[1] Thus we see that in Sartre's intuitive interpretation of existence even innocent plants are voracious monsters, revealing the world's repugnant absurdity. For Chateaubriand, even monsters reveal divine providence. "It seems to us," he writes, "that God has allowed these productions of matter in order to teach us what creation would be without him. It is the shadow which sets off lights."[2]

Here are two possible interpretations of the same nature: the one that a man chooses depends greatly on his emotional reactions. Criticism can only begin where reason finds a working point—in rational arguments.

As far as reason is concerned, one has to admit that the great rationalistic systems have not succeeded in deducing material facts by merely logical operations; and the failure of Hegel's and Schelling's systems of natural philosophy dooms such attempts forever. In fact, there remain in nature a large number of

[1] *La Nausée*, pp. 169, 177.
[2] *Oeuvres de Chateaubriand* (Paris, [1857]), I, 3, p. 149.

merely empirical elements, which have no logical necessity and
may truly be called contingent.

At the end of the nineteenth century Emile Boutroux wrote
his book on *The Contingency of the Laws of Nature;* [3] and
Boltzmann's kinetic theory of gases gave another blow to determinism. In 1927 the physicist Heisenberg stated that "the
mechanics of quanta has definitely established the invalidity of
the law of causality." [4] There are still laws of nature, but, as
Louis de Broglie says, "they are no longer causal laws but laws
of probability." [5]

In spite of these blows to determinism the laws of nature still
offer sufficient regularity to make possible certain predictions and
to exclude certain possibilities, especially as far as the macrocosm
is concerned. [6] As a practical matter, in most cases the probability
of our new statistical laws of nature hardly differs from certainty.
There exist in our society powerful professional groups whose
activities rest entirely on the regularity of our physical laws: the
physicists, chemists, engineers, geologists, industrial workers, etc.
Since this is so, it is a great exaggeration to speak, as does Sartre,
of a complete contingency of nature and of a complete absence of
physical laws.

We may speak of contingency in an absolute sense, because
the whole of physical laws cannot be deduced logically from the
whole of being. Their being is no more necessary than the being
of the whole universe. Even so rationalistic and theistic a thinker
as Whitehead had to admit the contingency of the presence, called
God, of a rationalistic selective principle in reality. According to
Whitehead, this principle simply is there, since itself is the only
reason for anything being there and being what it is. Besides,
there is another contingency in Whitehead's highly rationalized

[3] E. Boutroux, *De la Contingence des Lois de la Nature* (Paris, 1874).

[4] W. Heisenberg, "Über den anschaulichen Inhalt der quantentheoretischen
Kinematik und Mechanik," *Zeitschrift für Physik* (Berlin, 1927), Vol. 43, p. 197.

[5] L. de Broglie, "Déterminisme et Causalité dans la Physique contemporaine,"
Revue de Métaphysique et de Morale, XXXVI, 4 (Paris, 1929), p. 441.

[6] See A. Stern, "Causalité, Incertitude et Complémentarité," *Revue de
Synthèse* (Paris, 1937), pp. 133-148.

reality, since the universe might have been different without being less rational. It, seemingly, might have been morally more satisfactory. Consequently, if there is this universe and none other, this is contingent.

Nevertheless, I believe that if there is no absolute necessity, there is enough relative necessity left between the parts of our reality to guarantee the regular recurrence of phenomena in nature. In saying that nature has no laws, only habits which may change tomorrow, Sartre obviously throws out the baby with the bath.

Another of Sartre's affirmations is that all of us are superfluous and that persons who try to hide this from themselves, pretending that they are necessary, are *salauds* of "bad faith" (*de mauvaise foi*). This concept of bad faith will be analyzed more thoroughly, because it has a basic meaning in Sartre's philosophy. In his Existentialist psychoanalysis we will see that he tries to detect in various forms of human activity hidden attempts of men to justify themselves contrary to their better knowledge.

In his novels Sartre has tried repeatedly to show that all of us are superfluous, supernumerary (*de trop*), and that nobody is really necessary. This sometimes leads him, the author of a book entitled *Existentialism Is a Humanism*, to the most inhuman statements. When World War II was about to break out, Mathieu, the hero of *Le Sursis* ("The Reprieve"), had the following conversation with his brother Jacques:

Mathieu: "Peace or war! That does not make any difference. . ."
Jacques: "No difference? Tell this to those millions of men who are preparing to be killed!"
Mathieu: "And so what! They carried their death in themselves since their birth. And when they have all been slaughtered to the last, mankind will still be as full as before; without a gap; without one missing."
Jacques: "Minus twelve to fifteen million men."

Mathieu, the Existentialist professor of philosophy, answers that "this is not a question of numbers"; with or without those men the world will continue to go "nowhere." [7]

7 *Op. cit.*, p. 168.

Some of Sartre's heroes recognize that they are superfluous, such as Henri, a Frenchman of the resistance, who, caught by the Fascists and condemned to death, says to his friends:

I am not missed anywhere, I do not leave any empty spot. The subways are crowded, the restaurants full, the heads crammed to bursting with little problems. I slipped out of the world and it remained as full as an egg.[8]

However, there are other people who are not big enough to recognize their supernumerary character. They believe they are necessary to their families, their countries, their professions, and claim rights in this world. They are told by Sartre that they are "stinkers" and that "nobody has rights." [9]

We think that, here again, Sartre shoots beyond the target, putting absolute measures on relative things. To be sure, for the whole of the universe nobody is necessary, nobody will be missing when he disappears. But every son will be missing to his mother, every loved one to his beloved.

Is a father a "stinker" simply because he thinks that he is necessary to his wife and children, since nobody will take care of them if he dies? I do not think so. A George Washington was necessary to his nation to win its independence, and a Georges Clemenceau was necessary to his country to drive out the invader. If these men had the conviction of their necessity, were they therefore "stinkers"?

Of course, one may ask whether America's independence and France's freedom are absolutely necessary for the whole universe, including all planets and fixed stars, and this question, certainly, cannot be answered. But one cannot deny that the independence of these nations is relatively necessary for the continuance of civilization, and civilization is relatively necessary to mankind.

Although it is impossible to prove the absolute necessity of the existence of mankind, existence is relatively necessary to mankind. For if mankind had not felt this necessity, it would

[8] *Morts sans Sépulture* (Paris, 1949), p. 47.
[9] *La Nausée*, p. 171.

have already finished with existence, according to Schopenhauer's recommendations.

As we shall see later, in discussing Existentialist ethics, Sartre rejects all given, constituted values as limitations of our liberty, and grants everybody the freedom to invent his own system of values, without any possibility of having it legitimized by any supra-individual authority. Of one of his heroes Sartre says: "There would be neither right nor wrong unless he invented them." [10] It is strange that a philosopher, who in this way has removed all basis for value judgments of supra-individual validity, is so profuse in uttering the most offensive value judgments, with the most apodictic certainty, on the moral behavior of other people, and claims universal validity for such "philosophical categories" as "coward" and *salaud*. Only by examining Sartre's theory of freedom and his philosophy of values can we understand the confusing fact that the same philosopher who wants to teach workers that not Marxism but Existentialism leads to true social revolution can, by proclaiming that "nobody has rights," implicitly condemn the men who gave France the *Droits de l'Homme et du Citoyen* and America the Bill of Rights.

If Sartre's heroes find existence unbearable because it does not offer absolute necessity, they show only that they are incurable philosophical absolutists. It seems to me that this is the real moral disease of Existentialists. Their philosophy, to be sure, is thoroughly irrationalistic, yet most Existentialists have a rationalistic temperament. Their philosophy must be called irrationalistic because it considers that the universe is not subjected to rational laws and is therefore not logically deducible. Existentialism is irrationalistic also because it ascribes to emotional states such as anxiety, sorrow, and nausea a power superior to that of reason, refuting the claims of reason and defeating the efforts of reason. And yet the Existentialist temperament is definitely rationalistic. In my opinion there are two kinds of rationalists: The first consists of those who, like Descartes, Spinoza, and Hegel, believe in the possibility of deducing the relations of

[10] *L'Age de Raison*, p. 249.

the material world as if they were formal relations of logic or mathematics. The second group of rationalists is formed by those who—like the Existentialists—do not believe in that possibility and yet uphold stubbornly their claim for such a world, demonstrated *more geometrico,* a world deducible with absolute necessity. Since they cannot have such a world they escape into sickness, their metaphysical disease which they call "nausea." Most Existentialists seem to be frustrated rationalists. "I want everything or nothing" (*"Je veux tout ou rien"*), Albert Camus writes literally in his *Mythe de Sisyphe,*[11] apparently without realizing that he only repeats the outcry of Ibsen's Pastor Brand, whose search for the absolute in religion was so tragically doomed to failure.

Already before Ibsen, Balzac had shown that the search for the absolute is doomed in other fields: in art, by the failure of his hero Frenhofer (in *Le Chef-d'Oeuvre inconnu*); in science, by the ruin of his hero Balthazar Claës (in *La Recherche de l'Absolu*); and in family life, by the tragedy of his *Père Goriot.* They are all ancestors of Ibsen's Brand, who is only a fictitious copy of Sören Kierkegaard, the founder of Existentialism. In my opinion Kierkegaard was the prototype of a philosophical absolutist and of a frustrated rationalist. He fought Hegel, but like Hegel he would have wished to have a world where "everything which is real is reasonable and everything which is reasonable is real." Recognizing the impossibility of such a world and such a reason, Kierkegaard revolted against both.

Kierkegaard's battle cry was best expressed in the title of his famous work *Either-Or!* Either God or the dragons, either everything or nothing! To accept the "absolute paradox" which he saw in Christ, he crucified reason. In the conflict between Christianity and modern civilization—upon which Feuerbach insisted —Kierkegaard was ready to sacrifice modern civilization in order to maintain Christianity in its absolute purity. Finding modern society not ready to accept this "either-or," Kierkegaard was in lifelong revolt against society, democracy, and his own Church,

[11] *Le Mythe de Sisyphe* (Paris, 1942), p. 118.

its bishop, and all Christian institutions, including marriage, because, according to his claim for absolute purity, procreation seemed to be "sinful."

In the same way Sartre's Roquentin is in a state of permanent revolt against the world, only because this world is not as it should be according to his absolute postulates. The fact that Kierkegaard was a theist and that Sartre is an atheist is of minor importance, because they have in common something much more essential: the claim of the absolute in a relative world, and the attitude of revolt against a world which does not comply with their absolute claims.

We have here an explanation of the strange fact that there are religious and anti-religious Existentialists—Catholic, Protestant, Jewish, and atheistic Existentialists, who, in spite of their different credos, understand each other and consider themselves as belonging more or less to the same school of thought. That which separates them is much less important than that which they have in common: the rejection of a world which does not correspond to their absolute claims and the attitude of sterile revolt.

Camus, author of *The Stranger,* whose whole life is a rejection of the world and of the links between things and their human significance, states explicitly that the only coherent philosophical attitude of man in an absurd world is revolt. "This revolt gives its price to life," he says; and he finds in it a new kind of "grandeur." [12]

I cannot find it. There was grandeur in Prometheus' attitude, because it was more than revolt. By bringing men the light from Olympus he caused a revolution. But revolt against existence has to remain sterile, because we cannot change existence. The true philosophical attitude toward that which we cannot change is acceptance. *There* is the true wisdom. Revolt against the unchangeable existential condition of man is a childish attitude, not an adult one.

If we recognize that we cannot have a world deducible with logical necessity, a world of absolute certainty, we have to accept

[12] *Ibid.,* p. 78.

the fact wisely and not to adopt the attitude of a child crying because he cannot have the moon.

Bertrand Russell said that the chief thing philosophy in our age can do for us is "to teach us how to live without certainty, and yet without being paralyzed by hesitation." [13]

There is no doubt that, in the last analysis, Existentialism, too, teaches that man has to *accept* his existential condition. We find this postulate in Heidegger, in Sartre and—most forcefully —in Jaspers [14] and Simone de Beauvoir. For Existentialists, however, this acceptance presupposes a radical conversion, a "resolute decision," while for most non-Existentialists it is a self-evident, almost automatic reaction. It may be that the authentic Existentialists truly overcome their nausea, but most of them keep on vomiting as long as they exist in this world devoid of purpose, where, according to Sartre, "all human activities are equivalent."

[13] *A History of Western Philosophy* (New York: Simon and Schuster, 1945), p. xiv.

[14] See especially K. Jaspers' *Tragedy Is Not Enough* (Boston: The Beacon Press, 1952), p. 105.

CHAPTER FIVE

HOW TO OVERCOME NAUSEA

The tragic absurdity of existence is not a new discovery. In modern times Schopenhauer, Nietzsche, Dostoevski, and Unamuno have probably been those who most profoundly felt it. Many attempts have been made to overcome this condition.

Sartre's Roquentin overcomes his nausea by escaping into the imaginary world of art. Sitting in an obscure tavern at Bouville he hears an American jazz song played on a record, with the refrain, "Some of these days you'll miss me, honey." And, strangely enough, listening to this vulgar song, he recovers from his nausea, because in the melody he finally attains something " which does not exist." He decides to give up history, since "it speaks of that which has existed, and one existing being can never justify the existence of another existing being." [1] He will dedicate himself to art; he will write fiction, a kind of story where "behind the printed words, behind the pages one must guess something which does not exist, which would be beyond existence." [2]

Schopenhauer already had found relief from the suffering of existence in the pure contemplation of Platonic ideas in art or in the revelation of the thing in itself in music. And Nietzsche stated that "only as an aesthetic phenomenon, existence and the world are eternally justified." [3]

This seems also to be Camus' position, when he says that the work of art illustrates the "renouncement of thought . . . and its resignation to nothing but an intelligence which fabricates appearances and covers with images that which has no meaning."

[1] *La Nausée,* p. 228.
[2] *Ibid.*
[3] F. Nietzsche, *Die Geburt der Tragödie,* in *Gesammelte Werke,* III (1920), p. 46.

And he adds that if the world were understandable, there would not be any art.[4]

However, for none of these thinkers did the escape into the imaginary "non-existing" world of art become a permanent refuge and a true means of salvation from the sufferings of existence. In the pure contemplation of Platonic ideas in art Schopenhauer found only temporary relief, and he decided that salvation from existence, true "redemption," could only be found in the negation of the will to live.

Similarly, Nietzsche overcame his period of "illusionism," in which he had placed the "artist's gospel," with its beautiful lies, above the dreadful truth of the scientist. He finally created the ideal of the "superman," the man who is strong enough to confront truth without needing to cover it with the beautiful veil of illusion.

Camus, too, warns against seeing in art a shelter against the absurd. Art in itself, he says,

is an absurd phenomenon. . . . It does not offer any escape from the evil of the spirit. It is, on the contrary, one of the signs of this evil. . . . But, for the first time, it causes the spirit to leave its confines and confront other spirits, not in order that it may lose itself in them, but in order to point, with a precise finger, to the road without escape, where we must travel.[5]

Thus, without succumbing to its illusions, Camus clings to art, giving to emptiness its colors, but without forgetting for a single moment that it *is* emptiness.

Here is the point where Sartre's ways deviate from those of Camus. Sartre goes beyond art. His Roquentin, overcoming nausea through evasion into the non-existing world of art, symbolizes only one station in the Calvary of existence. Art is only a temporary refuge from the absurdity of existence. The novelist Sartre, who in 1938 published *La Nausée,* becomes the systematic philosopher and metaphysician who in 1943 publishes his gigantic treatise *L'Etre et le Néant.*

Theoretical philosophy has, therefore, become a means to

[4] *Le Mythe de Sisyphe,* p. 135.
[5] *Ibid.,* p. 132.

overcome nausea, but not for the first time in the history of philosophy. Considered from the standpoint of their psychological motives, the philosophical systems may be divided into those belonging to the "theorogone" type and those belonging to the "pathogone."

Theorogone philosophy is motivated by observation of the world and the wish to explain what has been observed. (The antique θεωρός was an observer or a spectator at public games.) In this sense the philosophies of Aristotle, Descartes, Bacon, Hume, and Kant may be designated as "theorogone."

Pathogone philosophy, on the contrary, is motivated by the suffering which existence in the world imposes upon us, and the wish to overcome it (from the Greek πάθος, suffering). In this sense the philosophies of Epicurus, Pascal, Spinoza, Schopenhauer, Nietzsche, and Unamuno may be considered as "pathogone."

If Sartre's philosophy should have to be classified on this basis, it certainly would have to be ranged among the pathogone systems. It is nausea—his kind of suffering from the world's absurdity—which motivates Sartre's philosophical system.

A comparison between Sartre's and the most representative pathogone philosophy ever produced in history—that of Spinoza—will clarify the peculiar character of the former.

Wishing to overcome man's suffering from existence, Spinoza tried to demonstrate away contingency, absurdity, and anxiety. His means were rationalism and determinism. According to Spinoza a reconciliation with destiny becomes possible if it appears not as an arbitrary force, but as the necessary manifestation of universal reason. Confronted by that which is logically and absolutely necessary, every resistance becomes senseless, and so does every wish to influence destiny by our desires. Thus our anxiety in the presence of contingency disappears, as well as the delusive hope to change the world according to our personal desires.

In the presence of that cosmic necessity, which belongs to Spinoza's universe, there is only one right attitude: that of comprehension; not a comprehension from the aspect of individual, subjective imagination, but a logical comprehension, based on reason, or, as Spinoza says, a comprehension *sub specie aeterni-tatis,* under the aspect of eternity. In the serene regions of reason the individual's vision is diverted from the mean interests of everyday existence and directed toward the whole. The small discords of existence are then dissipated in the great harmonies of a universe full of reason. *Amor Dei,* the love of God and Nature, preached by Spinoza, becomes an *amor fati,* a love of our destiny, since for Spinoza our suffering is nothing but an error arising from the limited prospect of individual life, of Existence.

Sartre's pathogone philosophy is of a quite different type. For, unlike Spinoza's, Sartre's philosophy does not try to demonstrate away the contingency, absurdity, and anxiety of existence. On the contrary, Sartre's philosophy tries to demonstrate the necessity of contingency, absurdity, and anxiety. His means are opposed to those of Spinoza: not rationalism and determinism, but irrationalism and freedom.

But is it not somehow self-contradictory to demonstrate the necessity of contingency, to prove logically the absurdity of existence, to rationalize that irrational condition which is anxiety?

That is exactly the reproach made to Sartre by some of his friends, especially by Albert Camus. "In a world where everything is given and nothing explained," Camus writes, "the fecundity of a value or of a metaphyics is a senseless concept." [6] And he states that in this absurd world we have not to try to "explain" or to "resolve," but merely to experience and to describe.[7]

Another of Sartre's critical friends, the Surrealist Hubert Juin, writes:

[6] *Le Mythe de Sisyphe,* p. 186.

[7] In 1952 the friendship which, for many years, linked Camus and Sartre was broken by a violent polemic between the two writers. The occasion was Camus' dissatisfaction with a review published about his book *L'Homme révolté* in *Les Temps Modernes,* the literary magazine directed by Sartre. The polemic reveals that Sartre no longer shares Camus' concept of the absurd, nor his rather abstract revolt against existence. Declaring that, although not being a Marxist, he believes in the "profound truth" of Marx's philosophy, Sartre reproaches Camus for his hostility toward history and concludes that, in refusing to participate in history—especially in the struggle of the proletariat—Camus ceases to share the aims of his contemporaries and cannot see anything but "absurdity" in all human actions. (See *Les Temps Modernes,* No. 82 [Paris: August, 1952], pp. 317-353.)

It is true that anxiety annihilates the rational, and it is this, too, we are reproaching in Sartre. . . . Anxiety is not ink. It is the night, and when one emerges from the night, one does not write *Being and Nothingness*. One acts like Heidegger and re-descends.[8]

It is, however, a fascinating spectacle to see how Sartre rationalizes the absurd and how he proves the necessity of contingency, for he is doing it with the most brilliant philosophical craftsmanship. It is even more fascinating to observe how he tries to evade the depressing consequences of his gruesome philosophy in favor of a kind of optimism, which I should not qualify as "heroic," like Nietzsche's, but which I should, instead, regard as an optimism of defiance, an optimism "in spite of."

Sartre's doctrine teaches that man can overcome his nausea by recognizing his freedom, by which act he can give meaning and value to existence. But being responsible for his choice of meanings and values in a world in which he is the only moral lawgiver, the authentic man, who overcame his nausea, will always have to suffer from a tremendous "ethical anxiety." There *is* freedom in Sartrian existence, but anxiety is its price. And it is a high price, that few people are ready to pay. There are strings attached to Sartre's optimism.

[8] *Jean-Paul Sartre ou la Condition humaine* (Brussels, 1946), p. 79.

CHAPTER SIX

EXISTENCE AND ESSENCE

Existence is the first basic concept of Existentialism, *essence* is the second. If existence is the "here" and "now" of being, essence is the "what" of this being. In this sense medieval scholasticism had already defined essence as the *quidditas* of things, a somewhat barbarian noun derived from the Latin pronoun *quid*, meaning "what." Heidegger, who is fond of barbarian expressions, used, after Scheler, the corresponding German term *Was-heit*, or *Was-Sein*, in order to define essence.

Now the basic thesis of Existentialism is that *man's existence precedes his essence*. In other words, his being "here" and "now" precedes his being "something." [1]

The religious Existentialists affirm this thesis because human existence defies all prevision. Therefore, as Etienne Gilson says, they consider essences to be objects of an inquiry which is always open, instead of starting with them and deducing from them that which ought to exist.

Sartre and other atheistic Existentialists also affirm the thesis that man's existence precedes his essence; because, if God does not exist, there is no supra-human consciousness that could think the human essence. Practically, this means that "man exists first, springs up in a world and is defined afterwards." [2] What he will

---

[1] This thesis, however, characterizes mainly the French Existentialists. In a booklet published after World War II, Heidegger points out the differences between his and Sartre's philosophies, insisting that in his own main work *Sein und Zeit* the relation between essence and existence has never been determined. (See M. Heidegger, "Über den Humanismus," *Platons Lehre von der Wahrheit* [Bern: A. Francke A. G., 1947], esp. pp. 72-73, 79-80, 87.) He finds the name "Existentialism" adequate for Sartre's philosophy, but does not use it for his own.

[2] *L'Existentialisme est un Humanisme*, p. 21.

be defined to be will be his essence, according to Thomas
Aquinas' statement: *"Essentia proprie est id quod significatur
per definitionem."* [3]

It seems to me that Sartre's basic Existentialist thesis implies
a logical difficulty, for it is impossbile to *be* without being *something*. We have already mentioned that Sartre had been warned
by Professor Laporte against the kind of abstraction by which we
think of certain things as isolated which are not made to exist
isolatedly. Existence and essence seem to be such things. However this may be, according to Sartre's theory, we have to accept
the postulate that man is first "here and now" before being something.

But what is it that man will be?—he will be what he will
have made of himself. And thus he will be responsible for what
he is. He is not determined by any previously given essence or
human nature, since, according to Sartre's atheistic assumption,
there is no God, no supra-human consciousness that could preconceive it. Thus man is free, in the sense of not being predetermined—free and responsible for what he makes of himself. [4]

During his whole existence man is making himself, creating
himself an essence which becomes complete only at the moment
of his death. Armand Salacrou, who strongly influenced Sartre,
said: "Without a moment of rest man is a creator of things which
are definitive." [5] The sum of these definitive things created by
man is his essence. In this sense Sartre adopts also Hegel's statement: *"Wesen ist was gewesen ist."* ("Essence is what has
been.")

Thus Sartre can derive man's liberty from the Existentialist
thesis that his existence precedes his essence. For not being determined by a previously given essence, by any concept of human

---

[3] *Summa Theologica*, I. 29, 2 ad 3.

[4] Sartre's and Heidegger's philosophies have often been considered as atheistic in the same sense. Heidegger, however, insists now that his philosophy is
neither theistic nor atheistic. (See Heidegger, *op. cit.*, p. 103.) I am inclined to
call Sartre's philosophy *anti*-theistic, i.e., against any belief in God, and
Heidegger's atheistic, i.e., without belief in God.

[5] *L'Inconnue d'Arras* (Paris, 1936), p. 18.

nature conceived in God's mind, man is free. He exists only in the measure in which he created himself; "he is nothing but the sum of his acts," and there is no reality but in action.[6] Thus, in spite of his atheism, Sartre's Existentialism is not a materialism.

We see now how the atheistic, indeterministic metaphysics of Sartre's Existentialism corresponds to his basic emotional intuition of the universe. For not being determined by any concept of essence or human nature pre-existing to man in God's mind, man's existence lacks necessity; it is completely contingent and gratuitous.

In this sense man is the opposite of the artifact, the object created by man. If, for instance, a sculptor creates a statue or an engineer builds an apparatus, the concept, the "what," the essence of the statue or apparatus, precedes its existence, in the mind of the sculptor or engineer. Every part of the statue or of the apparatus will be absolutely necessary to the whole, and the whole of the artifact will be necessary, too, because it will be determined by the concept pre-existing in the human creator's mind. Consequently in the artifact nothing is contingent, nothing is gratuitous, nothing *de trop* (supernumerary).

On a theistic assumption man is such an artifact and therefore entirely predetermined by his concept, his essence, his nature, pre-existing him in God's mind. But for the atheist nothing in man is predetermined; everything is contingent, gratuitous.

For the atheist Sartre, man is derivable from nothing, he is "supernumerary for eternity."

We have to ask whether, from this standpoint, the difference between man and nature is that between freedom, contingency, and gratuitousness on the one hand, and deterministic necessity on the other. However, on Sartre's atheistic assumption, nature is not an artifact either. And we saw how, in his *Nausea,* he condemned nature as equally gratuitous with man.

[6] *L'Existentialisme est un Humanisme*, p. 55. Thirteen years before Sartre, André Malraux gave exactly the same definition of man in his book *La Condition humaine* (Paris, 1933), p. 270. Also Sartre's other definition of man, as the desire to be God, has been anticipated by Malraux (*ibid.*, p. 271).

Consequently the basic difference between man and nature must consist of something else. That which makes the difference between human consciousness and inanimate nature is the most important thing in Existentialist philosophy: it is *nothing,* or, to be more precise, *nothingness.* This problem is discussed in the next chapter.

CHAPTER SEVEN

BEING AND NOTHINGNESS

What is "being"? What is "nothingness"?

These are the most dynamic questions in modern Existentialism, as they were in ancient Greek philosophy, from the Ionic thinkers and the Eleatics on. The most enlightened discussion of being and nothingness was offered in Plato's dialogue *The Sophist*. After Hegel and Schopenhauer had renewed the discussion, Heidegger took it up, especially in his essay *What Is Metaphysics?* and in his book *Being and Time*. Finally, being and nothingness became the driving forces in the development of Sartre's work bearing this title.

Logically, both of these questions are hopeless. As far as being is concerned, Pascal, three centuries ago, in his treatise *On The Geometrical Spirit* made fun of those "scientists" who try to define a word by the word itself, saying for instance: "Light is a movement of luminous bodies," as if one could understand the word "luminous" without understanding the word "light." And Pascal continued with the very important statement:

One cannot attempt to define being without falling into that same absurdity; for one cannot define a word without beginning by saying *it is*, whether one expresses it or simply implies it. Thus, in order to define being, it would be necessary to say *it is*, and consequently to use the defined word in its definition.[1]

To this penetrating argument of Pascal's I should like to add another: Every definition is the determination of a concept by indicating its higher genus and the *differentia specifica*. But since being is itself the supreme genus, it is evidently impossible to find a higher genus in which it would be included; therefore any definition of being becomes logically impossible.

[1] B. Pascal, "De l'Esprit géométrique," *Pensées et Opuscules*, ed., Brunschvicg (Paris, [1946]), Op. III, p. 169.

As far as nothingness is concerned, it is evident that any definition of it would have to say "Nothingness *is* . . . this or that." But this would be a *contradictio in adjecto,* by which the verb affirms what the noun denies. Any such sentence belongs to those which, according to Carnap, are "grammatically correct and, nevertheless, meaningless." [2]

Plato's "stranger" already realized that

it is impossible rightly to utter or to say or to think of non-being (μὴ ὄν) without any attribute, that it is a thing inconceivable, inexpressible, unspeakable, irrational.[3]

Thus we have to agree with Plato's conclusion "that it is no easier to define the nature of being than that of non-being." [4]

However, instead of realizing that logic reduces the questions, "What is being?" "What is nothingness?" to the absurd, Heidegger drew the opposite conclusion when he stated that by its inability to answer these questions, logic is reduced to the absurd. And with solemnity he proclaimed the dethronement of logic and reason,[5] suggesting somehow the classic case of the lunatic who considers the rest of the world as crazy and himself alone as sane.

Sartre does not go so far as to dethrone logic, although as an Existentialism his philosophy too is basically irrationalistic and prerationalistic; for to him the cognitive mind is only a mode of human existence, something secondary. Vainly struggling to define being, Sartre finally states these three definitions: "Being is. Being is itself. Being is what it is." [6]

With these definitions Sartre, unwillingly, confirms entirely Pascal's statement that one cannot define being without falling into the nonsense of defining this concept by means of the concept which one has to define. In using the word "is" to define "being," Sartre obviously commits the fallacy of *petitio principii,* since he presupposes as defined that which he has to define. He

---

[2] R. Carnap, *Scheinprobleme in der Philosophie* (Berlin, 1928), p. 28.

[3] *The Sophist,* 238 C; Likewise *Theaetetus,* 189 B; *The Republic,* V. 476, E-477, 478 B-C, *passim.*

[4] *The Sophist,* 245 E-246.

[5] *Was ist Metaphysik?* (Bonn, 1929), p. 14; Amer. ed., *Existence and Being,* p. 372, *passim.*

[6] *L'Etre et le Néant,* p. 34.

cannot be blamed, for since being is the highest genus, he cannot
possibly find a higher one in which it would be included. The
only thing for which Sartre can be blamed is for having tried to
define being, following the erroneous path of his master Heidegger.

Nevertheless, Sartre should not be judged as severely as Heidegger, not only because of the difference in the political pasts
of the two thinkers but also because there are other reasons which
justify a neat distinction between them. In the seventeenth century the French writer Boileau spoke a very wise word: *"Ce que
l' on conçoit bien s' énonce clairement."* [7] In Sartre we find a con-
siderable clarity of expression, and his ideas are well conceived,
to the extent to which the irrationalistic matter of Existentialism
allows one to reach rational clarity and logical conceptualization.
Heidegger, however, surrounds his ideas with "that sort of luminous intellectual fog" which, according to Mark Twain, "stands
for clearness among the Germans." [8] Is it that Heidegger did not
refine his thoughts to full clarity, or did his intellectual presump-
tion push him to use a German vocabulary of his own invention
so that he would not have to share that of other people?

However this may be, Heidegger made of Existentialism almost an esoteric science. Before becoming exoteric and a living
force in our society, Existentialism had to be refracted through
the lucid crystal of a Latin mind. And this is Jean-Paul Sartre's.

When this thinker states that "Being is what it is," one would
suppose that he only expresses a presumptuous truism, in the
style of Heidegger's mannerism. However, not without success
Sartre denies the analytical character of the statement, "Being is
what it is," since the other region of being which he distinguishes,
and which he designates with Hegel's term of "being-for-itself"
(*l'être-pour-soi*), is what it is not and is not what it is. Sartre's
"being-for-itself" is human consciousness, while the being he designates with Kant's term "being-in-itself" (*en-soi*) is that of the
phenomena of the external world.

[7] "What is well conceived is clearly expressed," *L'Art poétique*, in *Oeuvres
complètes de Boileau*, X (Paris, [1872]), Chant. I, p. 303.
[8] *A Tramp Abroad* (Hartford, Conn., [1908]), II, p. 293.

What does Sartre mean when he says that the being-for-itself, or, in other words, *man*, is not what he is, while the being-in-itself, or nature, is always what it is? He simply means that man is not a "café waiter" or a soldier or a professor in the same sense as a mountain is a mountain. Café waiter, soldier, or professor is the subject which I have to be, which I imagine, and from which I am separated as the subject is separated from the object—"separated by nothing," says Sartre; "but this nothing isolates me from it, so that I cannot be it. I can only play at being it."

Being originally mere existence without an essence, man *is* not but *makes* himself; and he continues to make himself until he dies. Thus, as long as he is alive, man never coincides with himself, never coincides with the idea he has of himself. Sartre defines man as the "lack" (*manque*) of this coincidence.[9]

Thus man, the "being-for-itself," is full of negation. Being not what he is, man, according to Sartre, is not subjected to the principle of identity—unlike the "being-in-itself," nature, which being what it is does not include any negation and is "as full as an egg." [10]

Man is far from being as full as an egg; he is a "hollow which is always future" (Paul Valéry's *"creux toujours futur"*) and "the being by which nothingness comes into the world." [11] And nothingness comes into the world mainly by man's questioning, for a question always implies the possibility of a negative answer. But while for our logical conception negation is nothing but a quality of our judgment, for Sartre's and Heidegger's metaphysical conception negation has its origin in nothingness, which is a kind of metaphysical power that acts by "naughting" (Sartre's *néantiser* and Heidegger's *nichten*). "Nothingness . . . is the foundation of negation as act, because it is negation as being," Sartre says,[12] although it is obvious, logically, that if nothingness *is* negation as *being*, it is being and no longer nothingness.

We are familiar with Heidegger's preposterous statement,

9 *L'Etre et le Néant*, pp. 98-100, 516, *passim.*
10 *Le Sursis*, p. 52.
11 *L'Etre et le Néant*, p. 60.
12 *Ibid.*, p. 54.

"Das Nichts nichtet," [13] which Sartre transcribes, *"le néant n'est pas, il se néantise."* [14] To translate this nonsense one would have to say, "Nothingness is not, it 'naughts' itself." Thus these authors try to escape from the contradiction of saying "nothingness is." However, it is difficult to find any action either done or suffered by a subject which would correspond to the verb "to naught." This explains why "to naught" does not exist in English, just as the French language does not have the verb *"néantiser,"* nor the German *"nichten."* Besides, even in order to "naught" itself, nothingness would have to "be."

In his last attempt to save a desperate situation, Sartre tries to find his salvation in the passive voice by saying: *"Le néant n'est pas, il est été,"* or *"il est néantisé."* This is a new linguistic monster which must be translated by the nonsense, "nothingness is not, it *is* been," or "it is naught." However, Sartre does not seem to realize that even in order to undergo an action it would be necessary to be something and not a mere nothing. How right was Parmenides, who declared, twenty-five hundred years ago, that one can neither know nor express that which is not: "Never let this thought prevail, saith he, that non-being is; but keep your mind from this way of investigation." [15]

Heidegger and Sartre did not heed the warning of the philosopher of Elea and were drawn into a whirlpool of contradictions.

The fact that nothingness resists every rational attempt to comprehend it does not mean for Existentialists that it does not exist. According to Heidegger, we have an *emotional* proof of the reality of nothingness: it is our anxiety. And Sartre shares his opinion, although he puts more emphasis on Kierkegaard's freedom as the source of anxiety. But, as we shall see later, freedom will also be defined as a manifestation of nothingness.

Since the time of Kierkegaard, anxiety, because of its objectlessness, has constituted the Existentialists' decisive argument against reason. Benjamin Fondane, varying Heidegger's words,

[13] *Was ist Metaphysik?* p. 19.

[14] *L'Etre et le Néant,* p. 53.

[15] Plato, *The Sophist* 237; see also H. Diels, *Die Fragmente der Vorsokratiker* (Berlin, 1934), I, "Parmenides," Fragments 2, 6, 7, 8.

says: "Anxiety reveals to us nothingness, which universal reason tries to conceal from us." [16]

However, the Existentialists do not realize that deducing from anxiety that nothingness is its cause is a logical inference, and hence an act of that odious reason they condemn so scornfully. Moreover, this inference is a logical operation which does not imply any certainty, since it is a conclusion from the effect to the cause. When we see a house burning we cannot infer from this effect a single possible cause of it, but only many different possible causes. The same is true of the conclusion from the effect of anxiety to its presumable cause, nothingness. Freud, for example, saw in the state of anxiety a reproduction of the trauma of birth; [17] and one may easily imagine other inferences of more or less probability.

Sartre says that when questioning "a being as to its being and its manner of being . . . there remains always a possibility that it reveals itself as a nothingness." [18] But when taking this for an *absolute* nothingness, he disregards entirely the clear distinction which Schopenhauer has established between *absolute* nothingness (*nihil negativum*) and *relative* nothingness (*nihil privativum*). Here is what Schopenhauer says: "Every *nothing* is thought of as such only in relation to *something* and presupposes this relation, and also this something." Consequently, Schopenhauer is right in concluding that, logically, and considered more closely, "no absolute nothing, no proper *nihil* is even thinkable, but everything of this kind, when considered from a higher standpoint . . . is always merely a *nihil privativum*." [19] Thus, logically, the Existentialists have no right to consider the not-being or not-being-here as an absolute nothingness.

As a matter of fact, nothingness is only a grammatical substantive expressing a logical relation between a particular subject and a particular predicate, and not at all a designation

---

[16] "Le Lundi existentiel," *L'Existence* (Paris, 1945), p. 35.
[17] *The Problem of Anxiety*, pp. 93, 123, *passim*.
[18] *L'Etre et le Néant*, p. 59.
[19] A. Schopenhauer, *Die Welt als Wille und Vorstellung* (Leipzig, 1892), I, 4, pp. 523-524.

of a substantial being. Identifying linguistic forms with the structure of things expressed by these linguistic forms, Existentialists follow the fallacious path of their teachers, the phenomenologists. Seeing the whole of reality through the network of language, Existentialists have transformed the grammatical substantive "nothingness" into a metaphysical force which acts by "naughting," and can be "present" or "absent" like a thing.

Hypnotized by Heidegger, Sartre operates with the concept of "nothingness" as if his great compatriot Bergson had never written those classical pages in which he reveals nothingness as a "pseudo-idea, a mere word." We speak of "nothing" when we expect to encounter a certain thing and find another in its place, be it mere air. The word "nothing," then, expresses only the disappointment of an expectation, a feeling rather than a thought. Bergson showed that "nothing" concerns the absence not so much of a thing as of a utility.

If I bring a visitor into a room that I have not yet furnished, I say to him that "there is nothing in it." Yet I know the room is full of air; but, as we do not sit on air, the room truly contains nothing that at this moment, for the visitor and myself, counts for anything. In a general way human work consists in creating utility; and as long as the work is not done, there is "nothing"—nothing that we want.[20]

As for "absolute nothingness," Bergson showed that suppressing a thing consists in replacing it with another, and that thinking the absence of one thing is only possible by the representation of the presence of some other thing. But if annihilation signifies substitution, "the idea of an annihilation of everything is as absurd as that of a square circle . . . , since the operation consists in destroying the very condition that makes the operation possible."[21]

According to the American physicist and logician Bridgman, a question has meaning if it is possible to find operations by which an answer can be given. As Bergson showed, there are no such possible operations in the case of nothingness. Consequently the problem of nothingness is meaningless.

[20] H. Bergson, *Creative Evolution* (New York, [1911]), pp. 297-98.
[21] *Ibid.,* p. 283.

However, Sartre believes in nothingness and uses this concept for his distinction between human consciousness and the world.

According to Sartre, there exist many realities, such as distance, absence, alteration, repulsion, regret, and distraction, which are not only objects of man's judgment, but are suffered, opposed, fought, and feared by human beings. They are "inhabited by negation in their inner structure, as a necessary condition of their existence." Sartre calls them *"négatités,"* which should be translated as "negatities." Here again, Sartre was strongly influenced by Heidegger, who wrote:

The permeation of *Da-sein* by nihilating modes of behavior points to the perpetual, ever-dissimulated manifestness of nothing, which only dread reveals in all its originality.[22]

But while in Heidegger there is also much emphasis on the fact that our existence (*Da-sein*) is suspended in nothingness (*die Hineingehaltenheit in das Nichts,* as expressed in one of Heidegger's barbarian neologisms), Sartre is more interested in the nothingness within being.

If nothingness can be given, it is not before and not after being, nor in general, outside being, but in the very womb of being, in its heart, like a worm.[23]

With the *question,* the basic negativity is introduced into the world. But a question presupposes a human being who asks and is basically a human process. The same holds for all the other negatities we mentioned before, so that it is through man, the being-for-itself, that nothingness comes into the world. His main activity is to "naught." This verb "to naught" (*néantiser*) constitutes one of the most obscure concepts in Existentialism. In Heidegger's *"nichten"* it is almost mystical. In Sartre it becomes a little clearer. Already in one of his earlier works, *L'Imaginaire,* Sartre says:

To imagine, to posit an image means . . . to hold the real at a distance, to free oneself of it, in short to deny it. . . . It is by placing himself at a convenient distance from his picture that the impressionist painter will disengage the whole of "forest" from the multitude of little touches which he has put on his canvas. . . . Thus to posit the world as a world, or to naught it, is one and the same thing.[24]

Here the verb "to naught" seems to be a synonym for "to deny," in the sense of "to abstract from." The same seems to be true in the passage where Sartre describes how he enters a café to look for his friend Pierre. He looks at all the tables, but he cannot find him. Sartre speaks, in this case, of a *"néantisation"* ("naughtization") by which all the objects and persons in the café who are not Pierre "are engulfed in the fullness of the background" where Pierre is supposed to appear.[25]

However, Sartre denies the abstract character of the proposition, "Pierre is not in the café," while admitting the abstract character of such statements as "Wellington is not in the café."

It seems that the difference between these two statements lies in the fact that the absence of Pierre has an Existential meaning for the friend who looks for him, while that of Wellington is a mere thought.

Thus, if we try to establish an analogy between the process of abstraction and Sartre's "naughtization," we have to keep in mind that the former is a logical process, while the latter seems to be an *Existential attitude*.

Gabriel Marcel says that "néantiser" means *"entourer d'une région de non-être,"* that is, to surround something with a region of non-being. Sartre himself speaks of a "muff" of non-being, created by "naughtization." If I think my past, I "naught" it in the sense that I place between it and myself a thick layer of emptiness, or non-being. But this does not mean to annihilate it, as Heidegger has already said.

"Naughtization" is a human process. And man is the being by which nothingness, in the form of negatities, comes into the world. Being never what he is, being always separated by a region of non-being from what he has to be according to his idea, being always in the making of himself, man never coincides with

24 *L'Imaginaire* (Paris, 1940), pp. 233-34.
26 *L'Etre et le Néant*, p. 45.

himself, but is "full" of negation, an ever-questioning and denying hollow projected toward the future. Consequently man, the
being-for-itself, is the opposite of nature, the being-in-itself,
which, free from negation, coincides with itself, is what it is, and
is the only object of the principle of identity.

According to Sartre, the negation, which is the prime property of consciousness, arises from the formation of a sort of "vacuum" within the plenitude of being. In this sense he distinguishes
"the mere in-itself," or nature, from "the in-itself surrounded by
that muff of nothingness, which we have designated by the name
for-itself," [26] or consciousness.

Thus that which makes the basic difference between human
consciousness and inanimate nature is, according to Sartre's philosophy, really nothing, or, to be more precise, the "nothingness"
which is in the heart of man.

[26] *Ibid.,* p. 716.

CHAPTER EIGHT

FREEDOM AND ANXIETY, CHOICE AND PROJECT

In a previous chapter [1] we have shown that human freedom follows from the Existentialist assumption that man's existence precedes his essence. This means that man is not determined by any previously given essence or human nature, since, according to Sartre's atheistic assumption, there is no God, no supra-human consciousness that could preconceive man's essence. Thus man is free, in the sense of not being determined.

But this is not the only reason for Sartre's considering man as free. In his main metaphysical treatise he tries to demonstrate that man's freedom coincides with the nothingness which is in his heart and compels him to make himself into something, instead of being something. This latter theory completes the former. Since man has not gotten anything on his way and "nothing comes to him from outside or from inside," [2] man can get an essence, create himself an essence, only by "engaging" himself, in this way or that.

A man who, like Sartre's hero Mathieu in *L'Age de Raison* and *Le Sursis*, is never able to engage himself remains always inessential. Only through engagement can we become essential and fulfill our freedom. Man is free to act, but he must act to be free and to become essential.

Since, according to Sartre, there is no reality but in action and man "is nothing but the sum of his acts," [3] he exists only in the measure he realizes his project; thus, himself. When his friend Brunot, a Communist, comes to see Mathieu to invite him to become a member of the Communist Party, Mathieu hesitates. He

---

[1] Ch. 6, "Existence and Essence."

[2] *L'Etre et le Néant*, p. 516.

[3] *L'Existentialisme*, p. 55.

does not want to engage himself, lest he lose his freedom. Then Brunot says to him: "You are free. But what is freedom good for, if not to engage oneself? . . . You are floating, you are an abstract, an absent one!" [4]

Orestes, in Sartre's grandiose tragedy *Les Mouches* ("The Flies"), had been taught by his tutor that the best thing for a man is to be free for all engagements, but he should never engage himself. At first, on arriving at Argos, Orestes enjoys this situation of a man who is committed to nothing—to no religion, no family, no country, no task. "There are men," he says, "who were born committed: they have no choice, they are cast on a road. . . . I am free, thank God!" [5]

But soon he shows that he is tired of his inessentialness and exclaims:

"Oh, if there were an act, you see, an act which would give me citizen's rights among them (the people of Argos)! If I could only take possession of their memories, their terrors, their hopes, in order to fill the emptiness of my heart, be it by a crime, be it by killing my own mother." [6]

Existentialism has to preach engagement because only by engagement can man, this empty shell, build up his essence. But since *any* kind of engagement fulfills this condition, there seems to be a complete moral equivalence of all possible engagements. Orestes is quite satisfied to become committed, even by killing his own mother, Clytemnestra.

This secondary essence, which man has not inherited but which is his own work and is petrified in his own past (Hegel's *Wesen ist, was gewesen ist*, "Essence is what has been"), would likewise determine him and thus hamper his freedom, if he were not able to separate himself from his past by "nothingness." Thus Sartre defines freedom as "the human being putting his own past out of action by secreting his own nothingness." [7]

If man were considered as fullness, it would be vain to search in him afterward for a region of liberty, just as it would be ab-

4 *L'Age de Raison*, p. 123.
5 *Les Mouches* (Paris, 1943), p. 24.
6 *Ibid.*, p. 26.
7 *L'Etre et le Néant*, p. 65.

surd to look for emptiness in a receptacle which previously had been filled to the brim. "What is important in a vase is the emptiness of the inside." Thus freedom is the nothingness in man's heart which compels him to make himself; it is man's possibility of secreting the nothingness which isolates him and thus of "naughting" everything which is given, including his own past.

In a kind of synthesis of the doctrines of Kierkegaard and Heidegger, Sartre declares that it is by *anxiety* that man becomes conscious of his freedom. This anxiety is understandable in the light of man's situation in a universe interpreted by Existentialism. Being undetermined by any previously given essence or human nature, each individual is what he makes of himself and, consequently, is responsible for what he is.

Man exists at first and "projects" himself toward a future, toward his own possibilities. Thus he is his own project, that which he has projected himself to be.

That is what Sartre, after Kierkegaard and Heidegger, designates as "man's choosing himself," and for him "freedom is freedom of choice." [8]

If we object that we do not have the consciousness to choose ourselves, Sartre replies that this consciousness expresses itself indirectly, by the joint feelings of anxiety and responsibility.

The Existentialist thesis that man chooses himself is certainly one of those which arouses the strongest opposition of common sense. Most of us would agree with Somerset Maugham's affirmation that "a man is not what he wants to be but what he must be." [9]

However, Sartre insists that our choice must not be confused with our will. For what we want to be is a conscious decision and usually subsequent to a more original project. If I want to become a professor, to write a book, to get married, etc., all of this is only a manifestation of a more original choice, "much more spontaneous than that which we call will." [10]

Schopenhauer had already said that only if a man is his own work are his deeds really entirely his and can be ascribed to him.

[8] *Ibid.*, pp. 561, 563, *passim.*
[9] *The Moon and Sixpence* (New York, 1935), p. 28.
[10] *L'Existentialisme est un Humanisme,* p. 24.

And when Schopenhauer continues by saying that "every man is what he is through his will," [11] we have only to replace the word "will" with the word "choice" in order to get Sartre's doctrine.

The difference is mainly terminological, since for Schopenhauer will is no more a conscious decision than is Sartre's choice. "I say," Schopenhauer writes, "that a man is his own work *before* all knowledge, and knowledge is merely added to enlighten it." Sartre would be able to subscribe entirely to this thesis, but he never refers to the father of modern pessimism with whom he shares so many views.

It is interesting to note that with their doctrine of the individual's responsible choice of his self, the Existentialists, as well as Schopenhauer, have a venerable ancestor: Plato. In the tenth book of his *Republic* the father of occidental Idealism tells us his myth of the spirits in the other world. Before being reborn they are told by a prophet of Lachesis to choose the pattern of their future lives. "Let him who draws the first lot have the first choice, and the life which he chooses shall be his destiny. . . . The responsibility is with the chooser—God is blameless." [12]

Does this Platonic myth not seem to contain Existentialism in a nutshell? But as far as the theory of values, and of essences in general, is concerned, Existentialism is—as we shall see later— the most radical anti-Platonism.

If man is what he is through his choice and choice is based on freedom, the responsibility arising from freedom becomes obvious; and this responsibility explains the anxiety linked to our consciousness of freedom. But in Sartre's philosophy this responsibility is even greater than one would suppose, because by his choice man not only engages himself but engages all men, mankind in its entirety. If, for instance, I choose to remain unmarried or to become a thief, I engage the whole of mankind to celibacy or crime; for by my individual choice I create a certain image of man I have chosen and am therefore responsible for myself and for all men.[13]

---

[11] *Die Welt als Wille und Vorstellung*, II, 4, p. 694.
[12] *The Republic*, X, 617 E.
[13] *L'Existentialisme*, p. 27.

"We are responsible to all for all." This sentence of Dostoev-ski's, which Simone de Beauvoir has chosen as the motto for her novel *Le Sang des Autres,* is the essence of the great Russian's ethics. He not only put it into the mouth of the Elder Zossima, in *The Brothers Karamazov,* but also emphasized it as his deep personal conviction in his *Diary of a Writer.* Sartre shares his conviction and tries to give it a philosophical foundation, by say-ing: I am responsible for myself and for all men, because by choosing myself I choose man as I want him to be.

There are moments in which man must ask himself: "Am I the one who has the right to act in such a way that all mankind adjusts itself to my acts?" [14]

This tremendous responsibility, resulting from our freedom of choice, is simply the responsibility for the values of mankind. We shall have to examine now the peculiar form which the prob-lem of values takes in Existentialism.

[14] *Ibid.,* p. 31.

CHAPTER NINE

FREEDOM AND VALUES: SARTRE AND NIETZSCHE

The problem of values is a part of the problem of essence, that is, of general concepts or categories and universal norms. According to the classic tradition, created by Plato, all concrete things exist only because they participate in universal ideas or essences. The Platonic conception was modified by Aristotle, the creator of traditional logic, but he, too, maintained the primacy of general ideas over individuals, stating that there is no science except of the general. In this sense traditional philosophy and science, influenced by Plato and Aristotle, have always been mainly a search for general concepts, universal categories and norms—in short, a search for essences. Thus traditional philosophy is based on the primacy of the universal, objective essences over the concrete, individual existents. We may therefore say that traditional philosophy is *essentialistic*.

Existentialism, on the other hand, proclaims the primacy of the individual, concrete, subjective, single existent over the general, objective essence; and considers that an individual existent is more than a mutilated general concept, since it exists, while the general concept does not exist. A norm is also a general concept or an essence; but since Existentialism denies the primacy of the essence over existence, of the general over the individual, it necessarily must deny that any individual value we express in our valuations is determined by a general norm. For, according to Existentialism, the essences are not given before the existents, but after them. This means that in evaluating we are not determined by any previously given essence or norm, by anything outside ourselves. We judge subjectively, without any objective support, and are responsible for our judgment or evaluation.

For Sartre the problem of values is conditioned by this basic anti-essentialism, by his atheism, and by his theory of freedom. He thinks that if God does not exist, man does not have presented to him any values or hierarchies of values to guide him, legitimize his conduct, or justify his preferences or repulsions and the significance he ascribes to things. Consequently man has to choose in complete aloneness the ways of his conduct and the significance he will ascribe to things, with the entire responsibility for the choice of these values resting on his own shoulders. Without values of universal validity, guaranteed by the authority of a supra-human being, there is no universally binding ethics. Each man has to act without a universal ethics to back him up; he has to act on his own responsibility, without excuse or justification, in complete solitude and dreadful freedom.

This ethical consequence of Sartre's metaphysics is a recurrent theme of his novels and plays. There is, for instance, Mathieu, the professor of philosophy, who finds himself in a dilemma:

He was free, free for everything, free to act like an animal or like a machine, free for accepting, free for refusing, free for shuffling. . . . He could do what he wanted to do, nobody had the right to advise him. There would be neither right nor wrong unless he invented them. . . . He was alone in a monstrous silence, free and alone, without help, without an excuse, condemned to decide without any possible recourse, *condemned forever to be free*.[1]

And, in a similar way, another of Sartre's heroes, Orestes, in the tragedy *Les Mouches*, exclaims:

Suddenly freedom dashed upon me and penetrated me. . . . There was no longer anything in heaven, neither "good" nor "evil," nor anybody to give me orders. . . . I am condemned to have no law other than my own. . . . For I am a man and each man has to invent his own way.[2]

Man is *condemned to be free*—this is the same formula Sartre adopts in his theoretical work.[3] Some may find this formula an exaggeration, for, according to a widespread belief, man loves

[1] *L'Age de Raison*, p. 249.
[2] *Les Mouches*, pp. 100-101.
[3] *L'Etre et le Néant*, p. 515, *passim*.

freedom passionately. Only a profound psychologist like Dostoevski was able to recognize that "nothing has ever been more
insupportable for a man and a human society than freedom."[4]
If a man is free, he is really "condemned" to be free. Sartre's
"moral anxiety" (*angoisse éthique*), the consciousness of man's
freedom in choosing values, is explained by the individual responsibility this choice implies. "My freedom is the only foundation of values," Sartre writes, "and nothing, absolutely nothing
justifies me in adopting this value rather than that, this hierarchy of values rather than another."[5]

From the standpoint of Existentialism, the French disciples
of Sartre who joined the underground were no more justified in
choosing the values of French democracy and fighting for them
in the FFI than the German disciples of Heidegger were in
choosing the values of Nazism and fighting for them in the SS.
"Every time," Sartre writes, "a man chooses his engagement and
projects in all sincerity and lucidity, whatever this choice may
be, it is impossible to prefer another to it."[6]

Placing the difference between "good" and "evil" in an inner
criterion—that of sincerity—Existentialist ethics has to admit a
kind of moral equivalence of all projects, because a Nazi can be
as sincere as a democrat, a murderer as sincere as a benefactor
of mankind.

This is certainly one of the greatest danger spots of Existentialism. Sartre tries to moderate this extreme moral individualism, according to which everybody has his own ethics, by stating: "We should always ask ourselves: What would happen if
everybody would do the same?" And he adds that only by a kind
of "bad faith" can a man evade this reflection when acting. The
one who lies and excuses himself by declaring that not everybody
does the same feels uneasy because the fact of lying implies a
universal value ascribed to the lie.[7]

    [4] F. Dostoevski, *The Brothers Karamazov* (New York: Modern Library,
[1929]), p. 262.
    [5] *L'Etre et le Néant,* pp. 75-76.
    [6] *L'Existentialisme,* pp. 79-80.
    [7] *Ibid.,* pp. 28-29.

Sartre's principle, "We should always ask ourselves: What would happen if everybody would do the same?" has a certain similarity to Kant's categorical imperative. In order to determine the rightness or wrongness of an action, Kant bids us to ask ourselves whether the idea of the proposed action would at the same time be willed as a universal law. But in Kant, rightness and wrongness have an independent, absolute validity, because they are backed up by a universal duty, imperatively demanded by a universal practical reason.

In Sartre's philosophy, on the contrary, there are no standards of rightness and wrongness before each man sets them up by his individual choice, according to the Existentialist principle that the individual existent precedes the general essence; and, even after the individual choice, the resulting moral standard exists only as long as we have not overthrown it by a new "naughting" free act, a new choice. For, according to Sartre, my freedom is the only foundation of values, and since *I am my freedom,* I am the being by which values come into being. Therefore I cannot be justified, because, besides the values which I have set up by my free choice, there are no other values which would justify me in my act of choosing values. Consequently, "I am the foundation without a foundation" of values, and this explains my ethical anxiety. The latter becomes even more acute when we realize that values cannot be established without being, at the same moment, put in doubt, since I keep the possibility of overthrowing, at any moment, the hierarchy of values I have chosen and of replacing it with another.

Thus Sartre's freedom has no limits other than itself, because "we are not free to cease to be free." [8] The *jump* into freedom is indeed a jump into limitlessness and gives us a feeling of anxiety, similar to that which we might have should we jump into an apparently limitless space.

I have not and cannot have recourse to any value when I am confronted with the fact that it is I who maintain the values in being: nothing can protect me against myself—cut from the world and from my essence by the nothingness I am, I have to achieve the sense of

8 *L'Etre et le Néant,* p. 515.

the world and of my essence: I make the decision concerning that sense, alone, unjustifiable, and without excuse.

This is the cause of my " ethical anxiety." [9]

Sartre teaches that man is the being through whom values come into being, and as soon as man realizes that it is he who posits all values, he will not want anything but freedom as the basis of all values. In this sense Existentialism is a *humanism*, because it makes man the only legislator in the realm of values. It is a humanism, also, in that it considers this world a *human* world and man as its "revealer," in so far as man is the means by which things are manifested. For it is man who sets up the relationships among things.

Further, Existentialism is a humanism in so far as it teaches that, having reached his age of reason, man has to recognize that he stands alone in the world and can rely only on himself. As Simone de Beauvoir says, the human individual is an "absolute value," and he alone has to lay the foundations of his own existence. "Every man needs the freedom of other men," she writes.[10] In its atheistic version, Existentialism is an attempt to redefine existence, not in subhuman, materialistic terms, not in suprahuman, theological terms, but in human terms, which are those of subjectivity.

From all these points of view Existentialism is a humanism. It is a humanism, however, only in the sense of the Sophists and their principle "man is the measure of all things," but no longer in the sense of the Stoics. For the Stoic idea of the universal man, or human nature, independent of space and time, subject to the same moral requirements—which form the basis of traditional humanism—has been replaced in Existentialism by the idea of the man here and now, the man of a specific historical epoch and a specific geographical environment.

While Sartre insists that Existentialism is a humanism, Heidegger has always rejected humanism. But after Germany's defeat in World War II, Heidegger rationalized his attitude by

---

[9] *Ibid.*, pp. 75, 77.

[10] *Pour une Morale de l'Ambiguité* (Paris, 1947), pp. 100, 218; Amer. ed., *The Ethics of Ambiguity* (New York: Philosophical Library, 1948).

writing: "I think against humanism, because it does not place man's humanity high enough." [11] Was this the reason that he joined the Nazi Party?

Sartre's axiological humanism—the idea that man is the only legislator in the realm of values—rests on his and Heidegger's Existentialist thesis that our knowing mind is only secondary to our existence, a mode of our existence, and that reason comes into being only through freedom. Consequently this freedom or this existence cannot be limited by any product of reason or knowledge, such as truth or significance, or by values and things recognized.

Things are determined by things. But being himself free, man is anything but a thing and can therefore not be determined by things. There are some people who realize this, who recognize their freedom and consider themselves as free creators and the unfounded foundation of all values. They assume responsibility for their value-founding choice and the anxiety arising from it. According to Sartre, they exist "authentically" and in "good faith."

The great majority of people, however, deny their freedom, hiding it from themselves with all kinds of deterministic excuses. They exist "unauthentically." They are "cowards" or, as far as they try to prove the necessity of their existence, they are "stinkers" (salauds). By denying this freedom, they try to flee from anxiety by grasping themselves from outside, as a thing. But we cannot overcome our anxiety, because, according to Sartre, " we are anxiety." I cannot flee from what I am. I can flee in order not to know, but I must know that I am fleeing. Consequently the flight from anxiety is only a way of becoming conscious of our anxiety. But that means apprehending anxiety "in bad faith."

Those who, in order to evade their freedom, responsibility, and anxiety, choose to consider themselves as things, determined by other things, will also consider values as given things by which they are being determined. They are possessed by what Sartre calls the "spirit of seriousness" (esprit de sérieux), designating the tendency to "consider values as transcendent data, independ-

11 "Über den Humanismus," *Platons Lehre von der Wahrheit*, p. 75.

ent of human subjectivity." [12] Dominated by this spirit, a person renounces his human condition by renouncing his freedom to choose the values in which he will believe—the significance he will ascribe to things—because he is afraid of responsibility, afraid of anxiety. Heidegger says that most people have no "courage for anxiety" (*Mut zur Angst*).[13] But that is exactly what Existentialism requires of us: courage for anxiety. Those who do not have it, those who are dominated by the "spirit of seriousness," submit themselves to the hierarchy of values, standards, and significances set up in a given society and transmitted by education and convention. He who accepts these ready-made, thing-like values gives up his human personality. For, as Nietzsche had said already, the word "man" means "valuator." [14] But, at the same time, the spirit of seriousness will deliver man from the responsibility of a value-choosing freedom and help him to hide his anxiety from himself.

The man dominated by the spirit of seriousness is merely an overgrown child, because for the child every new thing "has already been seen, named, and classified by other people. Each object presents itself to him with a label; it is extremely reassuring and even sacred, because the look of adult persons still clings to it. Far from exploring unknown regions, the child skims through an album; he takes the census of a herbarium." [15]

As already mentioned, many persons remain all their lives in this axiological condition of children, accepting ready-made values and becoming something like value-registering automatons. This is their "spirit of seriousness," which Existentialism is fighting.

Only now are we able to understand why Sartre declares in *La Nausée* that "nobody has rights" and calls those who believe in them "stinkers". It is because rights are also a kind of given, thing-like, ready-made values: substantialized, guaranteed values which precede us and determine us as things determine

---

[12] *L'Etre et le Néant*, p. 721.

[13] *Sein und Zeit*, p. 254.

[14] *Also sprach Zarathustra* (Leipzig, 1899), p. 86.

[15] Sartre, *Baudelaire* (Paris, 1947), p. 60; Amer. ed., *Baudelaire* (copyright by New Directions [New York, 1950]).

things, hiding from us our freedom to set up new aims. In his essay "Matérialisme et Révolution" Sartre says that idealism mystifies the revolutionary worker "by binding him with already given rights and values and masking from him his power of inventing his own paths." And he adds that "materialism, too, mystifies him by robbing him of his freedom." [16]

This latter remark indicates the crux of Sartre's conflict with the Communists, whose philosophy is based on Marx's deterministic dialectical materialism. On the one hand, Sartre, who, too, pretends to be a revolutionary, argues that Communism involves the contradiction of seeking human freedom through its materialistic denial; on the other hand, the Communists argue that by teaching that he is free, Sartre betrays the revolutionary worker, since if he were free he would no longer need to liberate himself by revolutionary action. Besides, they insist that dialectical materialism, too, admits human freedom, in the form defined by Friedrich Engels as the recognition of necessity. As a Hegelian, Engels thought that "freedom does not consist in an imaginary independence of natural laws but in a knowledge of these laws and in the possibility thence derived of applying them intelligently to given ends." [17]

But we will not delve into the details of this controversy between two political philosophies which has no bearing on the universal questions we are examining here.[18] Let us only sum up that, according to Sartre, only those possessed by the "spirit of seriousness" believe in ready-made, constituted values and rights, which they can find in society as they find things in nature. He who is aware of his freedom has to invent new values, new rights.

There is still another reason why Sartre rejects constituted

---

[16] "Matérialisme et Révolution," *Les Temps Modernes*, II, 10 (July, 1946), pp. 13-14.

[17] *Landmarks of Scientific Socialism* (Chicago, [1907]), p. 147.

[18] The American reader can find a more thorough analysis of the political aspects of Existentialism in Marjorie Grene's remarkable book *Dreadful Freedom* (Chicago, 1948); in H. Marcuse's valuable review "Remarks on J. P. Sartre's *L'Etre et le Néant*," in *Philosophy and Phenomenological Research*, VIII, 3 (March, 1948); in Auguste Cornu's essay "Bergsonianism and Existentialism," *Philosophic Thought in France and the United States*, ed. by Marvin Farber (Buffalo, 1950), pp. 151-168, etc.

values: He does not believe that in any concrete situation they would help to guide our action or to determine our conduct.

Sartre describes the case of a young Frenchman who, during the German occupation, had to choose between staying with his mother, who needed his help, and going to England with the Free French Forces. Thus he had to choose between two values: his duty as a son and his duty as a patriot. Which one should he choose? Constituted ethics could not help him, for it prescribes duties toward our parents and duties toward our country without telling us which of these duties is superior in a concrete, conflicting case. Thus the young Frenchman had to choose on his own responsibility, without the backing of constituted ethics.

From cases like this Sartre infers that "there is no general ethics." [19] But in this I think he goes too far. In the case mentioned a choice had to be made between two *positive* values, filial love and patriotic duty; and in such cases we have really to invent a solution on our own responsibility, without being backed up by constituted ethics.

However, if a decision must be made between a positive and a negative, I think that traditional ethics of constituted values would guide us with perfect security. If our neighbor's house has burned down, the traditional ethics of constituted values commands us, with perfect clarity, to give him shelter. And if when confronted with the choice between the positive value of assisting a person who suffers and the negative value of abandoning him, we choose the negative one, our bad conscience indicates to us which of these values was the positive one and which the negative. In my opinion, in the case of choice between a positive and a negative value we need not invent our own solution but merely follow the imperatives of the constituted moral values.

So we would not say, like Sartre, that "there is no general ethics," but simply that there are cases in which general ethics is insufficient to guide us and where we have to invent our own paths, on our own personal responsibility.

Sartre described the case of one of his comrades in a German prison camp, who told him that after having had many failures

19 *L'Existentialisme*, p. 47.

in his life he had chosen to become a Jesuit priest, because in these failures he saw a sign from heaven that he should give up secular life and take holy orders. But, as Sartre says, it was this man who chose that kind of interpretation of his failures, and, without knowing it, invented his own path, on his own responsibility.

I think a similar situation can be found in Maxwell Anderson's beautiful play, *Joan of Lorraine,* where the heroine, desperate that she cannot prove the authenticity of her visions and voices, is told by St. Michael that the bishops, who demand such proof, are equally unable to prove the authenticity of their views:

> The Church itself is built on revelations and these revelations came out of darkness and went back into darkness like your own. . . . In all the articles of belief and creed not one is capable of proof.[20]

Consequently everybody has to choose his interpretation of facts and bear the responsibility for his choice, with all the anxiety arising from the fact of his not being backed up by anything. Thus we can understand Sartre's affirmation that "even if God existed, this would not change anything. . . . It is necessary that man find himself and convince himself that nothing can save him from himself." [21]

If Sartre wished to teach that action is a response to a unique situation and is a unique creative response, he could have referred to Aristotle's *Nicomachean Ethics,* where we are told that in the matter of action the general concepts are empty, since every action is related to a special situation and requires special concepts.

However, Aristotle is not the only predecessor of Sartre; it must also be shown how much Sartre owes to Nietzsche, to whom he refers very seldom and never in any essential matter. Nevertheless, it is the essential which Sartre's philosophy shares with that of Nietzsche.

Let us begin with individualism of values and of ethics based on atheism. Here Sartre writes:

[20] *Joan of Lorraine* (New York, 1948), p. 128.
[21] *L'Existentialisme,* p. 95.

Since I have abolished God, the father, there must be somebody to invent values. . . . Life has no significance a priori. Before you were alive, life was nothing; it is up to you to give it a significance, and value is nothing but that significance you are choosing.[22]

And Nietzsche, after having proclaimed that "God is dead," [23] declares of values:

Verily, men have given unto themselves all their good and bad. Verily, they took it not, they found it not, it came not unto them as a voice from heaven.

Man merely assigned values to things in order to maintain himself; he created the significance of things, a human significance! Therefore, calleth he himself "man," that is, the valuator.

Valuing is creating: hear it, ye creating ones! Valuation itself is the treasure and jewel of the valuated things.

Through valuation only is there value; and without valuation the nut of existence would be hollow. . . .[24]

Comparing these two enunciations, one will find that they say exactly the same thing; only Nietzsche made his sixty years before Sartre and did it with more distinction and poetic ardor.

The "spirit of seriousness" (*esprit de sérieux*) also had been discovered by Nietzsche sixty years before it was uttered by Sartre. And the name Nietzsche chose for it is very similar to the one chosen by Sartre, that is to say "the spirit of gravity" (*Geist der Schwere*). Nietzsche, too, opposed it, as vigorously as Sartre. Here is how Nietzsche characterized the spirit of gravity:

Almost in the cradle are we apportioned with heavy words and worths: "good" and "evil" so calleth itself this dowry. For the sake of it we are forgiven for living . . . so causeth the spirit of gravity.

And we—we bear loyally what is apportioned unto us, on hard shoulders, over rugged mountains! And when we sweat, then do people say to us: "Yea, life is hard to bear."

But man himself only is hard to bear! The reason thereof is that he carrieth too many extraneous things on his shoulders. Like a camel kneeleth he down, and letteth himself be well laden.

22 *Ibid.*, pp. 89-90.
23 *Zarathustra, Prol.*, p. xii.
24 *Ibid.*, "Von tausend und einem Ziele," Pt. I, p. 86.

Especially the strong load-bearing man in whom reverence resideth. Too many *extraneous* heavy worths loadeth he upon himself—then seemeth life to him a desert.[25]

And in another paragraph, Nietzsche says:

. . . I also found again mine old devil and arch-enemy, the spirit of gravity, and all it created: constraint, law, necessity and consequence, and purpose and will, and good and evil.[26]

This is exactly the "spirit of seriousness" by which Sartre characterizes a man who passively accepts values invented by others, kneeling down like an animal to be loaded with them, like Nietzsche's camel, renouncing his liberty of inventing his own values, his own standards for good and evil.

If Sartre is opposed to those who believe in already given rights, so that they need not create new ones, Nietzsche expressed a similar idea. In his *Will to Power* he wrote: "The belief that the world as it should be really exists, is the belief of unproductive men who do not want to create a world as it should be." [27]

We have seen the intimate link between freedom and responsibility in Sartre's philosophy. However, sixty years earlier, Nietzsche had already asked: "What is freedom? That one has the will to self-responsibility." [28]

In her novel *Le Sang des Autres* ("The Blood of the Others"), Simone de Beauvoir resumes the problem of values as it had been posed—or reiterated—by Sartre. She writes: "I believe that your error is to imagine that your reasons for being should fall to you ready-made from heaven: it is up to you to create them." [29]

We already know that Nietzsche taught the same thing sixty years before Madame de Beauvoir when he wrote that "man merely assigned values to things . . . he created the significance

[25] *Ibid.*, "Vom Geist der Schwere," Pt. III, p. 283.

[26] *Ibid.*, "Von alten und neuen Tafeln," Pt. III, p. 289.

[27] *Der Wille zur Macht*, in *Werke* (Leipzig, 1922), XVI, 3, 4, Buch 585 A, p. 84.

[28] *Götzendämmerung*, in *Gesammelte Werke* (Munich, 1926), XVII, 38, p. 137.

[29] *Le Sang des Autres* (Paris, 1945), pp. 67-68.

of things, . . ." etc. He was even prepared for the objection made
by Madame de Beauvoir's heroine, who says: "But if we know
that we ourselves create these reasons for being we can no longer
believe in them! That is nothing but a way of duping ourselves." [30]

To this Nietzsche replied, by anticipation, in his *Will to
Power:* "Reject the humble expression, 'Everything is subjective!' Say rather, 'It is our work! Let us be proud of it!' " [31]

Thus Nietzsche's theory of the subjectivity and individuality
of all values, his thesis that they are not given but are created by
man, his affirmation that there is no universally binding ethics,
etc., are integral parts of Sartre's Existentialism. And since Sartre himself never gave to Nietzsche the credit he deserves, we
have had to do it.

On the other hand, we must emphasize an important distinction between Nietzsche's and Sartre's theories of values: While
Nietzsche requires that the individual remain faithful to the values freely created and the norms freely set up by himself, Sartre
teaches that everybody can posit his values and norms differently, on different occasions.

Boris, an important figure in those novels of Sartre which
have been integrated in *Les Chemins de la Liberté,* gives the following definition of freedom:

The individual's duty is to do what he wants to do, to think whatever he likes, to be accountable to no one but himself, to challenge,
again and again, every idea and every person.[32]

We would be inclined to consider this a caricature of Existentialism, as the concept of freedom of an idiot. For, in spite of his
being described as a student of philosophy at the Sorbonne and
as a former pupil—and a preferred one—of Profesor Mathieu
Delarue (for which read, "Professor Jean-Paul Sartre"), Boris is
not very bright, and his moral and spiritual horizon (*sit venia
verbo*) is no broader than that of the average Parisian gigolo.

30 *Ibid.,* p. 68.
31 *Wille zur Macht,* IV, 1059, in *Gesammelte Werke* (Munich, [1926]), XIX,
p. 368.
32 *L'Age de Raison,* p. 143.

However, in Sartre's main theoretical work we find some passages which seem to justify Boris. See, for instance, the following:

Since freedom is being-without-any-support, without any springboard, the project must be renewed permanently, in order to be. I am choosing myself perpetually . . . otherwise I should fall back into the mere existence of a thing-in-itself.[33]

But if I have to choose myself perpetually to avoid being debased to thinghood, what guarantees that I will always choose myself in the same way? Sartre recognizes this danger and says:

We are perpetually threatened by the naughtization of our present choice, perpetually threatened by choosing ourselves, and, consequently, becoming other than we are.[34]

Thus our choice and valuation of the whole world would be different, since by choosing himself man chooses the world.

We know Sartre's thesis—in conformity with Nietzsche's—that value does not reveal itself to a contemplative intuition which would grasp it as being a value, for this would restrict human freedom. Value is only revealed to an active freedom which makes it exist by the mere fact of recognizing it as such. It seems that Sartre is afraid that even the values which we set up by a free creative choice would, in the long run, become for us ready-made things, and thus hamper our freedom; ready-made by ourselves, to be sure, but nevertheless ready-made with respect to a present or future moment of our existence. Freedom, according to Sartre, is the possibility of "naughting" the past, my own past and all the values created by myself in that past.

In its radicalism this philosophy of freedom tries to avoid our becoming slaves not only of values set up by other people, but also of values set up by ourselves. In Sartre's philosophy Bergson's idea of life as an eternal renewal finds its most perfect expression.

On the other hand, Existentialism dissolves the classical unitary universe of values not only into a multiplicity of axiological

[33] *L'Etre et le Néant*, p. 560.
[34] *Ibid.*, p. 543.

microcosms, into millions of creative egos, each of which has its own world of values; it goes so far as to dissolve each ego into thousands of momentary egos, each of which has its own world of values and its own ethics. And while for Nietzsche the value-creating moral individualism is only the privilege of certain exceptional beings (He who cannot command himself has to obey, he says), in Sartre's philosophy all men can attain freedom if they make the necessary effort. In his system moral pluralism has reached its utmost extreme.

It is true that in Simone de Beauvoir's *Ethics of Ambiguity* we find something of Nietzsche's postulate to remain faithful to one's creative choice of values. "To will," she says, "means to commit myself to persevere in my will." [35] And in Sartre's more recent writings on literary and political subjects we find a tendency toward fidelity to one's original choice. This tendency, however, is not substantiated by his theoretical philosophy as explained in *L'Etre et le Néant*. In dealing with the concrete problems which he encounters as an editor of a monthly magazine, Sartre puts more and more water in his wine. But here we wish to examine the pure essence of his philosophy.

[35] *Pour une Morale*, p. 39.

CHAPTER TEN

SECOND CRITICAL INTERMEZZO

The dissolution of the ethical universe in Sartre's philosophy means an utmost axiological atomism, not only in space but also in time. In Sartre's world everyone should invent one's own values and norms and is free to invent them differently on different occasions. However, I do not see how in such a world any community would be possible, not even a community of two persons, for even this would suppose a certain continuity of evaluation.[1]

The strangest thing in Sartre's philosophy of values is the fact that a constituted value or right, by the mere fact of its being constituted, is an anti-value, or a "stinker's" right. But cannot a constituted value be a positive value, a constituted right be a valuable right? One would think so, since, after all, this seems to depend only on the contents of the value or right. No, says Sartre, a constituted value or right cannot have any positive character because a value or right, by the basic fact that it is constituted, limits our freedom and masks our power of inventing our own paths.

We have here another proof Sartre's uncompromising absolutism, so typical of the Existentialist temperament. It compels him to place the criterion of values in their state of aggregation rather than in their contents, so that only a value *in statu nascendi* would be a positive one, no matter what it expresses.

We have our doubts whether this radical axiological individualism of Sartre's is truly sincere. For if, in addition to the values we set up by our individual choices, there are no other values, why should we then suffer from that "ethical anxiety" which pervades the whole of Sartre's work? In our opinion "ethical anxi-

[1] John Dewey was right in insisting that to form a community "there must be values prized in common." *Freedom and Culture* (New York, 1939), p. 12.

ety" presupposes the belief in absolute standards, independent of our choices—standards which we are afraid of violating by our individual choices of values. Is it not that Existentialists believe in such absolute standards emotionally, while denying them intellectually? Only under this assumption does the concept of "ethical anxiety" appear meaningful.

Stating that "the revolutionary philosophy must always be a philosophy of transcendence," going beyond any state it has reached, Sartre's philosophy implies the idea of a permanent revolution against all constituted values and rights, even those constituted by one's own revolution. Thus the revolutionary would never be able to enjoy the values and rights he had fought for; and we may ask ourselves, why then should he fight for them? Miss Marjorie Grene is right when she says, "Here revolution for freedom implies revolution against freedom"; [2] and sees in this a hint of a much more profound difficulty in Existential theory: that freedom as such does not appear to be an adequate replacement for more substantive conceptions of values. John Dewey had already insisted on the merely negative character of freedom.

Maintaining that by accepting constituted values and rights man loses his freedom and is debased to thinghood, Sartre's philosophy seems to be inconsistent with any society; for every society, even a socialist one, is built on certain constituted values and rights.

In his attempt to rehabilitate subjectivity Sartre took into consideration only the subjective side of values. But in addition to expressing the appreciation of some subject and thus a subjective feeling, most values have objective validity and transcend the subject.

How can these two characteristics be reconciled? How can a sentiment be independent of the subject who feels it?

These questions have been answered by Emile Durkheim, the brilliant French sociologist, in the sense that our appreciation is objective by the reason of its being collective. There are social judgments which in comparison with individual judgments are

[2] *Dreadful Freedom,* p. 115.

objective. The hierarchy of values is thus found to be separated from the subjective and variable sensibilities of individuals.

The latter find outside themselves a pre-established classification which is not their work, which expresses something completely other than their personal feelings, and to which they are forced to conform.[3]

This fact is explained by Durkheim's whole conception of society as something other than a simple collection of individuals; the system formed by the association of individuals represents a definite specific reality that has its own traits. Naturally nothing can come from the collectivity if individual minds do not exist. But, according to Durkheim, this necessary condition is not sufficient. These minds must be associated and combined in a certain manner for a society to exist. From this combination social life follows; and it is this combination which explains it. In aggregating, interpenetrating, and fusing, the individual souls give birth to a being that constitutes a psychic entity of a new kind. Durkheim calls it "collective consciousness" and considers it as distinct from the individual minds which constitute it.[4]

Of course, this collective consciousness, resulting from the fusion of individual consciousnesses, must also have values which are different from those of the individuals. This explains why the individuals find outside themselves a pre-established hierarchy of values which is not their individual work, which expresses something other than their personal feelings, and to which they are forced to conform.

Durkheim has shown that this pressure, which is exerted on each by the whole, is the criterion of any social phenomenon, of any society. In rejecting this pressure as an attack on individual freedom, Sartre simply rejects society, in spite of all his protests; and his philosophy of values seems to me much closer to anarchy than to socialism, for which Sartre pretends to fight.

Since social life transcends infinitely the life of the individual

[3] "Jugements de Valeur et Jugements de Réalité," *Sociologie et Philosophie* (Paris, 1951), pp. 122-123.

[4] *Les Règles de la Méthode sociologique* (Paris, 1895); Amer. ed., *The Rules of Sociological Method*, trans. by S. A. Solovay and J. H. Mueller and edited by G. E. G. Catlin (Chicago, 1938).

in time and in space, it seems to me that its values cannot simply be rejected in the name of a strangely conceived rehabilitation of subjectivity.

In fighting all established values and rights, Sartre uses also the Marxian argument that "the system of values current in a society reflects the structure of that society and tends to preserve it." [5] However, even this argument would not refer to all values without any distinction. The fact that every value is a relation between an object and an appreciating subject permits the designation of all values as "subjective"; and this seems to confirm Sartre's doctrine. However, in my opinion, subjectivity of values does not necessarily mean individuality of values, because, in spite of their being relations of objects to appreciating subjects, values can be independent of the individual peculiarities of the appreciating subjects.

In one of my books I have made the following distinctions: individual values are those which depend on the individual peculiarities of the appreciating subjects, while objective values are those which, in spite of their being relations between objects and appreciating subjects, are independent of the individual peculiarities of the appreciating subjects. These objective values can be divided into collective and universal values. Collective values, I define as those which depend on the collective peculiarities of the social group that affirms them; and universal values, as those which, in spite of their being likewise relations between objects and appreciating subjects, are independent of both the individual and the collective peculiarities of those who affirm them.[6]

If we apply this distinction to Sartre's argument, it seems that only the system of *collective* values current in a society reflects the structure of that society and tends to preserve it; while this can be affirmed of neither the individual nor the universal

---

[5] "Matérialisme et Révolution," *Les Temps Modernes,* I (1946), p. 12; K. Marx and F. Engels "Manifesto of the Communist Party," II, *Capital, The Communist Manifesto and other Writings by Karl Marx,* M. Eastman (New York, [1932]), p. 338.

[6] See A. Stern, *Philosophie du Rire et des Pleurs* (Paris, 1949), pp. 207-31; "Society and Values," *The Personalist* (Los Angeles), XXIX, 3 (Summer, 1948), pp. 242-51.

values, such as, for instance, those of logical and mathematical truth.

But Sartre makes no distinction among individual, collective, and universal values; thus his struggle against constituted values refers to all of them, indistinctively. This makes clear that his philosophy of values is a theory which lumps together all values.

On a closer analysis, Sartre's postulate, that each person has to invent his own system of values, is quite inconsistent, since it arises from a disregard of past history and civilization. The average individual born in this world has to accept a tremendous quantity of empirical and scientific truths, which have been constituted by a long historical evolution and form the patrimony of human civilization. Of course, everybody has the right to question any of these truths if he has serious reasons for believing that they are not truths but errors. The great reformers of science have done it, for the benefit of mankind. But it would be foolish to request—not in the name of truth but in that of freedom—that each individual perform again all scientific experiments and re-invent all scientific theories, disregarding totally the achievements of four thousand years of civilization, *not* because these achievements are considered *erroneous,* but simply because they are *constituted.* It seems to me equally foolish to request, in the name of freedom, that each individual re-invent all his moral and aesthetic values, again disregarding those constituted by civilization's four thousand years, not because they are unreasonable but only because they are constituted. If Nietzsche tried to "transvaluate" our moral values, he did so because he believed that these values were wrong, that they were based on a false principle, but *not* because they were constituted.

On one hand, the re-invention of all moral and aesthetic values by each individual would be practically impossible; on the other hand, it would be extremely unjust toward the history of civilization, that is to say, toward the work of the hundreds of generations that have lived and striven before us. Sartre may easily say, "We do not believe in progress";[7] but this does not sweep away the tremendous body of moral values, and orders of

[7] *L'Existentialisme,* p. 79.

moral values, set up since the instructions of Ptah-Hotep (4000 B.C.), by Moses' Ten Commandments, the teachings of Buddha, Confucius, the Stoics, Christ, Spinoza, Kant, and the modern social moralists. The same is true for the body of aesthetic values and standards set up since Myron, Polycleitus, and Praxiteles through Michel Angelo, Delacroix, and French Impressionism up to Surrealism; or from Homer to Shakespeare, Goethe, and Verlaine; or from Palestrina to Debussy. To disregard these bodies of constituted moral and aesthetic values, *only because they are constituted,* would mean to disregard four thousand years of civilization, of human history; and it would mean for each man to begin civilization *ab ovo,* to become an artificial primitive.

"I am of bad faith," Sartre says, "if I choose to declare that certain values existed before me." [8] But I think Sartre is of bad faith in denying them, and thus denying history, civilization, and our spiritual heritage, which he himself uses so extensively.

Of course, the individual should not accept all constituted values *blindly,* as if they were things found in nature. For value is a correlative concept which always supposes subjective valuation. As soon as the latter disappears and is replaced with values which impose themselves not by their dignity but by the mere fact of their being constituted, the concept of value itself will disappear, and axiology will turn into ontology. I think I have shown that this is one of the consequences of the phenomenology of values of Max Scheler and Nikolai Hartmann.[9] In this respect Sartre's struggle against the "spirit of seriousness" is justified to a certain extent, just as is Nietzsche's war on the "spirit of gravity."

If, following Aristotle's maxim, we try to find the middle road between the extremes of Sartre's Existentialist and Scheler-Hartmann's essentialistic conceptions of values, we should say: Values should not be *rejected* for the mere reason of their being

---

[8] *Ibid.,* p. 81.

[9] See A. Stern, "Le Problème de l'Absolutisme et du Relativisme axiologiques," *Revue Internationale de Philosophie* (Brussels, 1939); "The Current Crisis in the Realm of Values," *The Personalist* (Los Angeles), XXXI (Summer, 1950), pp. 245-59.

constituted; they should not be *accepted* for the mere reason of their being constituted. What we should do is to *re-evaluate* the constituted values, accepting those which we find compatible with our moral and aesthetic conscience, rejecting those which are not, and invent new values where we find it necessary. In some of my books I have tried to show on what principles our moral, aesthetic, or, in short, axiological, conscience is built; but the arguments need not be repeated here.[10]

By the proposed re-evaluating of constituted values we would still have enough freedom left to invent new axiological paths, especially in those cases where constituted values turn out to be insufficient to guide our conduct. In such cases, where action becomes a unique creative response to a unique situation, our value-inventing freedom can manifest itself in full.

However, in those cases where there are systems of constituted values to guide us, we should re-evaluate them and try to understand why they were precious to our fathers and forefathers. Then we may accept or reject them according to their merits. It is in this sense that we should understand Goethe's admonition: "What thou hast inherited from thy fathers, acquire it to make it thine."

[10] See A. Stern, *Die philosophischen Grundlagen von Wahrheit, Wirklichkeit, Wert* (Munich-Basle, 1932), esp. pp. 322-430; *La Filosofía de los Valores* (Mexico City, 1944), esp. pp. 181-215; "The Current Crisis in the Realm of Values," *The Personalist* (Los Angeles), XXXI (Summer, 1950), pp. 245-259, *passim*.

CHAPTER ELEVEN

LITERATURE AND FREEDOM

Freedom is the all-powerful, triumphant idea in Existentialism. We have already seen how this idea shaped Sartre's ontology, his axiology, and his ethics. Now we shall see that the idea of freedom also dominates Sartre's concept of literature and politics.

In his book, *What Is Literature?* [1] Sartre propounded the theory that literature, and any other kind of art, is a social phenomenon. It is not just a way of individualistic self-liberation of the writer, and Sartre denies that the author writes for himself. He writes for the reader and needs the reader for the complete performance of his work, just as the painter needs the spectator and the composer the listener. All the words of a book could be read one by one and still the meaning of the work would not emerge were it not that the reader's mind gives it meaning. In other words, the meaning of a novel or a poem must be a meaning to the reader; the image suggested by the writer must be formed by the reader's mind; the thought that the author wants to convey must be the reader's thought, the result of the reader's intellectual and emotional activity. Without it, there would not be any literature, any art. Sartre calls this mental and emotional activity of the reader or spectator a "re-invention" and says: "It is the conjoint effort of author and reader which brings upon the scene that concrete and imaginary object which is the work of the mind. There is no art except for and by others." [2]

Sartre recognizes that the author guides the reader's and spectator's mental activity, "but all he does is guide him. The land-

[1] *What Is Literature?* (New York, [1949]).
[2] *Ibid.*, p. 43.

marks he set up are separated. . . . The reader must unite them.
. . . In short, reading is directed creation." [3]

It is astonishing that Sartre presents this doctrine as if it were
his own, although it had been propounded several decades before
him by Benedetto Croce. Sartre, however, never mentioned Croce
as the real inventor of the aesthetic doctrine of collaboration of
the artist and his public.

Croce had pointed out that in order to have aesthetic experience, the spectator or reader must be actively creating.

Everyone of us is something of a painter, something of a sculptor,
something of a musician, something of a poet: but how little in comparison with those who are so called just because of the higher degree
in which they possess the most common dispositions and energy of
human nature! [4]

Furthermore, he says, "the little dose of inventive imagination I
possess requires the aid of Shakespeare to intensify it to the
point of forming within itself the whole tragedy of Othello's
passion." [5]

There are different possible explanations of Sartre's adoption
of Croce's aesthetic theory without mentioning its author: He
might not have known Croce's aesthetics and have arrived independently at the same conclusions as the Italian philosopher. Or
he might have read Croce's aesthetic theories a long time ago and
have assimilated them so fully that he finally believed they were

[3] *Ibid.*, p. 45.

[4] B. Croce, *Estetica* (Bari, 1928), p. 14.

[5] *Problemi di Estetica* (Bari, 1923), p. 471. Croce's aesthetic doctrine has
been widely criticized. In his excellent *Introduction to Aesthetics* (New York,
1952), esp. pp. 145-147, Hunter Mead insists on the reciprocal influence between
the artist's idea and the material in which it is expressed. In the process of
artistic expression, which requires the solution of many technical problems, the
artist is often forced to modify his original idea. Professor Mead denies that any
appreciating layman can possibly reproduce these creative experiences of the
artist, so that appreciation cannot be considered a subform of creation. Mead's
objection mainly refers to painting, sculpture, and music, but—though to a lesser
extent—also holds good for literature; language too has its material and formal
problems, unknown to the reader, which the writer has to solve. While the spectator, listener, and reader cannot truly reproduce the artist's creative experience,
I think that they must at least perform those mental and emotional processes
which the painter, musician, or writer suggests by his work.

his own. The analysis of his relation to Nietzsche has already shown that Sartre has a tremendous power of assimilation of other people's thoughts. This gift has also its positive aspects, for it leads Sartre sometimes to an interesting development of the foreign ideas he has adopted. This is especially true of Croce's aesthetic doctrine.

Since the creation of the writer can find its fulfillment only in the reader's intellectual and emotional activity, Sartre concludes that the writer appeals to the reader's freedom to collaborate in the production of the work. With this conclusion Sartre goes beyond Croce. If the reader believes in the writer's story it is because of his free choice to believe in it, because of a kind of "will to believe," to use a term from William James, but without its theological implications. In developing his doctrine Sartre tries to show that the reader's feelings have their source in freedom and are, therefore, generous. "The author writes in order to address himself to the freedom of readers, and he requires it in order to make his work exist." [6]

On the other hand, the writer requires that the reader recognize his creative freedom, and thus reading becomes a pact of generosity between the author and the reader. They must trust each other, and this confidence springs from generosity. All apparent casualty in a work of art is based on finality. Sartre gives the example of a certain tree on the first plane of a painting of Cezanne's, which is in this place not because of natural causes, but because of a plan of the whole or a finality, the source of which is the artist's creative freedom.

With the concept of finality Sartre takes up a basic idea of Kant's aesthetics, in spite of criticizing it, and in many respects Sartre's aesthetics is a synthesis of Kant's and Croce's theories. Art, Kant says, should look "as if" it were nature; it must be the result of finality and thus of freedom, but this finality should not be noticeable; the work of art should be intentional, without appearing so. And Sartre says that the final goal of art is to recover the totality of the world "as if" it had its source in human freedom, which is about the same. Croce, on the other hand, de-

[6] *What Is Literature?* p. 51.

fined beauty as the successful expression of the artist's intuition and insisted on the necessity that this intuition be re-expressed by the spectator, reader, or listener. Sartre defines aesthetic joy as the feeling "that the work is achieved," and also insists on the conjoint effort of the author and the reader or spectator in the final production of the work of art. What Sartre adds is the idea that the work of art is an appeal of the creator's freedom to the freedom of the reader or spectator, so that the latter may become a re-creator.[7]

Existentialist humanism insists very strongly on the role of man as a "revealer" of reality, since it is man who sets up the relationships between the parts of reality. Art is a way of revealing and condensing these relationships, and Sartre thinks that one of the chief motives of artistic creation is to make us feel that, as revealers of its relationships, we are essential to the world.

From his thesis that writing is an appeal of the writer's to the reader's freedom and that reading is a pact of confidence and, consequently, of generosity between the two, Sartre draws important political conclusions. The author requires of the reader a free co-operation with his whole person, his thoughts and feelings, his passions and his scale of values. Now Sartre concludes that "the unique point of view from which the author can present the world to those freedoms whose concurrence he wishes to bring about is that of a world to be impregnated always with more freedom." [8] That means that it would be an abuse of the reader's confidence and generosity if the writer should try in his book to justify human injustice. It is impossible, Sartre thinks, that the reader could enjoy his freedom while reading a book "which approves or accepts or simply abstains from condemning the subjection of man by man." [9]

We find here one of the most interesting sociological aspects of Sartre's theory of literature. Literature has been defined by him as an appeal to pure freedom, and he infers that the reader cannot feel in himself a pure freedom when the writer invites

[7] *Ibid.*, pp. 48, 57-58, *passim.*   [8] *Ibid.*, p. 63.   [9] *Ibid.*

him to identify himself with a group of oppressors. "Nobody can suppose for a moment that it is possible to write a good novel in praise of anti-Semitism." [10] Sartre thinks that the same would be true of a novel advocating the oppression of the Negro or of the working class.

From this Sartre draws a very high moral imperative for the writer: that of winning an inner victory over his race, his class, his nation, and his passions in a perpetual effort to liberate himself and other people.

But Existentialism, like phenomenology, is a philosophy of the concrete. It rejects the idea of abstract, "eternal" freedom. Freedom *is* not, but wins itself in a victory over a concrete situation. According to Sartre, there is no freedom except in a given situation, for nobody can shake off fetters by which he has not been chained. These fetters are the given facts and external situations which man, this free project, encounters in his world. Freedom consists in overcoming any given situation.

In this sense also writing, like other human projects, should try to overcome a given situation, and the most powerful situations are those collective ones we call historical. Sartre thinks that literature has to overcome the historical situations given at a definite period and that each book has to propose a concrete liberation, conditioned by a concrete situation.

We see that this leads from the ancient concept of a literature of description and narration to a literature of action, a literature of praxis, engaged in definite projects of liberation. What the writer should do, according to Sartre, is reveal to the reader his power of acting, of creating and destroying in each historical situation. But to be able to fulfill this mission, the novelist must write for a public which has the freedom of changing everything, including the abolition of classes and the realization of the final goal of which Sartre dreams and which he calls a "socialist democracy." [11] Thus the ideal public which Sartre wishes is, according to his confession, not the bourgeoisie but the revolutionary

10 *Ibid.*, p. 64.
11 *Ibid.*, pp. 159, 290.

workers' class. Up to now, however, the latter has been very reluctant to accept Sartre as a literary leader.

To Sartre, literature is "the subjectivity of a society in permanent revolution," in constant renewal of its institutions and orders whenever they show a tendency to petrify. This conception corresponds to that ideal of fluidity and creative evolution which, according to Bergson, is one of the features of life, and which Existentialism tries to stimulate in everything touching human existence.

In the eleventh of his famous theses against Feuerbach, Karl Marx had declared that up to now, "the philosophers have only interpreted the world, in various ways; the point, however, is to change it." [12] Sartre, obviously, adopted this battle cry when he wrote: "We are no longer with those who want to possess the world, but with those who want to change it," [13] summoning the writers to engage themselves in the task of disclosing the world in the perspectives of a possible change. He also adopts Marx's ideal of a future "classless society" which would liberate literature.[14]

All this leads certain people to think of Sartre as very close to Communism, but they overlook the deep dissensions between the philosophy of Communism and the philosophy of Existentialism. Sartre rejects the materialistic ontology of Marxism and its determinism based on Hegel's dialectical logic, which would deprive man of his freedom of choice and suppress his subjectivity.[15] He reproaches Marxism for not allowing the developments of different shades within itself and thus having become a kind of "Church." [16]

The Communists, on the other hand, accuse Sartre's philosophy of egocentrism, nihilism, anti-humanism, idealism, lack of integration of man in society, etc. One of Sartre's Communist

[12] *Theses on Feuerbach*, p. 99.
[13] *What Is Literature?* p. 238.
[14] *Ibid.*, cf. pp. 158, 263-64, etc.
[15] "Matérialisme et Révolution," *Les Temps Modernes*, I (June, 1946), 14, 22, 25, etc.
[16] *What Is Literature?* pp. 149-150.

critics, the Frenchman Auguste Cornu, now a professor of comparative literature at the University of Leipzig (in Germany's eastern sector), summarizes these reproaches by writing:

Sartre's Existentialism . . . appears, in sum, as the ideological expression of the decadent bourgeoisie at the period when capitalism is breaking up. It translates this decadence into the escape from the real, the isolation of the individual, and the affirmation of the ego's absolute autonomy and superiority to the world. . . . [17]

George Lukacs, Hungary's leading Communist philosopher, recognizes Sartre as an "authentic thinker of high class," but reproaches him for "sketching a caricature of Marxism and winning an easy victory against it." [18]

Existentialist anxiety is described by the Communists as an historical and class phenomenon, a symptom of the decomposition of the bourgeoisie, and Sartre does not deny it. Moreover, he insists that this decomposition can disclose certain aspects of the human condition.

At any rate Sartre is *persona non grata,* not only in Rome, where his atheism and anti-universalism are severely criticized, but also in Moscow.[19]

---

[17] "Bergsonianism and Existentialism," *op. cit.,* p. 166.

[18] *Existentialisme ou Marxisme?* (Paris, [1948]), pp. 144, 148.

[19] In July 1952, an article of Sartre's in *Les Temps Modernes,* entitled "The Communists and Peace " (No. 81, pp. 1-50) stirred up much controversy. Its thesis is: "The USSR wants peace and proves it every day" (p. 12). Sartre considers the Communist Party as the "only political organization" which represents the proletariat in the French parliament (p. 1) and affirms the right of the workers of his country to demonstrate for peace. There is no doubt that in recent years Sartre's ideas have moved toward the left. While in his novel *La Mort dans L'Ame,* published in 1949, he had accused the USSR of having "thrown death into the soul" of the French proletarian by concluding a pact with Nazi-Germany (p. 265), his article of 1952 criticizes this pact only mildly by saying that it "lacks delicacy" (p. 17). Some American correspondents interpreted Sartre's article "The Communists and Peace" as proof that its author has "virtually come into the Stalinist camp." They overlooked, however, the deep philosophical abyss which separates the French Existentialist from the Dialectical Materialists, in spite of Sartre's admiration for Marx and Lenin. As far as the struggle between East and West is concerned, Sartre is a "Neutralist," and Neutralism is an attitude adopted by many non-Communist French intellectuals, such as, for example, the Catholic philosopher Etienne Gilson.

CHAPTER TWELVE

EXISTENTIALISM AND RESISTANCE

After victory day in Europe, when the steel curtain which the Germans had lowered around France had disappeared, the world discovered there an intellectual and literary landscape quite different from the one that it had known before the ordeal. The most striking of these new features of postwar France certainly was Existentialism. And since this philosophy and its literature reflect many problems created by the experiences of the Resistance movement against the German invader, many people considered, and still consider, Existentialism as a philosophy and literature of the French Resistance. This point of view is surely too narrow, even though it implies a certain portion of truth.

On the one hand, we have to realize that Existentialism was created in the middle of the nineteenth century by the Danish Protestant theologian Sören Kierkegaard and that it later bloomed in twentieth-century Germany during the period between the two world wars, in the books of Jaspers, Heidegger, and others. Even in France, Existentialism appeared a long time before World War II, especially in the writings of Gabriel Marcel. And Sartre himself published his Existentialist novel *La Nausée* in 1938, one year before the outbreak of the second world conflagration.

On the other hand, we must also realize that up to that time interest in Existentialism was restricted to a few specialists. When, on the eve of World War II, I devoted some of the lectures in one of my philosophy courses at the Sorbonne to an analysis of Heidegger's Existentialism, the majority of my students manifested no more interest in this theory than in the other movements I discussed in that series of lectures. Sartre's novel *La Nausée*, which at this time was already published, did not stir up much philosophical attention; and in comparing it with Sartre's later works we see that, although it posed some Existentialist problems, it did not find any definite solutions. Most people did not even understand the position of the problem of existence in *La Nausée,* because it was posed outside any definite historical situation which they could have shared.

All this changed radically when, after other European countries, France fully realized that the period since the victory of 1918 had not been one of peace but only of a "reprieve" between one world war and a second, more terrifying one. Sartre, very ably, compares this discovery to that of Charles Bovary in Flaubert's famous novel, who, finding after his wife's death the letters she had received from her lovers, suddenly saw slipping away twenty years of conjugal happiness he had already lived. "Frenchmen were stupified on discovering their historicity," Sartre writes.[1] Suddenly they found themselves geographically and historically "situated" as neighbors of a country where an extreme situation had developed, which, sooner or later, would engulf them.

In order to understand the relations between Existentialism and Resistance, we have to realize that the former is a *philosophy of extreme situations,* flourishes in extreme situations, and produces a literature of these extreme situations. In average situations man takes existence for granted. He does not question it, because it is as unproblematic and tasteless as the ever present saliva in our mouths. As Paul Valéry once said, it is only by chance that we think of the permanent conditions of our life.

In extreme situations, however, the whole trend of our consciousness is changed. In those extreme situations that we call *crises,* man asks himself anew the ultimate questions of the meaning, the essence, and the value of human existence. This questioning and the answers it produces are Existentialism, which thus can be defined as *a philosophy of crisis.*

The crisis which brings about the philosophical meditation on existence can be individual, as in the case of Kierkegaard's personal drama, or collective, as in the tragedy lived by Sartre and

[1] *What Is Literature?* pp. 211-212.

his comrades in the French Resistance movement. When provoked by a collective crisis, the Existentialist movement has much more social dynamism, as a comparison between Sartre's and Kierkegaard's philosophies easily shows. While the latter needed almost three-quarters of a century to be taken into consideration, the former became known throughout the world within two or three years.

There are different kinds of extreme situations which may bring about a crisis of existence in an individual or in a collective group. In his novel *The Plague*, Albert Camus showed how a terrifying epidemic brings people to new reflections on, and new insights into, the essence, meaning, and value of human existence. But among the crises of collectivities, the historical ones have a privileged philosophical character, for they are produced by man and yet find him hopelessly subjected to their destructive forces.

In Germany the extreme situation bringing about a crisis of existence began in 1933, when Hitler rose to power. Soon we found there a revival of Kierkegaard's Existentialism, which started the opposition against Nazism in that sector of the German Protestant Church which was close to Karl Barth.

In France the extreme situation provoking a crisis of existence arose in 1940, with the invasion of the country by Hitler's soldiers, the breakdown of the Third Republic and the system of values attached to it, and with the enslavement of the whole nation. In this extreme situation Existentialism, as a philosophy calling into question the whole of human existence and its values, received its strongest impulse in France. During this crisis it ripened into a philosophy which was everybody's business, and it found its answers in an effort to overcome this crisis of existence.

But does this not mean that philosophy, by its very nature a quest of eternal, timeless truth, becomes subjected to historical relativity? Does it not constitute a new kind of historicism based on the principle of *veritas filia temporis?*

We have already seen that Existentialism rejects the concept of eternal truth and resists any kind of evasion from existence here and now into timeless entities. To Existentialists, the contemplation of eternal Platonic ideas is a kind of escapism, a running away from the problems of concrete existence, which is always imprisoned in a definite time and a definite space. Nevertheless, Existentialism is no kind of historicism. In an earlier discussion of Sartre's axiology we found an astonishing disregard for past history and the values it produced during its evolution. It is history already made and no longer interesting to Existentialists, because it no longer "exists." What Sartre, following Heidegger, calls historicity is present history, the history we have to live, into which we are forced by circumstances, whose meaning we have to choose, and which we have to overcome, to surpass, and to transcend in a supreme effort toward freedom.

Furthermore, the historicity of Existentialist philosophy and literature does not mean a subjection of the philosophical quest of the absolute to historical relativity. Sartre clarifies this point in *What Is Literature?* when he says that "the war and the occupation, by precipitating us into a world in a state of fusion, perforce made us rediscover the absolute at the heart of relativity itself." [2] And in another passage of this same book he speaks of the task "to create a literature which unites and reconciles the metaphysical absolute and the relativity of the historical fact." [3] With the term "metaphysical" Sartre designates an effort to embrace human existence and human condition in its totality. That is what French Existentialism tried to do during the crisis created by the extreme historical situation of the German occupation and, especially, of the resistance against it.

Developed during that period of dreadful oppression, Existentialism in its French version is basically a philosophy of freedom, the most radical ever conceived since Fichte, who—and not by pure chance—wrote his philosophy of freedom during the occupation of Prussia by the French troops of Napoleon I.

But the Existentialist concept of freedom is intimately linked to that of situations, as we have seen in the preceding chapter,

2 *Ibid.*, p. 215.
3 *Ibid.*, p. 222.

and as we shall see later in a more detailed way in a subsequent chapter.[4]

We said previously that for Existentialists freedom *is* not, but wins itself in a victory over a concrete situation, which, in many cases, is an historical one. We saw that, according to Sartre, there is no freedom except in a given situation, and we tried to clarify this thesis by using the metaphor that nobody can shake off fetters by which he has not been chained. These fetters are all the facts and external situations man encounters in the world, in the being-in-itself. Freedom, as we saw, consists in surpassing and transcending these given situations, or the whole of given facts and obstacles which Sartre calls "facticity." We have to surpass it, projecting ourselves toward goals we have chosen. As Simone de Beauvoir defines ethics, it is "the triumph of freedom over facticity." [5]

All of this helps us to understand why the extreme historical situation of 1940–1945 had so strong an influence on the development of Existentialist ethics and the theory of freedom in France. It was the "test case" of Existential freedom, so that Sartre could make the following statement, which only in appearance is paradoxical:

We were never more free than during the German occupation. We had lost all our rights, beginning with the right to talk. Every day we were insulted to our faces and had to take it in silence. Under one pretext or another, as workers, Jews, or political prisoners, we were deported en masse. . . . And because of all this we were free. Because the Nazi venom seeped even into our thoughts, every accurate thought was a conquest. . . . At every instant we lived up to the full sense of this commonplace little phrase: "Man is mortal." And the choice that each of us made of his life and his being was an authentic choice because it was made face to face with death, because it could always have been expressed in these terms: "Rather death than. . . ." All those among us who knew any details concerning the Resistance asked themselves anxiously, "If they torture me, shall I be able to keep silent?" Thus the basic question of liberty itself was posed, and we were brought to the verge of the deepest knowledge that man can have

[4] Ch. 18, "How Free Is Our Project?"
[5] *Pour une Morale*, p. 64.

of himself. For the secret of man is not his Oedipus complex or his inferiority complex: it is this limit of his own liberty, his capacity for resisting torture and death.[6]

What Sartre says here in dry words is exemplified in pathetic action and sacrifice in his grandiose tragedy *Morts sans Sépulture* (in America, "The Victors").

Telling us that "even the pincers of the executioner do not deliver us from being free,"[7] the philosopher seems to justify those who see in Existentialist freedom an inner freedom, similar to the Stoic freedom to say "yea" and "nay," when we are confronted with the overwhelming determining power of the external world. The rapid spreading of Existentialism in a France occupied by the Germans is often explained, especially in America, by the hypothesis that under the brutal totalitarian oppression free human action toward the world had become impossible, so that the frustrated freedom had to flee into the interior of the human soul. Professor Larrabee, for instance, sees in Existentialism a kind of cult of inner freedom.[8]

Sartre, however, would not accept this interpretation. In his essay *Matérialisme et Révolution* he opposes vigorously the concept of inner freedom, designating it as an idealistic mystification. "Freedom," he says, "reveals itself only in action, is identical with action." According to him there is no interior or exterior of man, and freedom is engagement in action in order to change the present and to create a future.

Consequently, under the occupation, Existentialism was not a cult of inner, subjective freedom, but a philosophy of action, encouraging action by showing that there is no freedom except through action and that through action there is always another chance left, as long as we exist and are in the making. "We exist only when we are acting," says Jean Blomaert, the underground leader in Simone de Beauvoir's novel *Le Sang des Autres*.[9]

6 *The Republic of Silence,* ed. A. T. Liebling (New York, [1947]), pp. 498-99.
7 *L'Etre et le Néant,* p. 587.
8 H. A. Larrabee, "Existentialism Is Not Humanism," *The Humanist,* Vol. 8, No. 1 (Summer, 1948), p. 10.
9 P. 177.

Thus we realize to what extent the French version of Existentialism is linked to the moral situation of the Frenchman of 1940, who, as the title of one of Sartre's novels hints, had "death in his soul" and needed a doctrine which would help him to overcome this moral death.[10]

Sartre described the "literature of resistance" which this period produced as an example of a literature the purpose of which was not the enjoyment of the reader, but his torment. What it presented was not a world to be contemplated, but to be changed. In the previous chapter we could see Sartre's tendency to generalize this concept of the literature of resistance into that of a literature of historicity and action, which rejects *l'art pour l'art*. It seems doubtful, however, whether that type of literature can be maintained outside extreme situations.

In the novels and dramas which the Resistance produced, we do not find characterization. Existentialism rejects the concept of character, as we shall see in studying its psychoanalysis. The heroes we find in the dramas and novels of the Resistance are free human projects, trapped in certain situations, in extreme situations, which they have to overcome by action, thus winning genuine freedom in the midst of the most terrifying oppression. We see this in Sartre's tragedies *Morts sans Sépulture* ("The Victors") and *Les Mouches* ("The Flies"), and especially in the three novels of *Les Chemins de la Liberté* ("The Ways of Freedom") which, up to now, have been published. In the first two of these novels, the action of which takes place before the outbreak of World War II, there are no extreme situations; and so we find its hero Mathieu Delarue unable to commit himself. But in the third novel, *La Mort dans l'Ame,* the extreme situation of France's defeat has occurred. And, for the first time, we see Delarue commit himself in an action of military resistance against the invader, in the summer days of 1940, when on the rest of the front the resistance of the French army had ended. Militarily, this solitary action of a handful of French soldiers who volunteered under the command of a lieutenant is mean-

[10] *La Mort dans L'Ame* (Paris, 1949); Amer. ed., *Troubled Sleep* (New York: Knopf, 1951).

ingless. Morally, however, it is extremely meaningful; for by his decision, engagement, and action the hero overcomes an overwhelming situation, winning his liberty, affirming himself as a free human project—a being-for-himself—denying that man is a thing—a being in-itself, entirely subjected to the facticity of a situation. He wins a victory of existence over being.

We find a similar evolution in Jean Blomaert and Hélène, the heroes of Simone de Beauvoir's novel of the Resistance, *Le Sang des Autres.*

All of this shows that the purpose of the French Resistance movement was not only military and political—although it wanted to harm the enemy's military operations and create a spirit which would make political collaboration impossible; the Existentialists insist, indeed, that the main purpose of the Resistance was philosophical and moral. Simone de Beauvoir, for instance, writes: "The Resistance did not pretend to have a positive efficiency; it was negation, revolt, martyrdom, and in this negative movement freedom was positively and absolutely confirmed." [11]

In addition to this philosophy of freedom, the French Resistance also needed a new, subjectivistic philosophy of values. This, too, was offered by Existentialism. To understand the necessity of such a philosophy at that time, we have to realize that during the four years of German occupation the young Frenchmen lived in a "vacuum of values." They could no longer believe in the hierarchy of values in which they had been educated—that of the Third Republic; for these values had proved too weak to impede their country's catastrophe. But they were also unable to believe in the new values proclaimed by the German invader and his French lackeys, led by the collaborator Pétain. Could they believe in the values propagated through the London radio by the exiled General de Gaulle? But he had been condemned to death as a traitor to his country by France's official courts, and every "patriot" was forbidden to listen to his speeches as though they were the devil's gospel.

The transvaluation of all values in which the young French-

[11] *Pour une Morale,* p. 184.

men had been educated created total bewilderment. From one day to the next the negative value of freedom and the positive value of servitude were proclaimed; the negative value of equality and the positive value of a hierarchy of superior and inferior races, of masters and slaves. One proclaimed the negative value of the idea of a brotherhood of nations and the positive value of treason to an allied nation and one's own nation. Furthermore, the negative value of intelligence was proclaimed and the positive value of instinct; the negative value of law and the positive of violence; the negative value of democracy and the positive of dictatorship, which presented itself with the quavering voice of a kind old grandfather who wants to protect his poor immature grandchildren. Those who, on the eve, had been stigmatized as traitors, were now praised as heroes, while the heroes of yesterday were stigmatized as traitors. The "good" of yesterday became the "evil" of today; the "evil" of yesterday, the "good" of today.

I lived this period in France as a soldier in the French army, and I was a witness to the total axiological bewilderment of my younger comrades, who no longer knew what to believe. In this tragic situation only two alternatives were left to these young Frenchmen: either to believe no longer in any value and to become nihilists; or to choose a system of values of their own, using their liberty of choice, in complete isolation, without backing by any recognized, official ethics, and assume total responsibility for their choice.

The nihilists became epicures, purveyors of the black market, and agents of the enemy. Those who used their axiological freedom to set up new values and norms in which they would believe joined the underground and became soldiers of the Resistance. Their lot was "total responsibility in total solitude," one of Sartre's definitions of freedom.

It *was* a total solitude; for the society surrounding them—a nation officially collaborating with the enemy—refused to back them up, either because of fear or because of compliance. And it *was* a total responsibility; for when they chose to go to the Maquis and to fight the government of their own country, the lives of these men and of their comrades were at stake—perhaps, also, their honor as Frenchmen. For who guaranteed them that *they* were right and Pétain, the revered hero of Verdun, who once had saved the country, was wrong? What if they had been mistaken in their choice of democratic values and this choice would now cause imprisonment and torture to members of their family, torture and death for the comrades under their orders or for themselves? We understand easily the terrifying anxiety arising from this responsibility, which nobody was ready to share with them. Not only did the official moral code *not* back up their lonely choice of values, it condemned it vigorously. Only through total engagement in action could these young men overcome their feeling of forsakenness.

Thus, life in France from 1940 to 1944 turned out to be a practical school of Existentialism for the best elements of the nation. By terrifying experience the fighters of the French Resistance learned that man "is condemned to be free" in his valuations and decisions, that he has to act to be free, and that it is through anxiety that he becomes conscious of his freedom. It was the life of the Maquis that taught them the basic principles of Sartre's ethics: There is only one *good* for the individual—to recognize his freedom and act while recognizing it; there is only one *evil*—to deny one's freedom in order to evade the responsibility it implies; and, finally, that in choosing freedom for himself, every "Maquisard" chose the freedom of all.

But if, during the occupation, the men of the Resistance formed a community, which Sartre calls the "Republic of Silence," it was only because they remained faithful to the values they had chosen in their aloneness. And thus they were, perhaps, more Nietzscheites than Sartreites.

Psychologically speaking, the German occupation of France was divided into two phases. In the first, the invader tried to use the velvet touch in a vain effort to win over the French people and to make them accept slavery under the euphemism of collaboration. In the second phase, when this hope had faded, in the middle of 1942, and the Resistance had grown stronger, the monster used its claws in the bloodiest tortures man can imagine. To these two periods correspond two different kinds of literature of the Resistance and, to a certain extent, even two different philosophies. Typical of the first period was Vercor's novel *Le Silence de la Mer,* while Sartre's tragedy *Morts sans Sépulture* seems to be the most representative literary expression of the second period of German occupation and French Resistance.

But even in the philosophical interpretation of the two phases of French history from 1940 to 1945 we may distinguish two different points of view. In 1943, Sartre published his main philosophical work, *L'Etre et le Néant,* which must have been conceived partly before the war and partly during the first period of the occupation. In this work we find the relativistic theory of values which we discussed in a previous chapter [12] and which was applied by many members of the Resistance. This relativistic axiology Sartre never revoked. However, in a retrospective appraisal of the second period of the German occupation, he developed certain ideas which are entirely incompatible with his relativistic axiology. This was done in his book *Situations II,* published in France in 1947, two years after the liberation, and in the United States in 1949, under the title, *What Is Literature?* Describing the devilish tortures suffered by the members of the Resistance who were captured by the Nazis, Sartre writes: "We heard whole blocks screaming, and we understood that 'evil,' fruit of a free and sovereign will, is, like 'good,' absolute." [13]

Now if good and evil are absolute values, then we have returned to Platonism and Sartre's relativistic axiology is void. I would, however, not draw this conclusion; for axiological relativism is an inescapable consequence of atheistic Existentialism, and the latter was never revoked by Sartre. There has been no change in his theoretical philosophy, and I am inclined to consider this contradiction as one of those inconsistencies in his work which show that, emotionally, Sartre is an axiological absolutist. Let us not forget Pascal's dictum: *"Le coeur a ses raisons que la raison ne connaît point."* [14]

[12] Ch. 9, "Freedom and Values."
[13] *What Is Literature?* p. 219.
[14] "The heart has its reasons which reason does not know." *Pensées,* IV, 277, p. 458.

CHAPTER THIRTEEN

OUR "BEING-FOR-OTHERS" AND THEIR "GAZE"

Agnes was a pretty girl, living in a small American town. Her father put her on a train, gave her fifty dollars, and promised to send her the same amount monthly, for a time. She was supposed to go to Birmingham, Alabama, to study shorthand at a business college. But she never took the courses; instead, she became a manicurist in a cheap barbershop. Men came to the shop, put their hands down the neck of her dress and squeezed her. Soon she was "making more money on the outside after hours" than at the table. All of her family—Papa, Mama, and the others— know that she lives in a cheap hotel in New Orleans and that she is not a stenographer. But when she goes home, once a year, at Christmas, they do not say anything. They just sit and look at her all the time.

Agnes becomes desperate, almost hysterical: "Once a year, at Christmas, they sit and look at me, but none of them ever says anything about it. They all sit in the parlor saying to themselves, 'We are looking at you, Agnes.'"

This story, "We Are Looking at You, Agnes," is told by Erskine Caldwell [1] with masterly simplicity and gives an impressive idea of the inexorable feeling of guilt and shame the "gaze" of other people can arouse in us. Did Erskine Caldwell realize that the basic thesis of his story had been expressed at the beginning of the nineteenth century by Hegel in the *Phenomenology of the Spirit?* There Hegel says: *"Das Selbstbewusstsein ist an und für sich, indem und dadurch, dass es für ein Anderes an und für sich ist: das heisst, es ist nur ein Anerkanntes."* [2] In other

[1] "We Are Looking at You, Agnes," *We Are the Living* (New York, 1933), pp. 17-25.

[2] "Herrschaft und Knechtschaft," *Phänomenologie des Geistes*, ed. G. Lasson (Leipzig, [1907]), p. 123.

words, our self-consciousness exists only because it exists for another person. Thus self-consciousness is basically "acknowledgment" by another person; and our being-for-others is a necessary condition for the development of our self-consciousness, our being-for-ourselves. Or, as Sartre puts it, "the way to interiority passes through the other person." [3] The other person is interesting to me only to the extent that he reflects myself, that is to say, to the extent to which I am an object to him. Since I am an object only in so far as I exist to the other person, I have to obtain from that other person the acknowledgment of my being. The other person is the mediator between me and myself. Thus my being-for-myself depends on my being-for-others. "By its very nature shame is acknowledgment; I acknowledge that I am as the other one sees me." [4]

We see that Hegel's theory of the lack of independence of our self-consciousness has become an important part of Sartre's Existentialism, in spite of the fact that, historically, with Kierkegaard, Existentialism sprang from an opposition to Hegel's philosophy.

Hegel's thesis that self-consciousness is real only as long as it knows its echo in another person has been developed and completed by Sartre's theory of the "gaze." If I exist for the other person, I do so through his gaze. Consequently my fundamental relation to the other person is determined by the permanent possibility of being seen by him. The gaze of the other self reveals to me not only that I am an object to him, but also that the other self is a subject. "It is my shame or my pride which reveals to me the gaze of the other self. . . . Shame is . . . shame of oneself; it is the acknowledgment that I am that object which another self looks at and judges." [5]

Thus we see that in his short story "We Are Looking at You, Agnes," Erskine Caldwell expressed a fundamental Existentialist thesis—and this in 1933, years before Sartre started with Existentialism. As a matter of fact, this American writer is recognized

[3] *L'Etre et le Néant*, p. 292.
[4] *Ibid.*, p. 278.
[5] *Ibid.*, p. 319.

today as a kind of ambassador of Existentialism to the United States, and his stories are recited, in French, at the Existentialist club Zig-Zag, on the Rive-gauche.

Also, William Faulkner gave an impressive example of the gaze of other people as revealers of our moral being, and Sartre expressly referred to this brilliant American writer in his principal philosophical treatise. The French Existentialist mentioned especially a scene in the novel *Light in August,* where Faulkner describes the stabbing to death of the alleged Negro Christmas by Percy Grimm, the fighter for white supremacy. The victim does not resist, but before dying he "looks at" his murderer and his helpers.

He just lay there, with his eyes open and empty of everything save consciousness. . . . For a long moment he looked up at them with peaceful and unfathomable and unbearable eyes. . . . Upon that black blast the man seemed to rise soaring into their memories forever and ever. They are not to lose it, in whatever peaceful valleys, beside whatever placid and reassuring streams of old age, in the mirroring faces of whatever children they will contemplate old disasters and newer hopes. It will be there, musing, quiet, steadfast, not fading and not particularly threatful, but of itself alone serene, of itself triumphant.[6]

Sartre's own heroes sometimes express feelings similar to those of Faulkner's murderers or of Caldwell's Agnes, whose shame and guilt, aroused by the mere gaze of the members of her family, like the gaze of the Gorgon Medusa, petrify her into the being she really is. Everybody's gaze is the petrifying gaze of Medusa, changing the other for-itself into an in-itself and depriving it of its freedom. The most interesting human document of this kind is the letter that Mathieu receives from his false friend Daniel, in Sartre's novel *The Reprieve.* It reads, in part, as follows:

You must have experienced, in the subway, in the foyer of a theater, or in a train, the sudden and irksome sense that you were being looked at from behind. . . . Well, that is what I felt for the first time, on September 26, at three o'clock in the afternoon, in the hotel garden. . . . I became more compact and concentrated, I was both transparent and

[6] *Light in August* (New York, [1950]), p. 407.

opaque, I existed in the presence of a look. . . . Ah, Mathieu, what a discovery! I *was seen*, I struggled to know myself . . . and all the time I was seen, the inexorable look, an invisible steel blade, was on me. . . . Believe me, I first loathed this incessant violation of myself. . . . What anguish to discover that look as a universal medium from which I can't escape! But what a relief as well! I know at last that I am. I adapt for my own use, and to your disgust, your prophet's foolish, wicked words: "I think, therefore I am." . . . I say: "*I am seen, therefore I am.*" I need no longer bear the responsibility of my turbid and disintegrating self: he who sees me, causes me to be; I am as he sees me. . . .

Then, in spite of being a businessman who says he has never read Hegel, Daniel comes to the following Hegelian conclusions:

For one instant you were the heaven-sent mediator between me and myself, you perceived that compact and solid entity which I was and wanted to be in just as simple and ordinary a way as I perceived you. . . . I then understood that one could not reach onself except through another's judgment. . . .Without me you would be that same unsubstantial entity that I am for myself. It is by my agency that you can at times get an occasional and doubtless rather exasperating glimpse of yourself—as you really are. . . . [7]

This letter may seem psychologically improbable, when we realize that it comes from a greedy businessman without philosophical education, a low character and a pederast. However, philosophically, it is a very important document, and the readers of Sartre's novels who are not familiar with his ontology may be puzzled by it. But once seen within the system of this ontology, everything becomes clear. Let us sum up some of the basic philosophical implications of this letter:

In our previous chapters we have seen that Sartre distinguishes two modalities of being: "being-in-itself" and "being-for-itself." To this, now, a third modality is added: that which Sartre designates with Hegel's term "being-for-others" (*être pour-autrui*).

The being-in-itself, which is that of inanimate objects, was characterized as being what it is, as coinciding with itself, as being subjected to the principle of identity, as including no negation, as "as full as an egg."

[7] *The Reprieve*, pp. 405-407.

The being-for-itself, or human consciousness, was characterized as being what it is not and not being what it is. It *is* not at all, but is always creating itself; consequently it never coincides with itself, thus falling outside the principle of identity. It is through the being-for-itself that nothingness comes into the world. Being never what it is, being always separated by a region of nothingness from what it has to be, the being-for-itself, or human consciousness, is "full" of nothingness, of negation; it is an ever-questioning hollow projected toward the future, toward its possibilities, *"un creux toujours futur,"* as Paul Valéry says (in *Le Cimetière marin*). The being-for-itself is nothing but the pure naughtization of the being-in-itself; it is like a "hole in the womb of being." [8]

But we have seen that man's freedom, also, coincides with this hole, this nothingness which is in his heart and which compels him to make himself into something instead of being something. Thus being-for-itself is basically freedom, which also means that it is "transcendence"; for by its freedom the being-for-itself is able to transcend or to surpass itself, to go beyond itself, and also to surpass or transcend the being-in-itself, the brute inanimate things, by projecting itself toward its possibilities. Sartre speaks of a "transcendence which surpasses and naughts the given data toward an end." [9] The being-for-itself is always consciousness *of* something and therefore only consciousness of itself, so that it is always outside itself, transcending itself. It is a free projection toward its possibilities, it naughts any given datum, and it is defined by its ends. Sartre compares being-for-itself, or human consciousness, to a "gliding slope," on which we cannot sit down without being thrown outside, toward the being-in-itself. This, too, is a picture of transcendence, which, according to Heidegger, coincides with consciousness and existence, or *Da-sein*. "Projected into nothingness, *Da-sein* is already beyond what-is-in-totality. This 'being beyond' (*Hinaussein*) what-is, we call transcendence." [10] Thus, as Heidegger explains in *Vom*

---

8 *L'Etre et le Néant*, p. 711.
9 *Ibid.*, p. 597.
10 *What Is Metaphysics?* p. 370.

Wesen des Grundes, it is almost tautological to say "the human being transcends itself." To "exist" means, etymologically, *exsistere,* to stand out or to step out.

Now comes the third modality of being, the "being-for-others." At first the other person I see appears as a mere being-in-itself, a phenomenon of nature, no different from all the inanimate bodies I perceive around myself. It is through his gaze that the other person reveals himself to me as a being-for-itself; a subject; a consciousness; a free project of itself, able to transcend itself and to transcend all given data toward its own possibilities, its own ends. But this means also that by his gaze this other person can transcend me and change me from a being-for-itself into a being-in-itself, from a free project into a determined thing, into a solidified object—as I can change him by my gaze. "The people I see are congealed by me into objects, I am in relation to them what they are in relation to me." [11] By looking at other people, I measure my power, and by looking at me, they measure theirs. Thus being-for-others is, basically, *conflict,* a struggle of two transcendences, each of which tries to "outtranscend" the other.

Of course, it is not precisely the eyes, as physiological organs, which look at me: it is the other person as a subject, a consciousness. Thus the gaze of the other person includes all kinds of judgments and evaluations. Being seen by the other person means to grasp oneself as an unknown object of uncognizable judgments. A judgment, according to Sartre, is the transcendental act of a free person. The fact of being seen changes me into a being without defense against a freedom which is not my freedom. Being seen by the other person makes us slaves; looking at the other person, we are masters. I am a slave as long as I depend in my being on the freedom of another self, which is not mine but which is the condition of my being. And I am a master when I make the other self depend for its being on my freedom. It was Hegel who introduced this distinction between "slave" and "master" (*Herr und Knecht*) in the theory of knowledge. For him, there are two forms of our consciousness: *"die eine das selbstän-*

11 *L'Etre et le Néant,* p. 324.

*dige, welchem das Fürsichsein, die andere das unselbständige,
dem das Leben oder das Sein für ein anderes das Wesen ist: jenes
ist der Herr, dies der Knecht."* [12]

Sartre applies this distinction of Hegel's and thinks that it is
my gaze which would change the other person into a slave and
the other person's gaze which would change me into a slave and
make him the master of the situation. As a slave a person loses
all his possibilities and becomes a "transcended transcendence."

Thus by the appearance of the other person, the other self, a
new aspect comes into my situation, an aspect which I cannot
master, which escapes me on principle, since it is that of the
other person. This unforeseeable reverse side of reality is that
which André Gide calls *"la part du diable"* ("the devil's share"),
an aspect of existence which Sartre sees expressed especially in
the work of Franz Kafka.

Of course, I can regain my own freedom and transcendence,
using my gaze to transcend the other person's freedom and transcendence, changing his subjectivity into a petrified object, alien-
ating his possibilities. But then the other self can look again at
me and again transcend and enslave my freedom and transcendence. And so on.

One remembers a scene in Chaplin's remarkable picture *The
Dictator,* where Hitler and Mussolini, each sitting in a kind of
dentist's chair, are lifting their seats by means of cranks, so that
each in turn would rise above the level of the other and surpass
him. Robert Campbell sees in this scene a witty symbol of the
struggle between two transcendences.[13] And we agree with him.
However, the matter itself is far from being funny. Sartre realizes
this. It would be a vain effort, he says, for man to try to escape
that dilemma, "to transcend the other one or to allow one's self
to be transcended by the other one." And he concludes that the
essence of human relations is not Heidegger's *Mitsein* ("being-
with"), but *conflict.*

---

[12] *Phänomenologie des Geistes,* p. 127—"the one is the independent [con-
sciousness], to which the being-for-itself is the essence, the other is the dependent
one, to which life or the being-for-others is the essence: the former is the master,
the latter the slave."

[13] *Jean-Paul Sartre ou une Littérature philosophique* (Paris, 1947), p. 120.

And now Sartre tries to show that all possible relations between the own and any other self—even love—are only different forms of conflict. "Conflict is the original sense of the being-for-others." [14] All relations between different persons are attempts by each of them to subjugate or to possess the other's freedom. No ill will is the cause of this situation, but the mere fact of existence. As soon as I exist, I establish a factual limit to the freedom of the other person. I am that limit, and each of my projects draws that limit around the other self. Sartre concludes that "respect for the other person's freedom is a vain word." [15]

This is a rather sad confession from so passionate a fighter for human freedom as Sartre. Besides, his emphasis on conflict is too strong. Hayakawa tried to show—not without success—that co-operation, rather than conflict, is the great governing principle of society. Even organized competition among men would be impossible without a tremendous amount of co-operation taken for granted. We see this, for instance, in the case of a strike, which is a withdrawal of co-operation.[16]

While Sartre thinks that, owing to the inevitable conflict among men, the respect of other persons' freedom is a vain word, Simone de Beauvoir seems less pessimistic than her master, for she requires that we "must always respect the freedom of other people and help them to liberate themselves." [17]

Before closing the first part of this book, there is still more to be said about the petrification of the other subject by means of the gaze. Why is it that the gaze petrifies the other subject and changes it into an object? Well, we know that, according to Sartre's Existentialism, the being-for-itself, or subject, *is* not, but is always in the making, always becoming. But when I am looking at the other person, that is, when I am judging him, I do not judge him as far as he is becoming—because I cannot know his possibilities—but as far as he *is*, at the very moment of my judgment. Thus, I am perpetuating this moment of his evolution. It is just as though I should see the projection of motion pictures

[14] *L'Etre et le Néant*, p. 431.   [15] *Ibid.*, p. 480.
[16] S. Hayakawa, *Language in Thought and Action* (N. Y., 1949), pp. 117-18.
[17] *Pour une Morale*, p. 85.

showing a person walking toward a certain goal, and, suddenly, I should stop unrolling the film, before the man has reached his goal. He would then be perpetuated, or petrified, in the momentary position of having, for instance, one foot raised to take the next step, which he would never make. He would no longer give the impression of a subject projected toward its possibilities, but would appear as an inanimate object. Expressed in Sartre's terminology, this means that by the gaze of the other one, the being-for-itself is changed into a being-in-itself, into a thing. It is nailed down as it is in the moment of the judgment, as if it were what it is and were no longer in the making. But the being-for-itself can never coincide with itself. It is always in the making and, therefore, always "on reprieve," since its future is its free project. Only at the moment of the self's death, when the being-for-itself has changed completely into a being-in-itself and has lost all its possibilities, only then "the chips are down"—only then does this person coincide with himself.

Thus all our judgments on a living person are provisional; for by looking at him—with our physical or our mental eye—we change him into a being-in-itself and disregard his potential freedom, his future possibilities, which we cannot know and by which he may refute our present judgment. The gaze of Medusa, petrifying a person and obliging him to be forever what he is at a given moment, may thus be an injustice toward him. But this look will be a relief to those persons who want to be delivered from their freedom and their responsibility for continuously creating themselves.

It is this kind of relief which is expressed in Daniel's letter, when he wrote: "What a relief. . . . I need no longer bear the responsibility of my turbid and distintegrating self: he who sees me, causes me to be; I am as he sees me. . . ." [18]

By gladly accepting the calm and permanent being of an inanimate thing, delivered of freedom, responsibility, and anxiety, Daniel renounces his human condition and flees into "bad faith." We will meet more men of his type in our discussion of "Sartre's Existentialist Psychoanalysis."

[18] Sartre, *The Reprieve*, p. 407.

PART TWO

SARTRE'S EXISTENTIALIST PSYCHOANALYSIS

CHAPTER FOURTEEN

CHOICE AND COMPLEX

"Empirical psychoanalysis tries to determine the *complex*. . . . Existentialist psychoanalysis tries to determine the *original* choice." [1]

With these words Sartre defines the basic difference between Freud's psychoanalysis, which he calls "empirical," and his own. Does this mean that Sartre rejects the concept of complex? Not at all. We shall see later that he himself uses the concept of complex and even introduces two new complexes, which he calls the Acteon complex and the Jonah complex. He does not even deny the existence of Freud's Oedipus complex or Adler's inferiority complex. He only denies that these complexes are irreducible, that they constitute ultimate data. According to Sartre these complexes can be traced back to something more fundamental, which is man's original choice. As we consider the assumptions of his Existentialist philosophy, we shall understand easily the goal of his type of psychoanalysis.

We have only to remember the fundamental thesis of Existentialism: existence precedes essence. According to this assumption man exists first; he springs up in the world and is defined afterward. At the beginning he *is* not anything. He will become what he has projected to become, but there is nothing previous to his project of himself. And his project expresses his original choice. Since, according to Sartre's Existentialism, man *is* his choice, we understand why this philosopher had to establish a new discipline, Existentialist psychoanalysis, which should try to determine man's original choice, his fundamental project.

The first principle of Existentialist psychoanalysis is that man is a unified whole and not a collection, not an arithmetical

[1] *L'Etre et le Néant*, p. 657.

sum. In this respect Sartre's new discipline agrees with Freud's psychoanalysis, with Adler's individual psychology, and with other trends in modern psychology. Now if man is a whole, he must express himself entirely in even his most insignificant and most superficial conduct. There is no individual taste or tic which would not be revealing. Thus the aim of Existentialist psychoanalysis is to decipher the empirical behavior of man and to interpret it. Sartre wishes to reveal the apparently differing significances implied in each human act and then to trace all of them back to successively fewer and more inclusive significances, up to an ultimate significance. He recognizes that he has this starting point in common with Freud. "For Freud as for ourselves, an act is not limited to itself; it refers immediately to deeper structures." [2]

Like Freud, Sartre also considers the human act as "symbolic," as translating a deeper desire which has to be interpreted with reference to an initial determination. However, this determination is not a "complex," nor a "libido," nor a Nietzschean "will to power," nor an Adlerian "superiority goal." It is an original choice, a fundamental project, whereas all these other terms include secondary conditioning. The choice is a choice of one's position in the world and therefore involves the person as a whole just as the complex does. Furthermore, choice and complex are both previous to logic. It is the fundamental project that determines a person's attitude toward logic.

We know that Alfred Adler deduces the inferiority complex from the inferiority of the child's organs, even the organs of the healthy child, as compared with the organs of an adult. For Sartre the inferiority complex is a free project of a person's own being-for-himself in the world confronted with the other person. If I am that person, I myself have *chosen* that inferiority, which I recognize and against which I struggle. My inferiority complex is nothing but the projection of my initial plan of failure organized into a system of individual failures. One who suffers from inferiority has chosen to be the executioner of himself. He makes

[2] *Ibid.*, p. 535.

himself only the means to attain certain ends. A chosen humiliation, like masochism, for instance, can be used as a tool for delivering him from the existence as a being-for-itself; it can be an initially chosen project for getting rid of his own anxiety-inspiring freedom for the benefit of other people. In choosing inferiority our fundamental project may be to have our being-for-itself entirely absorbed by our being-for-others. According to Sartre the inferiority complex can arise in us only if it is founded on a free apprehension of our being-for-others. The inferiority we feel may be the chosen tool to make us similar to a thing, a being-in-itself free of responsibility.

Thus inferiority is a free and total project of myself as inferior to others; it is the manner in which I choose to accept my being-for-others, the free solution I give to the existence of the other person, that insuperable scandal.[3]

However, the fact that one chooses inferiority does not mean that he is content with *aurea mediocritas,* for in so choosing he creates the revolt and despair which reveal that inferiority. I may, for instance, persist in doing a certain type of work because I am inferior to the task, while in another domain I would be able to do a satisfactory job. A man may choose a fruitless endeavor *because* it is fruitless, perhaps because he prefers to be the last one rather than to disappear in the crowd. "But it is clear that I can choose as my field of action the domain in which I am *inferior* only if that choice implies the deliberate *will* to be *superior.*" [4] The man who chooses to be an inferior artist, Sartre says, necessarily chooses to *want* to be a great artist; otherwise the inferiority would not be felt or recognized. The choice of inferiority implies, according to Sartre, the permanent realization of the "distance" between the goal and the actual result.

All these Sartrian ideas sound strangely familiar to any student of Alfred Adler's individual psychology. But Sartre insists that man "chooses" inferiority, and in so doing, and maintaining it, he is of "bad faith"; for he is running away from the acknowl-

3 *Ibid.,* p. 537.
4 *Ibid.,* p. 551.

edgment of the true aims he has chosen, which he tries to hide from himself in order to escape the responsibility for his choice. We shall study later this concept of bad faith, especially in relation to the "unconscious," as that term is used by Freud and Adler and rejected by Sartre.

This short analysis of Sartre's interpretation of the inferiority complex shows that the French Existentialist is much closer to Alfred Adler than he may know or want to admit. For if, as Sartre maintains, the choice of inferiority implies the deliberate will to superiority, he falls in line with Alfred Adler, who said:

A thoroughgoing study has taught us that we can best understand the manifold and diverse movements of the psyche as soon as our most general presupposition, that the psyche has as its objective the *goal of superiority*, is recognized.[5]

It is well known that Adler interprets man's superiority goal as a compensation and hyper-compensation of an inferiority complex. Sartre's affirmation that the choice of inferiority implies the deliberate will to be superior is pretty close to Adler's conception. And if the Viennese psychiatrist insisted that the patient "is intensifying his feeling of inferiority *and yet freeing himself from responsibility* by attributing this inferiority to heredity, the fault of his parents or other factors," [6] he expressed an idea which, thirty years later, was exploited by Sartre in his much publicized doctrine of "bad faith." Sartre says: "The artist who wants to be great and chooses for himself inferiority, intentionally maintains that *distance;* like Penelope, he destroys during the night what he has done during the day." [7] This is a bright observation, but we have to remind Sartre that Alfred Adler wrote a whole study on "The Problem of Distance," in which he insisted that a person suffering from an inferiority complex "attempts unerringly to interpose a 'distance' between himself and the anticipated act or decision. . . ." [8] Adler even used the exam-

---

[5] *The Practice and Theory of Individual Psychology* (New York, [1929]), p. 7.

[6] *Op. cit.*, p. 104.

[7] *L'Etre et le Néant*, pp. 551-552.

[8] Adler, *op. cit.*, p. 104.

ple of Penelope;[9] but Adler did all this in 1914, and Sartre in 1943, without referring to his predecessor.

Sartre's Existentialist psychoanalysis starts from the premise that neither Freud's nor Adler's complexes, nor their instincts (*Triebe*), are really fundamental projects, original choices. In Sartre's eyes, Freud's libido and Oedipus complex and Adler's goal of superiority and inferiority complex are only "psycho-biological residues" lacking self-evidence; they cannot constitute the ultimate term of our analysis. One may easily conceive a man whose *libido* would not be his original and undifferentiated choice and who would not express himself by a will to superiority. According to Sartre, these instincts and complexes are not general character traits of all men and are not irreducible. They can be traced back to the "fundamental project," expressing our original choice which is the *being* of man, because, for Existentialism, there is no difference between existing and choosing oneself.

What is the difference between Sartre's "fundamental project" and any other project, such as those expressed in complexes and instincts or in other, less basic choices? The answer is that Sartre's "fundamental project" is a project which does not concern a man's relation to this or that particular object of the world. The fundamental project, which is what a man *is*, expresses his being-in-the-world as a whole; and since the world itself is revealed only in the light of a goal, the fundamental project posits as its goal a certain relationship to being in general which a man chooses to maintain. Existentialist psychoanalysis is a specific phenomenological method which aims to explain a man's fundamental project.

9 *Ibid.*, p. 105.

CHAPTER FIFTEEN

HOW ABOUT ADLER'S LIFE-PLAN?

There are many points on which Sartre's Existentialist psychoanalysis agrees with the empirical psychoanalysis of Freud and his followers. For instance, both of them take into consideration the *situation* of the person to be analyzed, since both deal with man as he lives in the world. Both try to reconstitute the life of the individual from birth to the beginning of the analysis, using any kind of objective material, such as letters, witnesses, etc. Each "historical" fact in the life of the individual is considered as a factor and a symbol of his psychic evolution.

On the other hand there are many basic problems on which the Viennese classical psychoanalysis and its Parisian existentialist apostasy are in complete disagreement. One of them is the deterministic character of Freud's theory. To be sure, it is not a "horizontal" determinism, which would explain an action merely by its temporal antecedents; it is a "vertical" determinism, explaining an act by its simultaneously existing, underlying desire, which, itself, rests on a still deeper complex. However, since, for Freud, complexes are acquired in early childhood and determine the child's subsequent life, this vertical determinism is actually based on a horizontal one. In empirical psychoanalysis the complex exists before its symbolic manifestations, so that it is constituted by the *past*. "Consequently," Sartre concludes, "the dimension of the *future* does not exist for [Freudian] psychoanalysis." [1]

Sartre is ready to adopt the method of Freud's empirical psychoanalysis when it tries to reveal the significance of an act by assuming that every action, even the most unimportant, is not the simple effect of the previous psychic condition, but is inte-

[1] *L'Etre et le Néant,* p. 536.

grated as a secondary structure in the wholeness of the individual. "But if we adopt the method of [Freud's] psychoanalysis . . . we must apply it in a reverse way. . . . Instead of understanding the considered phenomenon by its past, we conceive the understanding act as a return of the future toward the present." [2]

We must agree with Sartre that the dimension of the future does not exist for Freud's psychoanalysis. But how does this criticism apply to Alfred Adler's individual psychology? Was it not Adler who wrote, for example:

Let me observe that if I know the *goal* of a person I know in a general way what will happen. . . . If I am acquainted only with the *causes*, know only the reflexes, the reaction-times, the ability to repeat such facts, I am aware of nothing that actually takes place in the soul of a man.[3]

This was written in 1914, when Sartre was nine years old. Adler's whole life work was dedicated to the search for man's "goal" or "life-plan." Adler continues:

Every phenomenon, if it is to give us any understanding of a person, can only be grasped and understood if regarded as preparation to some goal. . . . As soon as the goal of a psychic movement or its *life-plan* has been recognized, then we are to assume that all the movements of its constituent parts will coincide both with the goal and the life-plan. . . . The properly understood part-movements must, when combined, give the integrated life-plan and final goal. Consequently, we insist that, without worrying about the tendencies, milieu, and experiences, all psychical powers are under the control of a directive idea and all expressions of emotion, feeling, thinking, willing, acting, and dreaming, as well as psycho-pathological phenomena, are permeated by one unified life-plan.[4]

Now, is not Sartre's *original choice* the counterpart of Adler's *goal*, and Sartre's *fundamental project* the replica of Adler's *life-plan?* And do goal and life-plan not imply the dimension of the future? Adler was little interested in the causes of certain illnesses, but very much in the *purposes* which the patient wished to achieve in "arranging" his symptoms. And it was under the

2 *Ibid.*
3 *Individual Psychology,* p. 3.
4 *Ibid.,* pp. 4-6.

angle of the *future,* anticipated by the patient in his goal, that Adler explained the patient's present. This is exactly the "return of the future toward the present," which Sartre claims to be one of the original features of his Existentialist psychoanalysis.

If Sartre insists that man's choice may be changed, Adler affirmed the same with regard to the life-plan when he wrote: "The psychotherapeutic treatment has for its object to show the patient . . . that he can change his life-plan. . . ."[5]

Sartre may reply that his *original choice* and *fundamental project* have a more basic philosophical meaning with ontological implications which cannot be found in Adler's *goal* and *life-plan.* We do not deny it, and shall later explain the deeper ontological significance of those Sartrean concepts. But being a psychiatrist and not a philosopher, Adler was not interested in giving an ontological foundation to his goal and life-plan concepts. Practically, however, these Adlerian conceptions have the same explanatory functions as Sartre's, and they were propounded thirty years before Sartre published his *L'Etre et le Néant.*

When Sartre wrote so many pages to explain in just which respects he disagrees with Adler, why did he not give a single acknowledgment to the basic ideas he has in common with that Viennese psychiatrist, and which, probably, he has borrowed from him? Should this not be considered as an example of that "bad faith" which Sartre so violently castigates in his books, and which he defines as lying to oneself and masking from oneself an unpleasant truth?

---

[5] "Individual-Psychological Treatment of Neurosis" (1913), *Individual Psychology,* p. 50.

CHAPTER SIXTEEN

EXISTENTIALISM IS A PERSONALISM

Among the teachers who left a strong impression on Sartre's mind, in addition to Heidegger and Husserl, we find Emile Chartier, better known under his pseudonym Alain. Now Alain was a strong believer in personal freedom. It was he who taught Sartre that what we call "character" is not an unchangeable stamp impressed upon an individual, but a kind of oath (*serment*), freely taken by the individual. He who says, "I am an irascible person," has neither inherited nor acquired this temperament, but has committed himself freely to anger. That is to say, anger is the free project of his being-for-others.

From this premise Sartre draws the very radical conclusion: "There are no characters, there is only a free project of myself." [1] Only for the other person do I appear as a character. For the other person who grasps me as an object, I am noble or vile, an irascible coward or a courageous character; and by the other person's gaze this aspect is reflected in me. That means that, as a being-for-itself, I do not have a character but am only my free project. As a being-for-others, that is to say, as an object, I appear to have a character. As long as I allow myself to be fascinated by the other person's gaze, I will grasp myself not as a subject but as an ego-object, just as he grasps me with his gaze. And I will see myself as endowed with a definite, invariable character, which is, in reality, nothing but a psychic substance. He who says, "I am now fifty years old, and it is too late for me to change," considers himself under the image of an invariable substance, a thing-in-itself.

To a philosopher of freedom and action—and in this respect Sartre is the most radical, not only since Bergson but also since

[1] *L'Etre et le Néant*, p. 637.

Fichte—substance must appear as an inhuman, subhuman concept. Therefore Sartre rejects substance in any form, be it called character, temperament, human nature, or what you will. Principles like heredity, education, environment, and psychological constitution are, in his eyes, nothing but "the big explanatory idols of our epoch," because they correspond to a substantialist interpretation of man.

On the other hand, Sartre does not want to crumble the individual down into a kind of psychic dust. What we call an individual *is* a unit, in his eyes also, but it is "a unit of responsibility." This unit may be "hateful or lovable, blamable or praisable, but nevertheless *personal*." [2]

Thus we may classify Existentialism as a *personalism*.

This personal unit, of which substance is only a "caricature," is considered by Existentialism as a free unification. And this unification comes before the diversity which it unifies. It is what Scholasticism called *unitas ante rem*. It is unification in the world, the unification of an original project, and this unification is a "non-substantial absolute."

It is in this sense that Sartre tried to write Baudelaire's biography, which, as he told me in a letter from Algiers, he considers a practical application of his Existentialist psychoanalysis.

The term "character" comes from the Greek word χαρακτήρ which means "coining" or "stamping." And we are accustomed to use this term in the sense of the stamped peculiarities a person possesses as a result of his heredity and environment. Geneticists and sociologists will not easily accept Sartre's thesis of the non-existence of characters, for their experimental research taught them a quite different lesson. However, utter disregard and even contempt for empirical science is one of the features of Existentialism. In it, science has been swallowed by moral philosophy.

Modern dramatic literature has been based on characters. Shakespeare's Hamlet, Goethe's Egmont, Racine's Phèdre are characters of definite structures which determine their actions in given circumstances.

2 *Ibid.*, p. 648.

One wonders how Sartre could become such a powerful dramatic author without using characters. His Goetz von Berlichingen, in *Le Diable et le bon Dieu,* shows no longer any of the features of a character. He has no definite coining, but is a sequence of three different beings, each of which has a different project. In the first part of the drama his fundamental project is to do evil for evil's sake, as a refusal of a world which rejects him. In the second part his basic project is to do good, because it seems to be impossible and because it is "the best way of being alone." [3] In the last part, after having liberated himself from the belief in God, Goetz's project becomes one of fighting in a revolutionary war for the liberation of the mutinous German peasants, that is, to do good by using evil in the form of violence. Each of these projects changes him into another type of person, and yet we feel that these types are united by a bond, for which Sartre's concept of "unit of responsibility" seems indeed to be an adequate expression.

The great tragedians of France's classical age, especially Racine and Corneille, were extremely anxious to comply with the rules of Tragedy established by Aristotle, and the French Academy watched rigorously that these rules be not violated. We are sure that nothing is farther from Sartre's mind than preoccupations of this kind. And yet—ironically enough—his conception of a characterless drama is in agreement with Aristotle's classical teachings. "In a play," the great Greek philosopher wrote, "they do not act in order to portray characters. It is the action, i.e., its fable or plot, that is the end and purpose of tragedy. . . . A tragedy is impossible without action, but there may be one without characters." [4]

We see that Sartre still has a chance some day to wear the green, gold-embroidered dresscoat, the sword, and the cocked hat of a member of the French Academy.

---

[3] "Le Diable et le bon Dieu," *Les Temps Modernes* (June, 1951), p. 2165.
[4] *De Poetica,* 1450 a. Bywater trans.

CHAPTER SEVENTEEN

THE UNCONSCIOUS AND BAD FAITH

"Existentialist psychoanalysis rejects the postulate of the unconscious." [1] With this categorical statement Sartre draws a clear line between his type of psychoanalysis and that propounded by Freud, Adler, Jung, and most of their pupils.

It is the concept of "bad faith" (*mauvaise foi*) which, in Existentialist psychoanalysis, replaces the notions of unconscious, censorship, and repression.

Now the unconscious is a psychological concept, while bad faith is a moral idea, implying a value judgment; and one may be surprised to see a modern philosopher replacing scientific concepts with moral ones. Ever since Spinoza proclaimed that in nature there is no good or evil, it has been considered one of the most important steps in human progress that man was able to separate the domain of facts from the domain of values and to eliminate the latter from the realm of science. As long as a person suffering from a mental disease was thought to be possessed by the spirit of evil, our society was a barbaric one. Only since the disease has been considered as a neutral fact and no longer as a moral value has mankind been civilized. Thus, by replacing hypothetical scientific concepts, such as the "unconscious" or "repression," with the moral concept of "bad faith," which implies a condemnation, Sartre seems to attack one of the most precious attainments of civilization. However, in this respect, as in so many others, he is only following Heidegger, who had frenziedly torn down all the partitions between facts and values, between logical structures and pre-logical emotions, between theoretical and practical concepts. We have to take this tendency as one of the features of Existentialism.

But now let us examine Sartre's concepts of bad faith, which

[1] *L'Etre et le Néant*, p. 658.

he uses in Existentialist psychoanalysis to replace the concepts of unconscious, censorship, and repression of empirical psychoanalysis.

Sartre establishes a basic relation between bad faith and the lie; bad faith is a lie of a specific type, a lie to oneself. A man is of bad faith if he knows the truth and tries to hide it from himself. A person of bad faith is conscious of his bad faith. Acting in bad faith, a person is the deceiver and the deceived at the same time. As far as I am the deceiver, I must know that I am deceiving myself; and as far as I am deceived, I believe in the lie I have manufactured, hiding from myself that I am the manufacturer. In bad faith I am running away from the truth, but I cannot really be ignorant of the fact that I am running away.

Now, according to Sartre, Freud replaces bad faith by a lie without a liar. In empirical psychoanalysis the liar, which is I, myself, is replaced with the concepts of the unconscious, the *id*, repression, censorship, etc., which are not I. I am an ego, but I am not the *id*, that unconscious instinct which compels me to steal. Freud's ideas of the unconscious *id* and of a censorship acting without our knowledge allow us to consider ourselves not as liars but as deceived persons of good faith. And for this reason Sartre rejects the Freudian concepts of unconscious, *id*, censorship, repression, etc., because they are nothing but vehicles of bad faith, means of practicing our bad faith in good faith.

Condemning the "mythological," personifying, metaphorical language of Freud, Sartre affirms that in order to do its job the "censor" in our soul must know the truth it is repressing into the unconscious. The censorship is a selective principle, allowing decent impulses to pass and repressing only indecent, illicit sexual impulses. How can the censor select and separate one from another without being conscious of them? How can censorship distinguish between repressible and nonrepressible impulses without being conscious of distinguishing them? Is it possible, Sartre asks, to conceive a knowledge which would be ignorant of itself? And here again he refers to Alain, who said, "To know is to know that one knows" (although this thesis had been refuted by Piaget's child tests).

Sartre concludes that censorship is conscious of itself. It is conscious of being conscious of the tendency to repress in order not to be conscious of it. Thus censorship is action in bad faith. In the eyes of our Existentialist psychoanalyst, Freud's empirical discipline does not help us to fight bad faith, because it introduces between the unconscious and the conscious an autonomous consciousness of bad faith which it calls "censorship." According to Sartre, Freud's distinction between the *ego, id,* and the *superego* [2] is nothing but a "verbal terminology."

According to Existentialist psychoanalysis, the very idea of "dissimulating" something implies the unity of one and the same psyche and, within this unity, a double activity aimed equally at locating the hidden something and hiding it. These two activities are complementary. In separating conscious and unconscious events by means of censorship, Freud has not succeeded, according to Sartre, in dissociating those two activities. How can the repressed tendency "disguise" itself without the consciousness of being repressed or disguised and without a project of disguise? Furthermore, Sartre asks, how can one explain the pleasure or anxiety accompanying the symbolic achievement of the tendency unless consciousness does have, in spite of censorship, an obscure comprehension of the aim to be reached, as simultaneously desired and forbidden? Having split the conscious unity of the psyche, Freud, according to Sartre, has always to suppose a kind of "magic unity," which binds together all psychic phenomena. What empirical psychoanalysis has done is to change bad faith into a fictitious intrusive person called "the censor," but this does not mean that bad faith has been eliminated.

But did not Sartre himself prove that the contrary of bad faith, sincerity, is merely a self-contradictory ideal which man cannot reach? He himself has shown that constitutionally man is not what he is, and is what he is not. Consequently man can never coincide with himself, and only complete coincidence with ourselves is sincerity. Being split into a subject and an object, man cannot coincide with himself and is therefore necessarily incapable of complete sincerity. Only things coincide with them-

[2] See e.g. Freud's *An Outline of Psychoanalysis,* N. Y., 1948.

selves, but things cannot be sincere because they have no consciousness. The only being capable of sincerity would be God, for he would be at the same time a being-for-himself (consciousness) and a being-in-itself (objective world). But Sartre does not believe in God.

The champion of sincerity requires that a lazy man be sincere in recognizing that he is lazy. But in achieving this sincerity and recognizing that he is lazy, the lazy individual admits that he is a thing which cannot change; he denies the very freedom which would allow him to change and to project himself toward becoming an industrious person. But denying one's freedom means to be of bad faith. Thus, in his very act of sincerity, an act of good faith, man is of bad faith. And in refusing to recognize his laziness as a definite thing-like constitution, in recognizing his freedom and its possibilities, the lazy man refuses to be sincere; but, at the same time, he escapes bad faith which would be the denial of his freedom. Admitting that "this contradiction is constitutive of the requirement of sincerity," Sartre was not entitled to reproach Freud, because in introducing the concepts of unconsciousness, censorship, and repression, he had not eliminated bad faith. Was Sartre really sincere when he required from empirical psychoanalysis the achievement of the ideal of sincerity which he himself had found incompatible with the very nature of human consciousness?

However this may be, in opposing Freud's hypothesis of the unconscious, Sartre sides with one of Freud's pupils, the Viennese psychiatrist Wilhelm Steckel, who had broken with his master. Steckel, in his study on frigid women, says: "Every time I was able to push my investigation far enough, I ascertained that the nucleus of the psychosis was conscious." He mentions, for instance, that many women whom matrimonial deception has made "frigid," only mask from themselves and from their partners the pleasure they actually find in the sexual act. Following Steckel, Sartre speaks of a "pathological bad faith" in these women, which Freud's empirical psychoanalysis would be unable to explain.

Existentialist psychoanalysis draws the conclusion that there is no such thing as an "unconscious," that everything psychic is conscious. But if this is so, it is hard to understand why Sartre needs to establish a new type of psychoanalysis. If nothing is hidden in the unconscious, why is it then necessary to analyze an individual? What other function can psychoanalysis have than to bring to consciousness certain tendencies which had been repressed into the unconscious, and thus to relieve an individual of this repressed material and its neurotic manifestations?

To this Sartre answers with the very subtle, but not very convincing, distinction between "consciousness" and "cognition," which is the basis of that compromise he tried to achieve between Descartes and Heidegger; it is expressed in his *cogito préréflexif*. Sartre's pre-reflective *cogito* differs from Descartes' *cogito* in that it is conscious, without having cognition. This assumption helped him to avoid Descartes' primacy of cognition and to affirm Heidegger's primacy of existence, without giving up the Cartesian subjectivity.

Applied to Existentialist psychoanalysis, this distinction signifies that "if the fundamental project is *lived* by the subject completely consciously, it does not at all mean that it must also be *known* by it; rather the contrary is true." [3] Our consciousness lacks the means which would permit both analysis and conceptualization. "It is penetrated with a great light, without being able to express what this light enlightens." [4] It is a "mystery in full light." Sartre's distinction between "consciousness" and "cognition" seems to coincide with Emil Froeschel's distinction between "not-expression-ripe" and "expression-ripe" psychic events, which is also supposed to replace Freud's correlation between "unconscious" and "conscious" factors.[5]

Sartre thinks that the individual, led by the psychoanalyst, would not be able to recognize the complex if it had been unconscious. But the individual does not only *accept* a hypothesis offered by the psychoanalyst, he sees what it is. This is only possible if he has never ceased to be conscious of the profound ten-

---

[3] *L'Etre et le Néant*, p. 658.
[4] *Ibid.*, p. 658.
[5] E. Froeschel, *Philosophy in Wit* (New York, 1948), pp. 13-30.

dencies of the complex, which are not different from its consciousness itself. Sartre concludes that the psychoanalytic interpretation only allows man to "take cognition" (*prendre connaissance*) of what he is, and not to "take consciousness" (*prendre conscience*) of that fact; because man never loses consciousness of what he is. For Existentialist psychoanalysis no psychic reality is unconscious; and it could not logically be otherwise, since Existentialism identifies consciousness with existence.

CHAPTER EIGHTEEN

HOW FREE IS OUR PROJECT?

We have seen that Existentialist psychoanalysis is a discipline aimed at uncovering a man's original choice, a man's fundamental project. Now we have to ask ourselves to what extent this project is free. In this respect Sartre admits very narrow limits of our freedom, which he designates by the words "situation" and "facticity." We choose the world, however, not in its context, but only in its significance, by choosing ourselves. We choose ourselves only in our way of being and not in our being itself and are thus responsible only for our way of being.

My factual "situation," for example, is characterized by my position in the world, by all the obstacles I meet and all the help I receive, all the resistance I have to overcome in order to reach my aim. However, this situation exists only in correlation with my project, my attempt to transcend the actual facts in my journey toward a goal. For actuality is revealed to me as resistance or aid only in the light of my free project. A big mountain, for instance, offers tremendous resistance if my free project is to build a railroad, for then I have to dig a tunnel through it. On the other hand it is a big help if my free project is to see the surrounding landscape. Only in the light of my free project is this mountain either an obstacle or a help; in itself, it is neutral.

Sartre concludes that man meets obstacles only in the field of his freedom, and there is no freedom except "in situation." Thus facticity, or situation, becomes a condition of freedom and not, as determinism affirms, an obstacle to it. Nobody can escape from a jail in which he has not been imprisoned. Man encounters everywhere obstacles and resistance which he has not created. This encountering is what Sartre calls "facticity" or "situation." However, the obstacles and resistance become obstacles and resistance only by virtue of, and through, man's free project.

We are free only with respect to, and *in spite of,* a given situation. "Without obstacle, no freedom!" Sartre says; and freedom becomes for him tantamount to escaping from being-in-itself. Our free action supposes a "naughtization" of an actuality. Taking into account situation, actuality, facticity, Sartre concludes that our freedom is freedom of choice and not freedom of obtaining.

To act freely does not mean for Sartre to act without a motive. However, the motive does not determine the action, and appears only by virtue of and within a chosen project. And the project is free. Only by virtue of and within his free project to become the ruler of all Gaul, did the power of the Occidental Church appear to Clovis as a motive for conversion. The motive owes its entire meaning to the project the person adopts; and that project is free.

Also my choice of myself meets with great opposition from facticity. "Can I choose to be tall if I am short?" asks Sartre, who is far from being a giant. He answers that in a comparative sense he himself chooses his body to be weak only if his project is to become a boxer or a baseball star. However, if he remains in the city—for Sartre that means in the café—and chooses nothing but discussions and literary work, his body will not be weak. It is weak only in the light of a certain free project, which he has not chosen, that of becoming a sportsman. Thus freedom creates its own obstacles and is limited only by itself.

We have here an example of that somehow sophistic skill with which Sartre changes compulsion into freedom and freedom into compulsion, necessity into choice and choice into necessity; and we understand a caustic remark on Existentialism in the satirical Parisian magazine *Le Canard enchaîné:* "I say *my freedom* as I say *my wife*. This does not prevent me from being a cuckold."

The only true limit to our freedom Sartre admits, is that arising from the existence of some other person. "I am a Jew, an Aryan, handsome or ugly. . . . I am all this for another person . . . without any hope of modifying it. . . . I am something which I have not chosen to be." [1]

[1] *L'Etre et le Néant*, pp. 606-607.

Theoretically, Sartre is not much worried about this situation. For since this limit of his freedom is the freedom of another person, he can maintain his thesis that freedom meets no limit but in freedom. However, practically, the fact that the one freedom is mine and the other is not mine makes a great deal of difference. Sartre does not deny it. We are "cast" into the world, face to face with the other person, and thus our existence is a limit to his freedom and his freedom is a limit to ours. It is in this that Sartre sees the origin of the concepts of guilt and sin in a world where there is no God. It is *vis-à-vis* the other person that man is guilty. And in his impressive play *Huis Clos* ("No Exit"), Sartre showed that the other person's "gaze," impeding our escape into behavior of bad faith, is the real meaning of the idea of hell.

Now, through the glance of the other I am, for instance, a Jew. He determines me as such; I am it for-the-other, without having chosen it. What attitude have I to take in order to recover my freedom in this situation? Here is Sartre's answer

A Jew is not first a Jew and afterward ashamed or proud; but it is his pride in being a Jew, his shame, or his indifference which will reveal to him his being-a-Jew. And this being-a-Jew is nothing besides his free manner of accepting it. . . . In fury or in hate, in pride or shame, in disgusted refusal or in joyful claim, I have to choose to be what I am.[2]

It is remarkable that Sartre published this statement in 1943, in Paris, under the Nazi occupation!

If his theory that freedom creates its own obstacles in the inanimate world reminds us of the theories of Fichte, his thesis of free acceptance of what we are reminds us of the ethics of the Stoics. Nevertheless, Sartre's doctrine has its personal note. He thinks that race, ugliness, and so on, can appear only within the limits of one's own choice of inferiority or of pride: that is to say, these features can appear only with the significance which my freedom ascribes to them. I do not choose to be for the other person what I am for him, but if I am for myself what I am for him, it is only because I choose myself as I appear to him. But I am

2 *Ibid.*, p. 612.

free not to choose myself as I appear to the other person. Only my own recognition of the freedom of the anti-semites, that is to say, only my own acceptance of my being-a-Jew for them, can constitute a true limit of my freedom. "If it pleases me, however, to consider them as *mere objects,* my being-a-Jew disappears immediately and yields to the simple consciousness of being a free and unqualifiable transcendence," for the being-for-itself cannot *be* anything. Paul Valéry already said: *"L'Esprit est le refus indéfini d'être quoi que ce soit. Ce qui n' est pas fixé n'est rien, ce qui est fixé est mort."* [3] As long as we are alive we become, and are in the making, even when we have reached the age of eighty.

This ability of freedom and of its most powerful weapon, the gaze, to change another subject into an object has been exemplified in Sartre's most moving tragedy, *Morts sans Sépulture* ("The Victors"). There, Lucie, a young woman who had joined the French underground, has been tortured and raped by the Fascists, who wanted to make her betray her comrades. She suffered every humiliation and did not speak; but she looked at her torturers and her look changed them into objects. They could violate her body, but not her freedom. "They have not touched me," she says, "nobody has touched me. I was of stone and I did not feel their hands. I looked at them and I thought: Nothing is happening. Nothing has happened." [4]

We are inclined to call this behavior "stoic." It is also Existentialist. In both teachings the ultimate freedom left to us toward a world which we cannot change is our freedom to have our "Yea" or "Nay," to accept or to refuse.

[3] *Tel Quel* (Paris, 1943), II, p. 193.—"The spirit is the indefinite refusal to be anything whatsoever. That which is not fixed is nothing; that which is fixed is dead."

[4] *Morts sans Sépulture,* p. 128.

CHAPTER NINETEEN

SEX AND LOVE IN EXISTENTIALIST PSYCHOANALYSIS

Trying to determine a man's original project, his fundamental choice, Existentialist psychoanalysis rejects Freud's libido theory, because Sartre does not consider sexuality a fundamental relation. A fundamental relation must be a project of being, must be more basic than sex.

In spite of rejecting Freud's pan-sexualism, Sartre's Existentialist psychoanalysis, nevertheless, gives an important role to sex, and most of his novels and short stories are almost pornographic. Should this be considered a typical feature of Existentialism? Apparently many Frenchmen feel that way. Sartre himself recounts that a French lady, who had used a lascivious expression, excused herself afterward, saying: "My goodness, I am becoming Existentialist!" But as a matter of fact, Existentialism in itself had no specific relation to sex until Sartre made it "sexy." Perhaps this is also one reason for the tremendous success of Sartre's version of Existentialism. In Heidegger's work there is no reference to sex, for he thinks that existence is the same for men and women. And interest in his type of Existenialism is restricted to professional philosophers.

But Sartre's Existentialism has aroused the interest of many persons who are not in any sense specialists in philosophy. Sartre does not believe that we are sexual beings because we have sexual organs. He thinks that, inversely, we have sexual organs because we are sexual beings. Infantile sexuality precedes the physiological maturity of sexual organs, and neither eunuchs nor women after the menopause cease to have sexual desires. Goethe was seventy-four when he fell in love with Ulrike von Levetzow. He wanted to marry this nineteen-year-old girl and sublimated his defeat as a lover into the heartrending "Marienbader Elegie."

For Sartre sexuality is not a contingent accident linked to our physiological nature; it is a *necessary ontological structure of our being-for-others.*

It is *desire* which reveals to us our own sexuality and that of the other person. But what is desire?

Trying to answer this question Sartre says that we have to give up the idea that our desire is lust, for this would not explain the fact that our desire always goes toward an object, that it leaves the limits of our subjectivity. Any subjective theory is unable to explain the fact that man desires a woman or woman a man and that neither of them simply desires lust. Thus, it is necessary to define desire by its transcendent object. Desire is consent to desire; it engages the whole personality. "I am an accomplice of my desire." [1]

But if that is so, we have to understand *love* as the basis of desire.

Love is one of the typical attitudes of the being-for-itself in its being-for-others.

We have already seen that, according to Sartre, the original sense of our being-for-others is *conflict.*

While I am trying to enslave another person, that other person tries to enslave me; and while I try to deliver myself from the enslavement of that other person, that other person tries to deliver himself of my hold. While the relations between the being-for-itself and the being-in-itself (the inanimate world) are unilateral, the relations involved in the being-for-others are reciprocal. Love shows it in the clearest form.

We have seen that it is by his gaze that the other person is revealed to us as a self: under the other self's gaze we feel our own being-for-others as a kind of being possessed. I am possessed by another self, whose gaze shapes my body and sees it as I will never see it. The one who looks at me possesses my secret, the secret, which I am as an object. Shame is the feeling of being an object, of recognizing myself in that dependent and congealed object which I am for some other person. The fear of being surprised in the state of nudity is explained by the fact that our

[1] *L'Etre et le Néant,* p. 457.

body symbolizes our objectivity without defense. To dress one-self means to dissimulate our object-character, to claim the right to see without being seen, the right to be a mere subject. When Adam and Eve recognized that they were naked, they were ashamed, feeling their degradation into mere objects to be looked at, each by the other.

Being "possessed" by the gaze of another self, I try to regain my being for myself. One way in which I can regain it is by absorbing the other person's freedom, which possessed mine, that is to say by *uniting* myself with the other person *as* a self. But this project is difficult to achieve. For Sartre calls our attention to the fact that it would not do for me to efface my object character by objectivizing the other person. This would only mean to get rid of my being-for-the-other-person, a project I can reach through indifference. What is required in love is that I get possession of the other person in so far as he or she is a self, a subject, a freedom endowed with a gaze, for only as such he or she possessed my being.

If love were nothing but the desire of physical possession of the other person, it would be easily satisfied. But we know that it is much more than this. Love wants to possess the other self's freedom *as* a freedom. For if through my gaze I change my love partner into an object, I have not reached my aim, and I stay alone. The lover does not want to possess the beloved as one possesses an object. He wants to possess her as a subject, a living freedom.

Now sexual desire must express this aspiration of love. Therefore the desire does not aim at possessing the beloved person's body in its physiological reality, but as the incarnation of the other person's freedom. Thus it is necessary that the other person's freedom, his being-for-himself, penetrate his whole body, even up to its surface, "so that in touching this body I am finally touching the other self's free subjectivity. This is the true sense of the word possession." [2] A caress is the expression of touching the other self's free subjectivity, as far as it is embodied.

Sartre does not deny that in sexual desire we try to possess

[2] *Ibid.*, p. 463.

another person's body, but we want to possess it as far as this body itself is possessed by the partner's freedom, that is to say, in so far as the other person's consciousness identifies itself with his body.

However, this project of desire, Sartre says, is condemned to failure, not only because the pleasure which characterizes the climax of sexual possession kills the desire, but because when this ecstasy of lust arrives, the consciousness of each partner is only consciousness of his own body; it is a reflexive consciousness, in which the transcendent character of desire has disappeared. In the climax of sexual possession, pleasure itself becomes the unique object of a person's consciousness; the whole of his attention is directed reflexively toward the embodiment of his own freedom, and that of the love partner is forgotten. Basically, desire is the wish to possess the other person and his self, his consciousness, incarnated in his body. But what desire finally achieves is only possession of ourselves. Sartre probably agrees with the French writer François Mauriac, who says: "We never find the body we have been seeking. . . . Voluptuousness is a battle without a victor." [3]

But though the project of desire is condemned to failure, how about love? In Existentialist psychoanalysis this human passion has to fulfill a great mission. We know already that, according to Sartre, man's existence is completely contingent, without any foundation. In love we try to discover a foundation of our being. By our partner's love, we try to become justified. Each of the love partners wishes to be the absolute choice of the other, not a relative contingent one. The lover feels himself offended, degraded, when the partner says that she has chosen him "among others." Only if both of them can say "We were created for each other," does the choice appear as an absolute one. Then the being-in-the-world of the beloved one is justified, and the one love partner becomes the real foundation of the other's existence. He becomes the absolute source of all values and is protected against any devaluation. He becomes the absolute center of reference for the partner, and her absolute value. How often do we hear that a

[3] F. Mauriac, *Fleuve de Feu* (Paris, 1923), pp. 124-25.

woman in love says of her beloved: "I would steal for him, kill for him!" This means that she has sacrificed traditional ethics to her partner and considers him as the absolute source of all values.

Before being loved, Sartre says, our existence was that of a "protuberance," completely unjustified and unjustifiable. But being the "absolute" choice of our love partner, having been "created" for him or for her, we feel that our existence is wanted in every detail by an absolute freedom—that of our partner. Thus we no longer feel ourselves to be supernumerary (*de trop*). "That is the basis of the joy of love: to feel our existence justified." [4]

Thus love would be the means to overcome our nausea, the feeling of the contingence and gratuitousness of our existence. In Sartre's Existentialism love has, as we see, a real metaphysical meaning. However love also is a project which is condemned to failure. In his first Existentialist film, *Les Jeux sont faits* ("The Chips are Down"), a work of high artistic value, Sartre shows the destiny of a man and a woman who, having met after death in a phantastic world of shadows, discover that they have been "created for each other." They are allowed to return to earth and to live their lives again. But only if their project of absolute love and mutual justification succeeds will they be allowed to stay on earth. Otherwise they will die again after twenty-four hours. And they die; because the project of love is condemned to failure. Why? Here are Sartre's general reasons:

We have seen that love is the project of recovering oneself from another self, of becoming the other person's absolute choice and thus of being justified by the other person's choice. This project can be realized only if the lover succeeds in being loved; for only then will he have conquered the other person as a self, as a freedom, as a subject, as a transcendence looking at him as he wishes to be looked at. "Thus it seems that love, in its essence, is the project to be loved." [5]

However, Sartre thinks that this project is a contradictory ideal. For each of the lovers wants the other to love him, without

4 *L'Etre et le Néant*, p. 439.
5 *Ibid.*, p. 443.

realizing that love is the wish to be loved; so that, for instance, in wanting my beloved to love me, I really only want her to want me to love her. Sartre concludes that the amorous relation is a system of infinite reflections, a fooling mirror game which carries with it its own frustration. Love is a kind of "dupery."

If our project were to abolish the other person's freedom and subjectivity, it would be hatred; love does not require the abolition of the other person's freedom, but only its enslavement by himself. But there remains always the possibility that my love partner may awaken from the self-enslavement of her liberty which is her love, and then use her newly conquered liberty to enslave mine, to change me into an object. And vice versa. From this springs the perpetual insecurity of lovers. Finally, Sartre thinks that love is always made relative by the presence of other people. In love each consciousness tries to shelter its being-for-others in the enslaved, and therefore benevolent, freedom of the love partner. However, as soon as the two lovers are seen together by other people, each of them not only feels his own objectivation but also that of the partner. Immediately the one partner is no longer the absolute transcendence which is the foundation and justification of the other partner's being, but a transcended transcendence, transcended not by the love partner but by other people. The coward deserter Garcin, in Sartre's dismal *Huis Clos* ("No Exit"), wants to shelter his being-for-others and, through it, his being-for-himself, in possessing and enslaving the consciousness of Estelle. If she loves him, his own repugnant picture will be reflected to himself in entire purity. And if he loves Estelle, she will see her own picture in his enslaved consciousness no longer as that of the infanticide that she is, but wonderfully transfigured.

Thus we see that love as an attempt to possess another person's freedom *as* a freedom, but as a self-enslaved freedom, is also one of those "avenues of flight" that man finds in order to escape into bad faith and an unauthentic existence.

In *No Exit*, the scene of which is hell, these attempts of Garcin and Estelle are frustrated by the permanent presence of a third person, Inez, representing other people. By her gaze both lovers are petrified into objects and compelled to be what they are in the eyes of other people, and, through them, in their own eyes. And we understand why, at the end of this grim drama, Garcin exclaims: "There is no need for red-hot pokers. Hell is other people!" [6]

But if love is a project condemned to failure, are we better off with hatred? Not at all. Hatred is resignation, for in it the individual abandons the attempt, made in love, to regain its being-for-itself by a union with another person. A man who hates tries to cease being an object for another person by destroying that other person. Hatred aims at the death of the hated subject. But what man wants to attain by the death of the other subject is, symbolically, the destruction of all other people. "The person I hate represents, in fact, all other persons." [7] By destroying all other consciousnesses I would be free of the possibility of being enslaved by others and would recover my absolute non-substantialized freedom as a being-for-myself.

But, like love, hatred also is condemned to failure. The man who hates cannot kill all people. And even if he kills the one he hates especially, he will not be able to eliminate the fact that the other person has existed. But in dying the other person has become a part of the world-in-itself. As long as the other person is alive, I can always try to buy back myself in his consciousness, to change the image which I am in his consciousness. But when his consciousness has disappeared, that which I have been for him is petrified by his death and will be that image irremediably in itself, in the past, without any possibility of ever reconquering my picture and changing it. The other one has taken the "key" of my alienation with him into the tomb. We know that, according to Existentialism, as long as a man lives he *is* not but only makes himself. Only at the moment of his death has his essence become completely crystallized, and only then he *is*, only then does he coincide with himself and become a being-in-itself. Thus by killing the man who despises me, I would change his contempt for me into a part of his eternal essence and thus perpetuate it.

---

[6] *No Exit* (New York, [1946]), p. 61.
[7] *L'Etre et le Néant*, p. 483.

This makes it clear why Sartre also considers hate as a project condemned by its very nature to failure.

We understand now why everything we have done to other people is perpetuated forever by their death. In Sartre's profound tragedy *Les Mouches* ("The Flies"), Egistus says:

Do you not know that the dead are pitiless? Their grievances are indelible because their account has been closed forever. Is it by good deeds, Nicias, that you will erase the evil you did to your mother? But what good deed can ever reach her? Her soul is a torrid noon, without a breath of wind; nothing moves there, nothing changes, nothing lives, a big fleshless sun, a motionless sun, consumes her eternally. The dead are no longer . . . and therefore they have become the incorruptible guardians of our crimes.[8]

Among the basic possible projects of our being-for-others Sartre also counts masochism and sadism, and he shows that they too are condemned to failure. But since no normal person would have any doubt about this, we need not go into it here.

As far as other possible relations with another self are concerned—collaboration, struggle, rivalry, emulation, engagement, obedience—Sartre does not examine them in detail but only says that "they all include sexual relations as their skeleton."[9] Thus we see that in spite of repudiating Freud's libido theory, Sartre gives quite an important place to sexuality. We already know that to him sexuality is a necessary ontological structure of our being-for-others. He even designates it as a "fundamental structure," but only of our being-for-others and not of our being-in-the-world, which is our very existence. It is in this respect that he seems not to go as far as Freud.

Sartre admits, with Freud, that there are no "innocent" children. He recognizes, with Freud, the sexual significance of certain objects surrounding the child. But he does not believe that an already constituted sexual instinct has given these objects and forms their sexual significance.

It rather seems to us that these matters and forms are grasped for their own sake and that they reveal to the child different *modes of*

8 *Les Mouches*, p. 47.
9 *L'Etre et le Néant*, p. 477.

being and relations to being of the being-for-itself which will clarify and shape his sexuality.[10]

Some Freudian psychoanalysts have noticed that most small children are attracted by all kinds of holes: holes in the sand, in a wall, holes in their own bodies or in the bodies of other persons. Many babies try to push their little hands into their mother's mouth or the mouths of other people. Freud, personally, insisted on the fact that the first phase of infantile sexuality is an oral one.

The baby's obstinate persistence in sucking gives evidence at an early stage of a need for satisfaction which, although it originates from and is stimulated by the taking of nourishment, nevertheless seeks to obtain pleasure independently of nourishment and for that reason, may and should be described as "sexual." [11]

We also know that the second phase in infantile sexuality, according to Freud, is called "sadistic-anal." In both the first and the second phase a hole in its own body is the center of the infant's sexuality.

Sartre denies that the child's attraction to these holes can be interpreted as a presentiment of the feminine sexual organ and the sexual act, for this would presuppose an experience the child cannot have. And, obviously, he does not believe in Freud's "archaic heritage" which a child brings with him into the world, "before any experience of his own, as a result of the experiences of his ancestors." [12] Sartre, on the contrary, thinks that it is the objective nature of the hole the child perceives in the world which will enlighten for him the objective structure of the anal zone and will give a "transcendent significance" to the erogenous zones which the child had only felt existentially.

For Existentialist psychoanalysis the hole is the symbol of a *mode of being*. It is the symbol of *nothingness* which we have to fill with our flesh. Therefore the child cannot help putting his fingers in the holes of his body. According to Sartre the hole represents to us the image of emptiness in man.

[10] *Ibid.*, p. 704.
[11] *An Outline of Psychoanalysis* (New York, [1949]), p. 28.
[12] *Ibid.*, pp. 49-50.

To stop the hole means originally to sacrifice the body so that full-ness of being may exist, that is to say, to yield to the passion of the being-for-itself to shape, to complete, and to save the wholeness of the being-in-itself.[13]

Also the opposite activity, that of boring holes, appears to Sartre as requiring Existentialist analysis, which, however, he has not yet tried.

But if the hole is the Existential symbol of nothingness, we understand that we spend a good deal of our lives in stopping up holes; stopping up holes means to achieve, symbolically, the whole of being. Putting his finger in his mouth the child tries to stop up a hole, to fill an emptiness; "he seeks the density, the uniform spheric fullness of the Parmenidean being." Thus, for Sartre, a baby sucking his finger is a kind of instinctive meta-physician. However, he still thinks that Freud supposes in the child an experience it cannot have. But does not Sartre himself presuppose more than experience in the baby, that is, an instinc-tive philosophical knowledge?

Also, when an adult is eating he stops up a hole, fights noth-ingness and makes fullness exist—not only the fullness of his belly but the fullness of being.

Only after establishing this basic ontological symbolism of the hole does Sartre's psychoanalysis pass to sexuality. He thinks of the feminine sex as basically obscene, like every gaping thing. For Sartre the vagina is a "call for being" like all other holes. "The woman calls for a foreign flesh which will transform her into a fullness of being by penetration and dilution." [14]

The woman feels her condition as a challenge, because she is "pierced." It is in this fact that Sartre sees the very origin of that inferiority complex which Adler finds in many women, ac-companied by a "masculine protest" against their feminine con-dition. Adler tells of a young woman who, one day, stood in front of the mirror and asked mother: "Did you too always want to be a man?" But according to Adler the "masculine protest" of cer-tain women against feminine strivings and sensations has its ori-

13 *L'Etre et le Néant*, p. 705.
14 *Ibid.*, p. 706.

gins in certain infantile situations, such as for instance, the uncertainty of her future sex role. Sartre sees the origin of that complex in the fact that the woman is "pierced."

To him the vagina is a mouth, a voracious mouth, which "swallows" the penis and symbolizes the idea of castration. In the sexual act the woman tries to castrate the man in order to fill the gap and change nothingness into the fullness of being.

Thus it is a presexual, existential, ontological relation which, in all these cases, is used to explain sexuality. And if I were to sum up the differences between the role of sex in Freud's empirical and in Sartre's Existentialist psychoanalysis, I should say: In Freud's empirical psychoanalysis sex is used to enlighten existence, whereas in Sartre's Existentialist psychoanalysis existence and its ontological implications are used to enlighten sex.

CHAPTER TWENTY

THE PHILOSOPHY AND PSYCHOLOGY
OF DEATH

Without death mankind would not have philosophized. This opinion of Schopenhauer's seems to be corroborated by the history of philosophy. While primitive mythology can be interpreted as an obstinate negation of the phenomenon of death as such, the main purpose of philosophy, from Socrates to Epicurus and the Stoics, was to dissipate man's fear of death. The rise of Christianity seems to have changed this tendency, for Saint Paul, Saint Augustine, and later Christian thinkers considered philosophical attempts to appease man's fear of death self-deceit and even sin, since in all these attempts human reason tried to create that which was supposed to result only from divine grace. Nevertheless, death continued to be an inspiring genius of philosophy. There is however, a great difference between the ancient philosophy of death and the Christian and modern atheistic ways of considering death. As long as we are alive, said Epicurus, death does not exist for us, and when death appears, we no longer exist. In Lucretius' *De rerum natura* we find a similar idea. On the contrary, the modern philosophy of death—the Christian as well as the atheistic one—rejects the ancients' attempts to dissipate the fear of death and tries to face death in all its dreadful reality. The whole Christian tradition from the early fifteenth century through at least the first half of the eighteenth century is filled with a strong horror and fear of death, a point of view taken very seriously by leading thinkers, such as Erasmus. This attitude toward death even affected men's actual dying, whether it be on the scaffold or the sickbed; and it also entered strongly into the literature of the age.

In the nineteenth century death became a central problem in

Schopenhauer's pessimism and in Sören Kierkegaard's Existentialist philosophy. Finally, in our epoch, Heidegger and Sartre have attracted much interest by their contributions to the philosophy of death, the latter also by his psychology of death. These modern philosophers—atheists as well as Christians—have realistically faced the issue of death and, unlike their Greek forerunners, none of them has tried to dissipate the fear of death. *"Philosophieren heisst sterben lernen"* ("To philosophize means to learn how to die"), says Karl Jaspers.[1] Now, Kierkegaard, Heidegger, Jaspers, and Sartre are Existentialists, and with Existentialism arises a new approach to death. It is characterized by a humanization and an individualization of death. Death is no longer considered as something beyond life, but as the last term of life, belonging to that series of events called life. "Man can only meet what is human . . . and death is a human phenomenon. It is the ultimate phenomenon of life, still life. As such it influences the whole life, countercurrent like."[2]

But even as a human phenomenon death is usually a general or collective concept. And a philosophy of death may still be a universal, abstract system based on the fact that all human beings have to die. However, Friedrich Schiller has already written: *"Diese Spinnweben von Systemen zerreisst das einzige Wort: 'Du musst sterben!'"* [3] ("These cobwebs of systems are torn to pieces by the single phrase: 'Thou must die!'"). Therefore Existentialism not only tries to humanize death but also to individualize it, replacing the general problem of death with the individual problem, "I have to die."

Sartre's philosophy of death is in many respects opposed to that of Heidegger. Since the French Existentialist's ideas were developed in a polemic against his German mentor, we must first consider the latter's philosophy of death.

Death, as the end of our being-in-the-world, belongs to existence; it "limits and determines the possible wholeness of exis-

[1] Quoted from I. M. Bochénski, *Europäische Philosophie der Gegenwart* (Bern, 1947), p. 198.

[2] *L'Etre et le Néant*, p. 616.

[3] *The Robbers*, Act V, Sc. 1.

tence." Consequently, Heidegger writes, our existence is "being toward death" (*"Sein zum Tode"*). Since existence is freedom, project, anticipation, it does not suffer anything passively but must be the anticipation and the free project of its own death, as "the possibility of no-longer-being-able-to-exist." [4]

The fact of being "cast into death," Heidegger continues, is revealed by anxiety. From this anxiety most human beings try to escape into the triviality of the anonymous crowd, which says: *"One* has to die some day." But this *Gerede* (idle chatter) that *"one* has to die" tries to give the impression that death concerns the "one," the anonymous crowd, not the speaker himself. "The one," Heidegger says, "is no one." [5] Thus existence in the anonymous crowd (*das Man*) is a perpetual evasion from the certainty of death as individual death, a lack of "courage to face the anxiety of death." This evasion Heidegger calls "inauthentic being for death." [6]

However, our existence becomes "authentic" through the resolute decision to free ourselves from the illusions of the anonymous crowd and to accept our death as our most personal possibility, one which can arrive at any moment and which we have to expect. In accepting freely the anxiety of death as a death which nobody else can die for us, we acquire what Heidegger calls "freedom for death." [7]

This, in a nutshell, is Heidegger's philosophy of death. I have never understood how these truisms could arouse the astounding admiration not only of many German philosophers but also of distinguished thinkers in France, Spain, and Latin America, for there is no originality in any of these Heideggerian ideas. The matter of having to be prepared to die at any moment is the very theme of the *ars moriendi* books, and it appears in Tudor and Stuart literature in innumerable places. One of the best known examples is the description in *Macbeth* of Duncan's queen as a good and pious woman who "died every day she lived." [8] Great

[4] Heidegger, *Sein und Zeit,* pp. 234, 250.
[5] *Ibid.,* p. 253.
[6] *Ibid.,* p. 259.
[7] *Ibid.,* p. 266.
[8] *Macbeth* IV, iii.

philosophers like Pascal and Nietzsche—who often are called Existentialist philosophers—expressed these ideas long before Heidegger, but in the unpretentious form of aphorisms. Thus we find in Pascal's *Pensées,* the following:

We like to rest in the society of our fellowman. . . . Being miserable like us, impotent like us, they will not help us. *We shall die alone.* Consequently we should act as if we were alone. . . . We should seek truth without hesitation.[9]

We have here, in a few unpretentious words, the essence of Heidegger's philosophy, written three centuries before him. What is missing in Pascal's aphorism to achieve Heidegger's philosophy, can be found in Nietzsche, who, sixty years before Heidegger, arrived at the conception and the words, "freedom for death." Read what Nietzsche says in the chapter of *Zarathustra* called "On Free Death."

My death, praise I unto you, the free death, which cometh unto me because I want it. . . .
    Free for death, and free in death; a holy Nay-sayer, when there is no longer time for Yea: thus understandeth he about death and life.[10]

And, in his *Götzendämmerung,* Nietzsche says likewise: "Out of love for life we should want death in a different way: free, conscious, without hazard, without sudden attack." [11]

But there is one element, and the most unsound, in Heidegger's philosophy of death which cannot be found in Nietzsche: a cult of anxiety about death. Nietzsche preaches philosophical serenity in the face of death: *"Seines Todes ist man gewiss: warum sollte man nicht heiter sein?"* [12]

Requesting that man live "authentically," by expecting his death at any moment and considering anxiety of death as the

---

[9] *Pensées,* III, 211, p. 429.

[10] "Vom freien Tode," *op. cit.,* pp. 106-107.

[11] *Götzendämmerung,* p. 144.

[12] "One is sure of one's death. Why should one not be serene?" *Bruchstücke zu den Dionysos-Dithyramben* in *Gesammelte Werke* (Munich, 1927), XX, 60, p. 233.

criterion of a life's "authenticity" (*Eigentlichkeit*), Heidegger places our whole life under the domination of death. His philosophy is a philosophy of *memento mori*. Such a philosophy might be fit for monks who sleep every night in their coffins and who, in life, have nothing to do but to prepare themselves for death. However, applied to a secular life, Heidegger's philosophy of *memento mori* would mean the end of any creative existence. If we want to perform great deeds in life, we must live under the fiction of immortality. When, in 1917, in the most critical moment of World War I, Georges Clemenceau was asked by his nation to lead her to victory, he was seventy-six years old. Had he not lived under the fiction of immortality, had he followed Heidegger's philosophy of intentional and permanent horror and fear of death, that man, who seemed to be so close to the grave, would have been paralyzed, unable to act. But he acted, disregarding the possibility of death at any moment, and led his nation to victory.

The reason was that he probably considered his life only a kind of vessel which had to be filled with values the validity of which goes beyond time. Only by participating in such timeless values can we accept our death as a natural event which does not affect these values.

Apparently Existentialists do not accept the idea that our existence is only a vessel to be filled with values. For this reason Existentialism gives too much importance to the vessel of existence and is always ready to deny the value of the contents of existence only because its vessel is fragile. However, we have to realize that the contents of that vessel called "existence" are not necessarily linked to any one specific vessel. If the contents are valuable enough then they survive their vessel and become part of the objective realm of values belonging to mankind. Homer, Plato, Shakespeare, Kant, and Lavoisier no longer exist. The vessels of their existence broke a long time ago. But the contents of those breakable vessels, the values with which they were filled, survive as part of mankind's objective spirit. Being unable to look beyond the tip of the nose of his own existence, the Existentialist—especially one of Heidegger's type—fails to recognize and appreciate the values of which his own existence is but the perishable vessel. Thus Existentialism easily degenerates into a mean egotism and egoism, tormented by the horror and fear of death.

Besides this general criticism of Heidegger's philosophy of death we have also a special argument against it. If there was anyone who had no right to preach a philosophy of individualism, which has to overcome submission under the slogans of the anonymous crowd, it was Heidegger. For when the Nazis became the masters of Germany, Heidegger, without hesitation, adopted all the slogans of the anonymous crowd and became a Nazi. What is Nazism, if not that *"Verfallenheit an das Man,"* that absorption of the individual by an anonymous crowd, which Heidegger had criticized so much? Finally, we see also that Heidegger had no philosophical basis for his condemnation of unauthentic existence and his recommendation of an authentic one, since his philosophy does not offer any foundation for value judgments, nor, being atheistic, can it refer to any theonomous axiology.

Sartre was certainly well inspired when he refused to follow Heidegger's ideas on death. He does not want to place life under the domination of death, because this would mean to meditate on one's subjectivity with the look of another self. For the being-for-itself never meets its own death, which only exists for the other self which survives. "The characteristic of a dead life is that it is a life of which another self has become the guardian." [13] Being dead is being-for-others and no longer being-for-itself; but being dead is also being-in-itself.

This theory of Sartre's needs more explanation. We remember his thesis that man is not what he is, because he is always in the making: he *is* not, but he becomes. However, this refers only to man as long as he is alive. As soon as man is dead, he is what he is, he coincides with himself. And what is man when he is dead? He is his past, and he is in-itself. But to understand this we must take into consideration Sartre's ideas of temporality.

[13] *L'Etre et le Néant,* p. 626.

The present is for-itself; it is the presence of the being-for-itself confronted with the being-in-itself. The present is a perpetual flight from being. "The present is not." [14]

The future is that which I have to be, in so far as it is possible that I may not be it. A being can be for-itself only under the perspective of a "not yet," a being whose complement is at a certain distance, beyond being. Thus everything that the being-for-itself is beyond being is the future. Human consciousness or human existence is lack, lack of coincidence with itself. Those things which each being-for-itself considers as lacking are his possibilities. Every man projects himself toward his possibilities, which are his values. But where are these possibilities?—In the future. As long as man is alive he projects himself toward his future in order to unite himself with what he is lacking and thus to become what he is. However, there is always a possibility that he would miss the future toward which he projects himself, and this is another source of anxiety. Man can be his future only in a problematic way, for he is separated from it by the nothingness which he is, by his freedom which always allows him to naught his former projects and project him toward another future.

Finally, we have the dimension of the past, and it is that which explains the "being" of the dead. While the present is for-itself, the past is in-itself, like inanimate things. It is always the past of a definite present. According to Sartre, I do not *have* my past. I *am* my past. The past is the always growing wholeness of the being-in-itself which we are. That is to say, as being-for-myself I am my present and my projection toward the future, while my past has become a part of the world-in-itself, something completely unchangeable, which is my essence and has the solidity of a thing. In this sense Sartre says that our past is the perpetually growing wholeness of the being-in-itself which we are.

Now, at the moment of my death, I shall be entirely my past and thus a part of the world-in-itself. By death the being-for-itself becomes entirely a being-in-itself, having ceased to be a present and a possible future and become totally past. And the past

[14] *Ibid.*, p. 168.

is the being-in-itself, the essence of a man, which, as we know, becomes crystallized at the moment of his death.

If as a living being I cannot slip back into my past, it is because this past is in-itself while I am for-myself. The past is that which I am, without being able to live it. If we say of a man that he is a drinker, or a composer, or a good father, we refer, and can refer, only to his past, because only in the past we are what we are in the form of an unchangeable being-in-itself. In the present, as being-for-ourselves, we *are* not but we become, we are projected toward an uncertain future, toward possibilities which can always be naughted by our freedom. But in the past, the world of the being-in-itself, there is no freedom. *Facta infecta fieri nequeunt* ("Things done cannot be undone"), as the Romans said; for things belong to the world-in-itself. And our past too belongs to this world, and cannot be changed by our freedom. This is the sense of Sartre's statement, *"Le passé c'est l'en-soi que je suis en tant que dépassé."* [15]

At the moment of death "the chips are down," no more bets can be made. Death petrifies us forever, from the moment it strikes us. Alive, I am a being-for-myself, as far as I am my present; a being-in-itself as far as I am my past; and a being-for-others, in so far as I am a transcended transcendence, but always able to transcend another self by my gaze and recover my freedom. Dead, I am no longer a being-for-myself, I have become entirely a being-in-itself; because my present has slipped away, my future possibilities have disappeared, and I have become entirely my past. Dead, I am also a being-for-others, but definitely transcended by the gaze of the other, because I am no longer a transcendence, a freedom able to dominate another freedom and to influence my being-for-others. "To be dead means to be the prey of the living ones." [16]

As long as we are alive, we are "on reprieve" (*en sursis*). The man who was a coward in his past, and is still alive, has kept his freedom to naught this past, to project himself toward a heroic future and thus give the lie to other people's opinion of him. A

---

[15] *Ibid.*, p. 162.
[16] *Ibid.*, p. 628.

living coward is a coward "on reprieve," who can still die a hero. But when he dies a coward, he is a coward forever, his essence has become crystallized as that of a coward. In this sense we say that death petrifies us forever as we are at the moment it strikes us. Our being is left in the hands of other people, like a cloak we abandoned to them at the moment of our disappearance. They can do with it what they wish. Death gives the final victory to the point of view of other people.

The heroes in Sartre's novels and dramas know this. There is, for instance, Sorbier, in the tragedy *Morts sans Sépulture* ("The Victors"), a man of the resistance, who, with his friends, has become a prisoner of the Fascists. The friends are waiting for their hearing, that is to say, for their torture and death. Sorbier has a heroic mind, but he knows that he has a sickly body, feeble nerves which may abandon him when they torture him in order to make him reveal the whereabouts of the other men of the underground. He fears not death, but physical pain and his own moral weakness under it. He says to his comrade Canoris:

"I tell you that I would betray my own mother. . . . It is unjust that one minute suffices to corrupt a whole life. . . . Oh, there are cowards like me, but they will never know it. They are lucky." [17] But he is only a coward on reprieve, and by a last free act he dies like a hero. The chips are down, he has become a hero forever, his essence has become entirely crystallized as that of a hero.

On the other hand there is Garcin, in *Huis Clos* ("No Exit"), a deserter and coward, who died as a coward and is now in a fictional hell with his essence irretrievably crystallized as that of a coward. "It was only a physical lapse," he says, "that might happen to anyone." Thus he flees into bad faith. But he does not believe his lie to himself, and knows that his surviving comrades consider him the coward he definitely is now, since his whole being has become his past and thus a being-in-itself. Being now the prey of his surviving friends, he exclaims desperately:

"Oh, if only I could be with them again, for just one day; I'd

[17] *Morts sans Sépulture*, pp. 61-63.

fling their lie in their teeth." [18] But it is too late, the chips are down, his life has become a part of the world-in-itself, it has been congealed, petrified into the past. *"La mort transforme la vie en destin"* ("Death changes life into destiny"), says André Malraux in his novel *Espoir*. It is in the past that we are what we are. In Hegel's words: *"Unser Wesen ist, was gewesen ist."* ("Our essense is what has been.")

There is no doubt that Sartre's philosophy of death is extremely interesting. However, it implies the paradox that *alive* man *is not; and dead*, he *is.*

"One always dies too soon or too late," says Inez, in *No Exit*.[19] Very seldom our death comes like the last sound of a melody, making an organic whole of our life. In general, death surprises us in evolution and what it leaves of us is an unfinished project, a sketch, not a detailed painting. Pierre Curie, who with his wife initiated the whole science of radioactivity, died in a Paris street accident. His existence, which had been projected as a perfect work of art, became a torso. The perpetual interference of chance with the individual's projects shows that death is not our free possibility but the negation of all our possibilities. Death is the project which destroys all projects, even itself; it is the destruction of all our expectations. Besides, since the dead are the prey of the living, death is the definite triumph of some self other than mine. Sartre summarizes his refutation of Heidegger's philosophy of death in this way:

We have to conclude, in opposition to Heidegger, that far from being my own possibility death is a *contingent fact*, which, as such, escapes me on principle and springs from my facticity. I can neither discover my death nor wait for it . . . for it is that which disarms all expectations. . . . Death is a mere fact like birth; it comes to us from outside and changes us into something which is outside. . . . There is no place for death in the being-for-itself: the latter cannot wait for it . . . nor project himself toward it. . . . Death is only a certain aspect of facticity and of being-for-others. . . . It is absurd that we were born, it is absurd that we die.[20]

18 *No Exit*, p. 52.
19 *Op. cit.*, p. 58.
20 *L'Etre et le Néant*, pp. 630-631.

This is a clear renunciation of Heidegger's philosophy of "freedom for death" and "being toward death." Consequently, Sartre also refuses to base his distinction between an "authentic" and an "unauthentic" existence on man's attitude toward death. His distinction between the "authenticity" and "unauthenticity" of our existence is based on man's attitude toward his *freedom*. He who recognizes his freedom as the source of all values and accepts the responsibility and anxiety arising from this knowledge exists *authentically*. He who denies freedom and flees from it into bad faith under the pretext of a determination which compels him, for instance, to be lazy, in the same manner as a stone is heavy—he who accepts ready-made values—exists *unauthentically*. Applying this concept to a definite situation, Sartre says, in his book on the Jewish question:

If it is agreed that man may be defined as a being having freedom within the limits of a situation, then it is easy to see that the exercise of this freedom may be considered as *authentic* or *unauthentic* according to the choices made in the situation. . . . And the Jew does not escape this rule: authenticity for him is to live to the full his condition as a Jew; unauthenticity is to deny it or to attempt to escape from it.[21]

The anti-Semite always exists unauthentically, for

He is a man who is afraid. Not of the Jews, to be sure, but of himself, of his own consciousness, of his liberty, of his instincts, of his responsibilities . . . of everything except the Jews. He is a coward who does not want to admit his cowardice to himself.[22]

Thus the difference between authenticity and unauthenticity has a more general meaning in Sartre's philosophy: it is an attitude toward freedom and responsibility, and not just toward death, as it is in Heidegger's philosophy.

To be sure, in his *Republic of Silence* Sartre says that during the German occupation "the choice that each of us made of his life was an authentic choice, because it was made face to face with death," [23] and thus gives the impression that he uses the

21 *Anti-Semite and Jew* (New York, [1948]), pp. 90-91.
22 *Ibid.*, p. 53.
23 *Op. cit.*, p. 499.

term "authenticity" in Heidegger's sense. However, only because
death was ever present for the fighters of the Maquis, was it the
test case of this situation.

In *Morts sans Sépulture* Sartre has, however, shown that
there are situations in which even when one is confronted with a
choice between life and death the authentic choice is not necessarily death but can be life. The group of French underground
fighters, imprisoned by the Fascists, is suddenly told by their
hangmen, that if they continue to be silent they will be shot, but
if they betray their leader they will be freed. Fortunately the
situation has changed, they can speak without risking the life of
their leader, because now they know the latter is in a safe place.
They deliberate, and Lucie, the young woman, wants to choose
death. She had behaved heroically, had not spoken nor cried
under torture. If she accepts death now, her life will end on a
heroic note and will enter the past as the life of a heroine. However, if she continues to live, another event may occur which will
find her less heroic, and she may spoil her eternal essence as a
heroine which she has won so hardly. Thus she chooses death, because she wants to escape the freedom and responsibility of tomorrow, which would make her a heroine on reprieve.

Another of the underground comrades, Henri, feels as Lucie
does. He also wants to choose death rather than life under the
responsibilities of a new freedom. He already has to bear the responsibility for the death of Lucie's fifteen-year-old brother
François, whom he had to kill because the boy was ready to betray his comrades in order to save his own life.

However, Canoris, a Greek anti-Fascist who has joined the
French underground, makes clear to his friends that it needs
more courage to accept life and continue to fight the German invader than to die under the bullets of the firing squad; that he
who decides to continue life under these circumstances makes an
authentic choice, because it is a choice of freedom and responsibility, while he who chooses death, makes an unauthentic choice,
because he chooses escape from freedom and responsibility.

We see, then, that while this kind of Sartrean authenticity is
contrary to that required by Heidegger, it is ethically far nobler.
But there is still another reason why Lucie and Henri prefer

death to life. Henri expresses it by saying: "I had already packed up my luggage, I was already on the other side. Now I must return. I shall see all that again. . . . I thought that it was for the last time." [24]

In short, Henri thought he was already in front of the *wall*, where life ends. This symbol of the wall, which is a recurrent theme in Sartre's novels and dramas, characterizes his interesting *psychology of death*. Let us say some words about it.

For Sartre, man is essentially freedom, the anticipation of his own possibilities projected toward his future. But as soon as man knows that he has to die at a definite, very near date, he can no longer "project" himself toward the future; he feels as if a wall had suddenly been erected in front of him, a wall beyond which he cannot go, think, feel, or plan. He is no longer a real man, because being man means being free to project oneself toward the future, toward one's possibilities; and this is just what he cannot do, because of the wall in front of him. This is the situation of a man condemned to death, or of one so ill that the physicians have told him he will not live to see the next year. Being no longer a man in the sense of a free project toward the future, the individual who stands before the wall has no longer any moral or spiritual community with his former fellow men. His kind now are only those who face the same wall.

That is, roughly, the idea Sartre expresses not only in his masterful book of short stories published under the title *Le Mur* ("The Wall"), but also in many of his other writings, especially in his great tragedy, *Morts sans Sépulture*.

In *Le Mur* we see, for instance, the Spanish loyalist, Pablo Ibbieta, in his death cell with two other republicans, awaiting execution by Franco's soldiers. Here are some of his reflections on his fellow prisoner Tom:

For twenty-four hours I had lived at Tom's side, I had heard him, I had talked to him, and I knew that we had nothing in common. And now we resemble each other like twins, only because we shall die together.[25]

24 *Morts sans Sépulture*, p. 185.
25 *Le Mur* (Paris, 1939), pp. 22-23; Amer. ed., *Intimacy and Other Stories* ([Copyright by New Directions, 1948], Norfolk, Conn., 1952).

Standing before their wall together, both are unable to project themselves toward their future, both have ceased to be real men; they understand each other, they form a community of situation. But they had nothing in common with the Belgian physician who came into their cell to see them and who was not condemned. "We looked at the Belgian, we looked at him, all three of us, because he was alive. He had gestures of a living being. . . . He could think of tomorrow." [26]

Thus those who stand before their wall no longer consider themselves living beings; they are virtually dead. Ibbieta continues:

I tell myself: afterwards, there will be nothing. But I do not understand what this means . . . I see my corpse: this is not difficult, but it is *I* who see it, with *my* eyes. . . . If I think that I shall no longer see anything, that I shall no longer hear anything, and that the world will continue for others. . . . [27]

Then, reflecting on his previous life, he says to himself:

I wanted to free Spain, I admired Pi y Margall, I belonged to the anarchistic movement, I had spoken in public meetings, I took everything seriously, as if I were immortal.[28]

This last sentence corroborates the idea we have expressed previously that in order to accomplish great things in life, we must live under the fiction of immortality. Ibbieta's reflections and his words, "I would not have been able to move my little finger, had I imagined I would die this way," are the best refutation of Heidegger's idea that in order to exist authentically, we must place our life under the permanent shadow of our personal death, ready to be stricken at any moment.

Ibbieta also thinks of his girl Concha, who will cry when she learns of his death. "However," he adds, "if she looked at me now, her gaze would remain in her eyes, it would not reach me. . . ." [29] Standing in front of his wall, he understands perfectly that he has no longer anything in common with those people who

[26] *Ibid.*, p. 23.
[27] *Ibid.*
[28] *Ibid.*, p. 25.
[29] *Ibid.*, p. 26.

are not prevented by anything from projecting themselves toward their future, even if it is the woman he loves.

This idea is expressed in a much more powerful way in *Morts sans Sépulture*. We know that Lucie is imprisoned with her underground comrades and that she and all of them have to die under a Fascist firing squad, all except John, the man she loved and adored. Now, standing before her wall, she has everything in common with her comrades who are in the same situation, but nothing in common with her beloved who, tomorrow, will leave the jail and can freely project himself toward his future and all its possibilities. And although this is not John's fault, Lucie's love for him has faded away. Listen to a part of their dialogue:

> *John*: Let me stay with you; I shall be silent, if you want, but I shall be here and you will not feel lonely.
> *Lucie*: Not lonely? With you? Oh, John, have you not understood yet? We have no longer anything in common.
> *John*: Have you forgotten that I love you?
> *Lucie*: It was another woman that you loved. . . .
> *John*: It is you.
> *Lucie*: I am another woman. I no longer recognize myself. . . . Well, you love me. And so what? . . . Our love is so far behind, why do you speak of it? It had really no importance.
> *John*: You are lying! . . . It was our life. . . .
> *Lucie*: Our life? Yes. Our future. I lived in expectation. I waited for the end of the war. I waited for the day when we could get married. . . . I waited for every evening. . . . Now I have no longer any future, I expect nothing but my death, and I shall die alone.[30]

These words, "I shall die alone" (*"je mourrai seule"*), are almost exactly the same as those pronounced by Pascal (*"On mourra seul"*), and express the ancient idea of individualization of death, dear to Existentialism.

What is love and marriage?—A shared human project. But if one of the love partners suddenly stands in front of a wall, the wall of death which stops him from projecting himself toward the future, he has no longer anything in common with the other partner, who still possesses his human condition, his freedom of projecting himself toward his possibilities. This powerful scene

[30] *Morts sans Sépulture*, pp. 146-149.

shows that, while for idealistic writers love always seemed to be stronger than death, for the realistic Existentialist Sartre death is stronger than love.

This psychology of death, symbolized by the wall, has certainly been developed very brilliantly by Sartre. However, we have to say that it is not new. The gifted Viennese writer Arthur Schnitzler had developed it as early as the end of the nineteenth century, without using the word "wall," to be sure, but in the same sense as Sartre. The difference is only that Schnitzler was a physician, living in a peaceful world. Consequently his *morituri* had not been condemned to death by the sentence of a war tribunal but by the diagnosis of a doctor. In Schnitzler's master tale *Sterben* ("To Die"), published in 1892, Felix, a young man, is told by his physician that he has but one year more to live, for consumption is slowly killing him. Suddenly placed before his wall, beyond which he cannot see, nor feel, nor think, he loses all moral and spiritual community with his friends, and even with Marie, his sweetheart, who, at first, intends to die with him. But when Felix has to die and will take Marie with him, she escapes in horror from his hands which try to strangle her. To imagine one's wall and to see it before one's eyes are two different things. For Schnitzler also death is stronger than love.

The basic idea of the wall, that the dying and living do not speak the same language and that there is little they can communicate to each other, is even more clearly expressed in Schnitzler's play *Die letzten Masken*, ("The Last Masks"), where the dying journalist Rademacher asks the physician at the hospital to call his former friend, the successful writer Weihgast, to his bedside. It is Rademacher's intention to relieve his embittered heart by telling Weihgast, in the most violent words, how deeply he despises him, and that Weihgast's own wife shares his, Rademacher's feeling, and had been his mistress. He even rehearses the tirade before Weihgast's arrival, with his roommate, Florian, who also will die soon. But when Weihgast arrives, Rademacher has nothing to tell him but trivialities. And when, afterward,

Florian asks him how the conversation went, the dying Rademacher answers:

What have I in common with him? Are his happiness, his troubles any business of mine? What did we have to talk about together? What have people like you and me in common with persons who will still be in this world tomorrow? [31]

This is Sartre's idea of the "wall" exactly, and Schnitzler published that play in 1902, three years before Sartre was born.

We meet Sartre's concept of the wall also in other connections, not related to death; however, it is in his psychology of death that its symbolism is most impressive. And even though we realize that in this field Sartre had a forerunner—Arthur Schnitzler—we must recognize that the French philosopher and writer developed that psychology with the penetrating logic and dramatic genius which characterize all his writings.

As far as Existentialist psychoanalysis is concerned, Sartre concludes that Heidegger's "fear of death, the resolute decision, or the flight into unauthenticity cannot be considered as fundamental projects of our being." Consequently, it is necessary to "go beyond the results of Heidegger's hermeneutics, toward a more fundamental project." [32] And we know that the search for the fundamental project, this original choice of man, is the very aim of Existentialist psychoanalysis. The next chapter will try to show what this fundamental project is.

[31] A. Schnitzler, *Die letzten Masken*, in *Gesammelte Werke* (Berlin, 1915), p. 390.

[32] *L'Etre et le Néant*, p. 651.

CHAPTER TWENTY-ONE

MAN'S FUNDAMENTAL PROJECT: TO BECOME GOD

In the last chapter we saw that man's fundamental project, the ultimate goal sought by Existentialist psychoanalysis, cannot refer to death. Neither can it be life, nor any particular characteristic of the human condition. "The original project of a being for-itself *can only aim at its being.*" But what kind of being? This will become clear when we recall some features of the being-for-itself.

Being-for-itself, or human consciousness, has been characterized as a vacuum within the plenitude of being, as negation or naughtization, as "lack." Being-in-itself, the world of inanimate objects, is fullness, and "lack" springs up only through human consciousness. Sartre thinks that the existence of desire is the best proof that man is basically "lack." If man were what he is, he would not need anything to complete him. But, being not what he is, man is incomplete. It is the full moon which confers upon the crescent its nature as a crescent. Thus we have to determine what it is that lacks. Sartre answers that this perpetually absent being, which haunts the being-for-itself and which represents value, is the being-in-itself.

We know that human consciousness never coincides with itself; that it never *is,* but is always becoming. Now, Sartre thinks that for this reason man has the desire—or, better, he *is* the desire—to have at the same time the coincidence with itself of the inanimate world, called being-in-itself, and the translucidity of the consciousness, called being-for-itself.

We also know that, to Sartre, man's existence is entirely contingent, without foundation or necessity, gratuitous, absurd, and that it was this insight which gave Sartre's hero Roquentin his nausea. Now the being which is the object of the being-for-itself's deepest desire would be a being-in-itself, which is its own foundation, that which metaphysics call *ens causa sui*, and is no longer contingent, gratuitous, absurd. To attain it would mean to overcome the nausea linked to our existence.

Sartre's Existentialist psychoanalysis expresses this metaphysical desire of man, based on ontology, in the form of his nostalgia for the quiet, eternal, peaceful being of the inanimate world, just as, according to Freud's empirical psychoanalysis, man is nostalgic for his prenatal life. And these two desires certainly have something in common. Both can be interpreted as man's desire to escape from his human condition—into the quiet, passive, imperturbable being of a mountain, or, in Freud's case, toward the unconscious, vegetating life of a fetus. Again and again Sartre's heroes express this desire in one or another form. Consider, for example, Daniel's confession in *The Reprieve* (*Le Sursis*):

If I had been an insensible stone figure, incapable of sound and movement, blind and deaf—flies and earwigs and ladybirds would run up and down me, and I should stand, a fantastic, white-eyed statue, devoid of purpose, impervious to pain—I might then have coincided with myself. Not so as to accept myself, heaven forbid! but thus become the pure object of my hatred. . . . Just to be. In the dark, at random. To be a homosexual, just as the oak is an oak. To extinguish the inner eye. . . . Why can't I be what they see? [1]

What Daniel expresses is just flight from the human condition, evasion from freedom into bad faith and unauthenticity.

Mathieu also has that fundamental human desire of the being-in-itself, but as an Existentialist professor of philosophy, he realizes the impossibility of the synthesis aimed at in that fundamental project.

He reached out his hands and slid slowly over the stone parapet; it was wrinkled and furrowed, like a petrified sponge, and still warm from the afternoon sun. There it lay, vast and massive, enclosing in itself the crushed silence, the compressed shadows that are inside the objects. There it lay: a plenitude. He longed to clutch to that stone

[1] *The Reprieve*, pp. 133-134.

and melt into it, to fill himself with its opaqueness and repose. But it could not help him; it was outside forever.[2]

As a matter of fact, man does not simply desire his return to thinghood, to a simple being-in-itself. His fundamental project is to be at the same time in-itself, like a thing, and for-itself, like a consciousness; determined like a thing, but free like a man; solid and eternal like a rock, but conscious and sensible like a soul.

It is *as* a being which is what it is not, and which is not what it is, that the being-for-itself projects to be what it is. *As* a consciousness it wants to have the impenetrability and the indefinite density of the being-in-itself. *As* a naughtization of the being-in-itself and *as* a perpetual evasion from contingency and facticity it wants to be its own foundation.[3]

In short, man's lack, desire, fundamental project, ideal, supreme value is to become an *en-soi-pour-soi*, an "in-itself-for-itself," a self-conscious cosmos which would be the foundation of its own being-in-itself by the mere consciousness it takes of itself.

We realize that this ideal is beyond human possibilities, and as a matter of fact, that *ens causa sui*, or being which is its own cause and foundation, has always been identified with the concept of God. Sartre admits it openly by saying that the fundamental project of man is that of becoming God. "To be a man means to endeavor to be God. . . . Man is, fundamentally, the desire to be God." [4]

Sartre's term *en-soi-pour-soi* is obviously a translation of Hegel's *an-und-für-sich*. In Hegel it is the attribute of the Absolute, returned to itself in highest perfection. Sartre's en-soi-pour-soi is an individualization of that universalistic Hegelian concept of the Absolute.

If man's basic desire is to be God, if he cannot choose anything but to be God, is this not the total negation of his freedom of choice? Sartre denies it by saying that if the project of becom-

---

[2] *Ibid.*, p. 362.

[3] *L'Etre et le Néant*, p. 653.

[4] *Ibid.*, pp. 653-654. See the same definition in A. Malraux, *La Condition humaine* (Paris, 1933), p. 271.

ing God is the meaning of our fundamental desire, the concrete desire is never constituted by this meaning but is always a particular invention of aims in relation to man's empirical situation. The desire to be always realizes itself as a desire of a certain way of being. And this desire for the way of being is expressed as the meaning of those millions of concrete desires which constitute the web of our consciousness.

Now starting from that ontological premise, Existentialist psychoanalysis sees in a man's empirical desires a *symbolization* of his personal way of achieving that fundamental and general human project. It can be grasped only in and by means of those empirical desires. The way in which man tries in his concrete, empirical desires to realize the fundamental human project of becoming God characterizes, even creates, his personality. That fundamental desire expresses concretely in the world and in a person's definite situation a general abstract structure, which is the general reality of man in a person. This allows Existentialist psychoanalysis to state that there is a general human reality, not merely incomparable individualities. And freedom is expressed in the innumerable concrete forms in which humans manifest their choice of being and try to realize their being "in-itself-for-itself." Every concrete desire, that of eating, sleeping, creating a work of art, or helping other people, expresses the personal project of a man to realize his being-in-itself-for-itself, and thus characterizes in an individual concretion his whole personality. This is one of the basic ideas of Existentialist psychoanalysis.

Man's desire is not only defined by the relation "in-itself-for-itself," or the idea of God-man; but it is also relative to that brute and concrete being called object of desire. This can be anything—a piece of bread, an automobile, a woman. Man's desire is one of the aspects of his being-in-the-world. If I desire a painting, it means that I want to buy it in order to *have* it. If I desire to write a book, it means that I want to *make* it. If a woman uses rouge and lipstick, it means that she wants to *be* beautiful. Here are the three great categories of human existence: *to have, to make, to be;* and Existentialist psychoanalysis tries to study them.

Of these categories, that of having seems at first to be the most important in Sartre's Existentialist psychoanalysis; we have met it already under the name of "possessing." We remember that Sartre defined the essence of human relations, including love, as a mutual attempt of different selves to possess each other's freedom, to appropriate it, to enslave it. And now we shall see that the same frenzy of possession and appropriation also dominates man's relation to things, to the being-in-itself.

Heidegger has said that knowledge in the sense of the discovery of truth is *Raub,* that is, robbery or piracy.[5] Sartre adopted this primitive theory of knowledge of Heidegger's, which the latter had explained also in his booklet, *Vom Wesen der Wahrheit.*[6] For Sartre scientific research is nothing but an attempt at appropriation. A truth which has been discovered is *my* knowledge. It is a synthesis of the ego and the non-ego, expressed by the possessive pronoun "mine." The relation between the discoverer and the object discovered is that of a "rape by looking." This idea leads Sartre to establish the first complex of his Existentialist psychoanalysis, called the "Acteon complex." In Greek mythology Acteon was the hunter who peeped through the bushes in order to see the naked beauty of Diana as she was taking her bath. Sartre thinks that the scientist is a hunter who surprises a nude virgin and violates her with his look.

In knowing, consciousness also draws its object toward itself and incorporates it without destroying it, as the whale swallowed Jonah. Therefore Sartre's Existentialist psychoanalysis assumes a "Jonah complex," according to which "to know" is to swallow whole without consuming. Sartre supposes here that "the known object is not affected by knowledge," and this idea is the essence of his Jonah complex. But it would seem that the mechanics of quanta, with Heisenberg's uncertainty principle and Bohr's theory of complementarity, form a neat refutation of Sartre's Jonah complex; for these results of modern physics prove that—at least in the microcosmos—observation necessarily modifies the object observed.

[5] *Sein und Zeit,* p. 222.
[6] (Frankfurt am Main, 1943).

But what is essential for Sartre is the demonstration that knowledge or discovery of truth is a mode of appropriation and ownership. He sees in it an analogy to carnal possession, which offers us the seducing and bewildering image of a body which is "perpetually possessed and perpetually new, and on which possession leaves no trace." [7]

But on this point one may hold a different opinion, as did, for example, the hero of a novel by François Mauriac, who sees "traces of fingers" on a feminine body which "has served already." [8]

According to Sartre's Existentialist psychoanalysis, not only knowledge and love, but all other human activities, such as art, sport, charity, etc., are nothing but forms of appropriation, and thus modes of the category "to have."

Take sport, for instance. It is a form of play, and in that too Sartre detects an appropriative tendency. To be sure, play is in the first place the opposite of the spirit of seriousness. Seriousness is characterized by an attitude, which ascribes more reality to the world than to the self. Materialism is serious, and for this reason it is the doctrine of the revolutionists. The latter must be serious, since they feel themselves overwhelmed or oppressed by the world they want to change. The serious man is a man of "bad faith," denying his own freedom and considering himself as a consequence of the world. In Sartre's eyes Marx is the great pontiff of the spirit of seriousness because he is the author of the materialistic principle of the priority of the object; and man is serious when he considers himself as an object and not as a freedom, an initiative.

Now play in itself is subjective. It is an activity in which man makes the rules and where there cannot be any consequences but those following from man's freely posited principles.

Nevertheless, Sartre also states that play is never free of an appropriative tendency. It is, at first, a desire of "being" and then a desire of "having." The category of "making" is always transitory, and, basically, every desire is a desire of being or hav-

[7] *L'Etre et le Néant,* pp. 668, 678.
[8] *Fleuve de Feu,* p. 23.

ing. Sport is the free transformation of a milieu of the world into an element which would sustain action. Sartre studies especially skiing, which he seems to know fairly well. To see a snowfield, he says, means to possess it. The sense of skiing is not only to allow me quick displacements; it is also, and, basically, to *possess* the snowfield. Gliding down a slope assures one of the mastery of matter, of the domination of the snowfield. "Admirable image of power," he adds.[9]

Again we see that Sartre's fundamental project is close to Nietzsche's will to power and Adler's goal of superiority, as man's basic choice. "It is my snowfield, because I have crossed it a hundred times. It is mine." Sartre finds appropriation in climbing mountains, in swimming, in obstacle races, etc. A mountain I climbed for the first time and on which I raised a flag is "mine."

To this aspect of sportive appropriation Sartre adds that of "the difficulty we have overcome" in the free act of play. This again is one of Nietzsche's ideas. Nietzsche says, in his *Goetzendaemmerung*: "How is freedom measured?—By the resistance which has to be overcome, by the endeavor it costs to maintain oneself on top." [10]

In his essays on literature, published in the French original four years after his main treatise, Sartre declared that *"doing* reveals *being,"* and, as we know, he demanded a literature of doing, a literature of praxis, of action.[11] In *L'Etre et le Néant*, however, he puts more emphasis on the concept of *being,* when he writes: "Art, science, play, are activities of appropriation, be it totally, be it partly, and what people want to possess, beyond the concrete object of their quest, is *being,* the absolute being-in-itself." [12]

But what is possession? Fichte, under the influence of Rousseau, saw in ownership the result of a social contract, according to which a person renounces the use of the goods of all other people in exchange for the exclusive right to use one thing. "But he

---

9 *L'Etre et le Néant,* p. 673.
10 *Gesammelte Werke,* VIII, p. 149.
11 *What Is Literature?* p. 238.
12 *L'Etre et le Néant,* p. 675.

who has not received anything exclusively for himself, has re-
nounced nothing. . . . Not having been included in the compact,
he preserves his original right to do in every respect what he
wants." [13]

From this Marxism derives the right of the proletariat not to
recognize the property relations of the capitalistic world. Sartre,
on the contrary, who pretends to be a socialist, refuses to see in
property only a social concept. According to him property is a
basic ontological relation between man and the being-in-itself.
We assume that this is another reason for Sartre's conflict with
the Communists.

For Sartre, ownership is an internal link in being. We recognize the possessor in and by the object he possesses or possessed.
This is the significance of relics. We recognize Lincoln in an object which had belonged to him and is now in a museum.

This internal ontological link between the owner and the object owned is explained by a kind of unification. "To possess
means to unite oneself with the object possessed under the sign
of appropriation." [14] Thus the desire for a particular object is
not only a desire for that object, but it is also a desire to unite
oneself with the object and to achieve the unity called "posses-
sor-object possessed." Consequently the desire of *possessing* is
reduced to the desire of *being* in relation to a certain object.

The Existentialist Sartre is satisfied to have reduced in this
way the desire "to have" to a desire "to be." Nevertheless, the
desire "to be" continues to manifest itself in the form of a wild
desire "to have," to appropriate, to possess. This longing for
possession is the manifestation of the project to be an "in-itself-
for-itself," a God-man. In each case the appropriation is characterized by the fact that the object appears to us at the same time
as a subjective emanation of ourselves and as a relationship of
exteriority, independent of us. For Sartre the possessive pronoun
"mine" expresses an intermediary relationship between the absolute interiority of the ego and the absolute exteriority of the non-

---

[13] J. G. Fichte, *Der geschlossene Handelsstaat* (1800) in *Sämtliche Werke*
(Berlin, 1845), III, p. 445.
[14] *L'Etre et le Néant*, p. 678.

ego. It is in this syncretism of ownership that the non-ego becomes ego and the ego becomes non-ego. In this relationship we meet also a "value," or the ideal indication of the total being which would be achieved by the union of a man and his property. Consequently, appropriation is a relation between the being-for-itself, called man, and the being-in-itself, called thing. It is through ownership that man becomes God in this philosophy of Sartre's, which looks like an ontological foundation of capitalism.

This character of Sartre's philosophy seems to be even more accented by his theory of money. Appropriation is to him a kind of creation. In a primitive society I have to create the object which I want to possess. In modern society this creative function is only masked, not abolished: "The object I possess has been bought by me. *Money* represents my power." It is an instrument of possession.

Bacon said knowledge is power. But Sartre says "money is synonymous with power. . . . To have is to create."[15] He thinks the whole of my property reflects the whole of my being. The house, the car I possess, *is* I. Schopenhauer taught that what is important in man is not what he *has* nor what he *represents* in society, but only what he *is*. Sartre, on the contrary, states: "*I am what I have.*" Obviously, this union between the for-itself-I-am and the in-itself-I-have seems to attain the ideal of the in-itself-for-itself, man's project to be God. Divinity through ownership—is this not a strange formula for a socialist?

We must remember, however, that some of Sartre's basic ideas on ownership and money had already been expressed a century earlier by the founder of scientific socialism himself—Karl Marx—although Marx did it with critical intentions. Even Sartre's verbal expressions are similar to those used by Marx in his commentaries on passages from Goethe's *Faust* and Shakespeare's *Timon of Athens,* except that Marx wrote in German and Sartre in French. If we translate the two passages into English, their similarity becomes obvious.

In 1844 Marx wrote: "What I can pay, that is, what money can buy, *is* I myself, the owner of the money. My power is as

[15] *L'Etre et le Néant,* pp. 679-680.

big as the power of money. . . . If money is the bond which links me with human life, society, nature, and man, is then money not the bond of all bonds?" [16]

In 1943 Sartre wrote: "I am what I have. . . . Money represents my power. . . . it represents my magic bond with the object." [17]

It is unnecessary to add that in analyzing the concepts of ownership and money Sartre did not refer to his predecessor Marx.

Sartre comes to the result that appropriation is nothing but the symbol of the self's ideal, or "value." In identifying ownership with value he seems to efface the difference between value and price, which Kant separated so ingeniously.

However, Sartre insists on the *symbolic,* ideal character of all these relations, and not on their utilitarian aspect. No gesture of utilization really achieves the appropriative pleasure, but only refers me to another, as Schopenhauer had already remarked. Sartre thinks that beyond its symbolic value appropriation does not amount to very much. Ownership only indicates one supreme pleasure: that of being the owner's own foundation, but this is always beyond any appropriative attitude destined to achieve it.

Now Sartre thinks that this insight into the impossibility of really possessing an object explains man's violent desire to destroy. To him to destroy means a kind of resorption of the in-itself by the for-itself, a relationship as profound as that of creation. This approach reminds us of Ernst Juenger's glorification of destruction as a basic human passion.[18]

Man is the foundation of the barn which burns and which he set on fire, Sartre says, hinting at a kind of divinity through destruction. "Destruction achieves appropriation, perhaps finer than creation, for the object destroyed is no longer impenetrable." [19]

Albert Camus certainly was inspired by this theory of Sartre's

[16] *Geld* ("Oekonomisch-philosophische Manuskripte," 1844), in *Marx-Engels Gesamtausgabe, Erste Abteilung* (Berlin, 1932), *Band* 3, p. 147.

[17] *L'Etre et le Néant,* pp. 679-680.

[18] *In Stahlgewittern* (Berlin, 1930).

[19] *L'Etre et le Néant,* p. 683.

when in his gruesome tragedy *Caligula* he made the Roman tyrant say the following words: "I live, I kill, I practice the frantic power of the destroyer, beside which that of the creator seems to be a grimace." [20]

Did Sartre wish to create a philosophy of tyranny?

Using something, and thus slowly destroying it, is also an appropriative activity. Besides all utilitarian advantages, usage creates a secret pleasure, because it is a partial destruction caused by us. This is the real reason of our pleasure in *consuming*. Consumption, for Sartre, means at the same time appropriative destruction and alimentary pleasure. Consumption is "destruction by incorporation." [21] Did Sartre not realize that he was describing not a new feature of his Existentialist psychoanalysis, but only Freud's *death instinct?* Freud referred to "the act of eating as a destruction of the object with the final aim of incorporating it." [22] Even the wording of Sartre's and Freud's statements is the same.

Sartre's Existentialist psychoanalysis goes farther in applying Freud's death instinct, the aim of which is, according to its author, "to undo connections and so to destroy things." [23] Generosity, for instance, is considered by Sartre not as irreducible, but as a primitive form of destruction. I destroy a thing not only by annihilating it but also by giving it away. While idealism always considered generosity as an unselfish ethical manifestation, Sartre thinks that the rage of destruction, which is at the bottom of generosity, is only a veiled form of the rage to possess. "Donation is a harsh and brief, almost sexual, pleasure: to give is . . . a destructive, appropriative contact." But also the being-for-others interferes with this relationship, for, according to Sartre's Existentialist psychoanalysis, generosity is an appropriation by destruction, because it uses that destruction "in order to enslave the other person." [24] Sartre concludes by saying that whenever

20 *Caligula* (Paris, 1947), p. 209.
21 *L'Etre et le Néant*, p. 684.
22 *Psychoanalysis*, p. 21.
23 *Ibid.*, p. 20.
24 *L'Etre et le Néant*, p. 685.

Existentialist psychoanalysis finds generosity in a person, it has to search for his original project and to try to find out why this person has chosen appropriation by destruction rather than by creation. This will reveal the original relation to being, which constitutes the person in question.

It is a general tendency of any science dealing with human things to reduce values to value-free facts. However, in dealing with generosity, Sartre merely reduces positive values to negative ones. In admitting psychology as such, we should be compelled to accept even this if only his demonstration were better founded. But I submit that Sartre's reduction of generosity to a desire to possess, to destroy, and to enslave is too farfetched and highly artificial.

We are accustomed to judge the rage to possess as a moral phenomenon. However, Sartre tries to give it a mere ontological meaning. If we want to possesss a certain object, it is as a *representative* of the being-in-itself, which we want to appropriate to ourselves in order to be our own foundation and to overcome the nausea of our contingency and gratuitousness.

Every appropriative project aims at changing the ego, or being-for-itself, into the foundation of the world—into the concrete wholeness of the world, the concrete wholeness of the being-in-itself—by means of an ideal identification between the being-for-itself and the being-in-itself.

To-be-in-the-world means to project to possess the world, that is to say, to grasp the whole world as that which lacks the being-for-itself in order to become in-itself; it means to become engaged in a totality which is the ideal, the value.[25]

This sentence is quoted from the ontological treatise which Sartre published in Paris during the German occupation, and we may be sure that the Nazis liked it. For it could easily be interpreted as a philosophical justification of their dream of possessing the world.

After Hitler's defeat Sartre may have felt the scandalous implications of this doctrine, for he reversed it completely in his

25 *Ibid.,* p. 688.

essays on literature, where, as the reader will remember, he affirmed emphatically:

We are no longer with those who want to possess the world, but with those who want to change it, and it is in the very plan of changing it that the secret of its being is revealed.[26]

This Marxian formula fitted very well into the "historical situation" of France in 1947, when it was first published; just as four years earlier, the rather Hitlerite formula, "to be in the world means to project to possess the world," reflected the situation of a Europe dominated by the Nazis. This contradiction may serve as an example of a philosophy "in historical situation," which has abandoned the traditional idea of timeless truth.

Man's desire to possess the whole world is only a logical consequence of Sartre's premise that man's fundamental project is to be God. For God is the being who possesses the world. My freedom, Sartre says, is "a choice of becoming God," and all my projects reflect this choice, in an infinity of ways of being and of having. Now Existentialist psychoanalysis aims at finding in all those empirical and concrete projects, the original manner in which each person has chosen his being. But this means that Existentialist psychoanalysis must also find out why one person chooses to possess the world by means of certain particular objects, while another person chooses to possess it by means of other objects. For, according to Sartre, the object is not irreducible. We are aiming at the being of the object by the detour of its manner of being, or its "quality." This leads Sartre to his psychoanalysis of objects and qualities, which we will examine in the next chapter.

26 *What Is Literature?* p. 238.

CHAPTER TWENTY-TWO

THE PSYCHOANALYSIS OF QUALITIES AND FOODS: VISCOSITY AND NAUSEA

For Existentialist psychoanalysis the material qualities of the objects we want to possess—the fluidity of water, the density of stone, the viscosity of candy—are different symbolic ways of representing being. What we choose in those objects is a certain way in which being reveals itself and can be possessed. Red and blue, the taste of tomatoes or green peas, are not considered by Existentialist psychoanalysis as irreducible facts, and neither are our preference for, or dislike of, these qualities.

Existentialist psychoanalysis first wants to reveal the "ontological meaning" of these qualities, and only then will it try to explain a person's preference for, or dislike of, those qualities. It is only in this way, and not by considerations of sexuality, Sartre says, that his new discipline will be able to explain the tastes of certain persons: for instance, why Peter and Paul like oranges but would vomit if compelled to eat oysters. Thus Existentialist psychoanalysis no longer maintains the old dictum *de gustibus non est disputandum* ("tastes are beyond discussion"). For tastes, or the preference of certain poets for certain metaphors— Poe's fluidity of water, Rimbaud's geological images—symbolize a certain way of choosing being. Existentialist psychoanalysis does not consider the preference for sweet, bitter, or viscous things as irreducible, but sees in these qualities certain aspects of being, and in the preference for these qualities certain fundamental choices of being characterizing certain persons. For a man "is" what he prefers.

Schopenhauer says that there are two kinds of thinkers: Those who became philosophers by observing the world and those who became philosophers by reading a book. Sartre, certainly, belongs to the latter group. He became a phenomenologist by reading Husserl, an Existentialist by reading Heidegger, and an Existentialist psychoanalyst by reading Gaston Bachelard—and also Freud and Adler, of course. For the basic idea of Existentialist psychoanalysis, and even a part of its development, can be found in some books of Gaston Bachelard, a gifted professor of philosophy at the Sorbonne, especially in his *Psychanalyse du Feu* and in his *L'Eau et les Rêves*.

But we do not mean to say that Sartre is merely a compiler. He has a remarkable creative talent, but one which always needs to be inseminated and stimulated by other people. Metaphorically speaking, his creative talent is feminine rather than masculine.

In *L'Eau et les Rêves* ("Water and Dreams"), Bachelard distinguishes between a "formal" and a "material imagination." The latter is a kind of physics and chemistry of our dreams, including the daydreams of the poets, which compel them to borrow their metaphors from certain realms of nature. Bachelard thinks that in all those images it is the matter which commands the form. The material things themselves have a significance, a symbolism, which has to be explained in relation to the personality of the one who chose it. In considering, for instance, the poetry and prose of Edgar Allan Poe, Bachelard thinks that there is a synthesis of beauty, death, and water in the metaphors.

Sartre does not like Bachelard's term "material imagination," because, according to him, Existentialist psychoanalysis is not interested in *images*, or metaphors, but wants to explain the significance of *things*. However, in spite of his term "material imagination," Bachelard too is interested in the material significance of things. This becomes clear, for instance, when he says

... that the voices of water are hardly metaphoric, that the language of water is a direct poetical reality, that the brooks and the rivers *sonorize* the mute landscapes with a strange fidelity, that the rustling water teaches birds and men how to sing, to speak, to repeat, and that there is ... a continuity between the word of water and the word of man. Conversely, we will insist on the fact ... that, originally, human language has a *liquidity* ... a water in the consonants.[1]

[1] *L'Eau et les Rêves* (Paris, 1942), p. 22.

Thus, as Sartre himself admits, the difference between him and Bachelard seems to be largely terminological. Sartre insists with vigor on the necessity of applying psychoanalysis not only to persons but also to things, and of creating a "psychoanalysis of things." The latter would have to determine the way in which each quality, each thing, and each matter is an objective symbol of being and in what relation it stands to man. It tries to determine what Sartre calls the "metaphysical contents" of every revelation of being. "What," he asks, "are the metaphysical contents of the qualities red, yellow, polished, rough?"

When we say that a man's shaking hands are "slimy," or when we speak of a "viscous" smile, we believe that we are just using a metaphor. "You are wrong," Sartre says, and he goes on to explain to us that viscosity, like any quality, is of an objective nature "which is neither material (and physical) nor psychical, but which transcends the opposition of the physical and the psychical by revealing itself as an ontological expression of the world as a whole. . . ." [2] For Sartre viscosity symbolizes being in a certain way; and it is not by analogy, nor by a projection of our feelings toward that quality that the latter acquires a symbolic character. He thinks that in order to establish a symbolic relation between viscosity and sticky meanness, we must already have felt meanness in viscosity and viscosity in certain forms of meanness. What he seems to have in mind is a kind of a priori link between the physical quality of viscosity and the moral quality of meanness, a link we may discover, but which we do not create. It is as though we sprang up in a world in which feelings and acts are really endowed with material qualities such as viscosity, softness, etc., and all material substances with psychical significances which make them repugnant, horrible, attractive, etc.

According to Sartre, we are confronted with a boundless universal symbolism, which expresses itself in our likes and dislikes for these or those objects whose materiality in itself is significant. If we find a feeling viscous or bitter, this is not an image, a metaphor, but *"une connaissance,"* a knowledge.

[2] *L'Etre et le Néant,* p. 698.

It seems to me that, in conceiving his psychoanalysis of qualities, Sartre was again strongly influenced by Edmund Husserl, and especially by the latter's idea of "material ontological disciplines" of an a priori character, whose task would be "to analyze the essences of nature eidetically." [3] What these material ontological natural sciences (to which Husserl wanted to subordinate the empirical natural sciences) look like in actual fact we can see from the *Realontologie* of his disciple, Mme Hedwig Conrad-Martius, which Husserl found worthy to be published in his yearbook of phenomenology, although it is composed of "revelations," such as the following:

Light-giving is a source of light in itself. It spreads light by virtue of being lit inwardly. . . . Pure light is in pure self-glorification. . . . Shining, as such, implies emergence and start, self-transcendence, devotion and revelation, purely and simply.[4]

I think that this phenomenology of light, the merely verbal character of which is obvious, has to be considered as a forerunner of Sartre's psychoanalysis of viscosity and other qualities. The difference is only that Sartre did his analysis with much more intelligence than the German woman philosopher, whose "intuitive revelations" on the "essence" of light are almost ridiculous. Both of them, however, use Husserl's phenomenological method. Sartre thinks that viscosity is discovered by Husserl's phenomenological "intuition" and that it is an "objective" quality, an objective structure of the world. Considering the great importance of the concept of viscosity in Sartre's philosophy and literature, we translate here some characteristic passages from his Existentialist psychoanalysis of this quality.

The viscous reveals itself essentially as suspicious, because in it fluidity slows down; it is the coagulation of liquidity, that is to say, it represents in itself a growing triumph of the solid over the liquid. . . . The viscous is the agony of water. . . . Water is more transient, but one can possess it, even in its flight. . . . A drop of water touching the surface of a sheet of water is immediately

---

[3] *Ideen zu einer reinen Phänomenologie* (Halle, 1922), p. 20.

[4] "Realontologie," *Jahrbuch für Philosophie und phänomenologische Forschung*, IX (1929), pp. 339, 341, *passim*.

changed into the sheet of water . . . it is like a spiritualization
and de-individualization of a particular being, which dissolves itself
in the great wholeness from which it sprang. . . . This symbol . . .
seems to have a great importance in the constitution of pantheistic
schemes; it reveals a particular type of relationship between being and
being. . . . However, in the viscous (which melts) there is at the same
time a visible resistance, like the refusal of an individual who does
not want to be annihilated in the whole of being. . . . In the unseizable
character of water there is a pitiless hardness which gives it a secret
sense of metal: it is like steel finally incompressible. The viscous is
compressible, and gives, at first, the impression of a being which can be
possessed. . . . The viscous is docile; only at the very moment in which
I think I possess it, it possesses me. In this appears its essential character. . . . I open my hands, I want to drop the viscous, but it clings
to me, it pumps me, it sucks on me. It is a soft, driveling, feminine
activity of aspiration. . . . There is a poisonous possessiveness; there
is a possibility that the in-itself absorbs the for-itself . . . and the in-
itself attracts the for-itself in its contingency, its indifferentiated exteriority, its existence without any foundation. . . . The viscous is the
revenge of the being-in-itself. . . . To touch the viscous means to risk
being diluted into viscosity. This dilution is dreadful, because it is the
absorption of the being-for-itself by the being-in-itself.[5]

We easily recognize in these words the deep symbolism of the
viscous and its prominent significance in the whole of Sartre's
philosophy. To demonstrate his Existentialist psychoanalysis of
qualities, he could have chosen any quality. If he chose viscosity,
it is because viscosity is the symbol of nausea and our whole
nauseous existence, in which the ego, the free being-for-itself, is
again and again threatened with absorption by the being-in-itself, the absurd, contingent, brute thinghood which stagnates and
solidifies the liquidity of our freedom. For the liquidity, or fluidity, of water is the symbol of our consciousness, our freedom; and
the slackening of this liquidity, its stagnation and growing solidification into the stickiness of the viscous, is the symbol of our
collapse into thinghood, the loss of our freedom and our human
condition.

However, thinghood would seem to be symbolized better by
the solidity and hardness of a stone than by the sticky structure
of the viscous. And, as a matter of fact, in expressing their yearn-

[5] *L'Etre et le Néant,* pp. 699-702.
   667-668

ing for the quiet, peaceful being of inanimate objects, the heroes
of Sartre's novels always dream of becoming hard like stone. We
saw in *The Reprieve* that Mathieu wanted to melt into the stone
of a balustrade of the Seine River, and Daniel wanted to become
a stone figure, a white-eyed statue, incapable of sound, blind, and
deaf.

But it is impossible for a man to attain this totality of thinghood symbolized by the statue, the brute and mere being-in-itself. As Kant has said, man is a citizen of two worlds (Bürger
zweier Welten): the moral world of freedom and the physical
world of determinism. When Sartre says that man is partly a
being-for-itself and partly a being-in-itself, this only translates
Kant's dualism into another terminology. For the being-for-itself
is freedom, and the being-in-itself is the deterministic world of
thinghood. But Sartre added something very important to this
Kantian dualism: the insight that man is never entirely the one
and never entirely the other; he has never entirely the fluidity of
water and never entirely the solidity and impenetrability of a
stone. On his way from the fluidity of his consciousness to the
hardness of a stone, man is coagulated into something interme-
diate, which is viscous. The human body, this soft, gelatinous
mass imprisoning freedom by thousands of sucking, clutching,
pulpy arms, is basically viscous and the source of a permanent
nausea. Only after studying the psychoanalysis of the viscous
can we understand entirely Sartre's novel *La Nausée*, reflecting
the lessening of the fluidity of our freedom, the solidification of
our consciousness, our slow debasement into the soft, formless-
ness of chaotic, inanimate nature, the "absorption of the being-
for-itself by the being-in-itself" which, for Sartre, characterizes
viscosity and in which he sees the symbolization of the "anti-
value" (*antivaleur*).

In an earlier chapter we saw that being-in-itself is represented
not only by the material world, but also by our own past. And in
Sartre's eyes, the predominance of the latter seems to be one of
the greatest dangers to freedom. In this connection he speaks of a
consciousness which wants to project itself toward its future, its
possibilities, but which is suddenly, sneakingly, held back by the

invisible suction of its past and slowly diluted into this past. The past is in-itself, while the present of consciousness is for-itself. Thus, the absorption of the present by the past is tantamount to an absorption of the being-for-itself by the being-in-itself, and this again, according to Sartre's definition, is viscosity. If the wealthy society woman and the labor leader, who fall in love in Sartre's screen play *Les Jeux sont faits* ("The Chips Are Down"), fail to make a new common start in life, it is also because they cannot free themselves from the octopus-like embrace of the arms of their respective pasts.[6]

When our consciousness becomes "viscous," our ideas become "sticky." The horror in viscosity is that time becomes "viscous," that facticity progresses continuously and sucks up our being-for-itself, our freedom. In that state of viscosity it is no longer the being-for-itself which would absorb the being-in-itself in order to become its own foundation and to achieve the supreme value. It is, on the contrary, the being-in-itself, the brute thing-hood, which absorbs the being-for-itself and its freedom, and draws it into complete exteriority and contingency. Consequently the victory of viscosity is exactly the reverse of man's project to possess the world and thus to become God, for viscosity is man's being possessed by the world. And since the realization of the project of man's possessing the world would mean the realization of absolute positive value, the victory of viscosity (symbolizing man's being possessed and absorbed by the world) necessarily symbolizes the absolute negative value, or what Sartre calls the anti-value.

If viscosity is the symbol of the absorption of the being-for-itself by the inanimate being-in-itself of things, what must Existentialist psychoanalysis think of a person who likes viscous substances in any form, and, especially, in the form of food?

Sartre answers this question only indirectly in his novels and dramas but, nevertheless, with sufficient clarity. A person who likes viscosity would allow his freedom to slow down and finally

---

[6] Gerhart Hauptmann speaks in this respect of the "specters" of our lives of yesterday and compares their function to that of a "backward pulling funnel." See *Gabriel Schillings Flucht*, in *Gesammelte Werke* (Berlin, 1912), IV, pp. 184, 197.

to stagnate and coagulate into the solidity of things. A person who likes viscosity would resign his human condition in favor of the world, he would give himself the opacity of a thing which is determined by other things. Such a person would ascribe more importance to the world than to his ego and would consider himself as a consequence of the world rather than a free power, transcending the world by his projects. He would accept ready-made values as though they were things and not the result of human freedom. Burying his freedom under the soft, viscous masses of his materiality in order to escape the responsibility and anxiety linked to it, he would be a man of bad faith, a slave to the spirit of seriousness, and his existence would be unauthentic.

These are some of the conclusions Sartre's Existentialist psychoanalysis would draw from the fact that a person likes viscosity. But are not these conclusions too far fetched to be drawn from such simple facts as that a person likes caramels, honey, or cream? These inclinations seem harmless to us, but not to Sartre who has recognized the devilish character of viscosity and thinks that "taste is assimilation." He insists that "the synthetic intuition of food is . . . an assimilatory destruction. It reveals to me the being with which I am going to make my flesh." [7]

This reminds me of Feuerbach's materialistic principle *"der Mensch ist was er isst"* ("man is what he eats"), which Nietzsche sarcastically applied in his criticism of German cooking, that "degeneration of pastries into paperweights," with the conclusion that "German intellect is indigestion." [8]

The materialistic principle that man is what he eats is used by Existentialist psychoanalysis in a new, antimaterialistic sense, for here man does not become what he eats, but is already what he wants to eat. "Man is what he prefers," Sartre says. "What I accept and what I reject with disgust is the very being of that existent, or, if one prefers, the totality of the food proposes to me a certain mode of being, which I accept or which I re-

[7] *L'Etre et le Néant*, p. 707.
[8] *Ecce Homo*, in *Gesammelte Werke* (Munich, [1928]), p. 193.

fuse." [9] Consequently, in accepting viscous food with pleasure or in rejecting it with disgust, I accept or reject the mode of being symbolized by viscosity. And the same is true for any other quality of food or drink: bitter, sweet, hard, salty or gaseous. Each quality presents to us a specific type of existence; and we will swallow it with pleasure or spit it out with nausea, not according to the structure of our stomach or some allergy, but according to our "original project." One cannot say that Existentialist psychoanalysis lacks imagination.

It is thus by no means insignificant to like oysters . . . or snails, or shrimps, if we only are able to unravel the existential significance of these kinds of food. In a general way, there is no taste and no inclination which would be irreducible. They all represent a certain appropriative choice of being.[10]

Up to now it was only considered dangerous for a person to tell his dreams in a society where there might be a Freudian psychoanalyst. From now on it also becomes dangerous to dine where there might be an Existentialist psychoanalyst.

Viscosity, according to Sartre, is the perpetual danger of, and threat to, consciousness and freedom, and no victory over it is definite. As a citizen of two worlds—the one of consciousness and freedom, the other of thinghood and determinism—man has always to fight in order to keep the higher part of his existence from being sucked up and swallowed by the lower part. This perpetual fight is masterly described in Sartre's novels and dramas, and Robert Campbell is right when he calls Sartre "the painter of human viscosity." [11] Since in Sartre's eyes viscosity is the antivalue, he has to paint it with the ugliest colors. This explains why, in his novels, the kisses are given between attacks of diarrhea and love is made between vomitings, as one of Sartre's critics put it, unfortunately without exaggeration. The French magazine, *France au Combat,* was even more violent and called Sar-

[9] *L'Etre et le Néant,* p. 707.
[10] *Ibid.*
[11] *Jean-Paul Sartre ou une Littérature philosophique,* p. 40.

tre's Existentialism an "Excrementalism." And Sartre himself quoted another similar remark by one of his critics, which hardly can be translated: *"Nous avions le mouvement dada, voici maintenant le mouvement caca."* [12]

Of course, vomits and excrements are repugnant. But in Sartre's work the viscosity they symbolize is even more repugnant: the loss of human dignity, man's debasement to thinghood. We doubt that this symbolism is a real objective structure of the world, as Sartre would have us believe. We would prefer to consider it as Sartre's very personal way of symbolizing moral relations.

We still remember his statement that man's fundamental project is to become God by possessing the whole world in the form of certain qualities. Only by uniting himself with the world possessed, can man achieve that being-in-itself-for-itself, which would be its own foundation, the *ens causa sui*, which religion calls God. We have also seen that viscosity symbolizes man's being possessed by the world and thus is diametrically opposed to the fundamental human project.

But even if man's project to become God by possessing the world were not thwarted by the opposite tendency of viscosity, the project would nevertheless be condemned to failure, for, as Sartre states, the idea of God is "contradictory." Thus man is a "useless passion." [13]

[12] *Pour et contre L'Existentialisme* (Paris. 1948), p. 187.
[13] *L'Etre et le Néant*, p. 708.

CHAPTER TWENTY-THREE

EXISTENTIALIST PSYCHOANALYSIS AND ETHICS

We have already spoken of that characteristic feature of Existentialism which consists of a mixture of scientific and moral concepts, disregarding the ideal of a value-free science which modern thought has tried to establish. Now while Freud's empirical psychoanalysis is such a value-free science, a psychological investigation which abstains intentionally from any value judgment, any moral condemnation or approbation, Sartre's Existentialist psychoanalysis wants to be considered as a "moral description, because it reveals to us the ethical sense of the different human projects." [1]

This new discipline vacillating among psychology, ontology, and ethics, tried, at first, to detect the origin of the concept of value, and found it in that which lacks the being-for-itself, in order to be in-itself-for-itself and to be its own foundation. Revealing thus the ideal significance of all human attitudes, Existentialist psychoanalysis rejects any utilitarian interpretations of human behavior and is the enemy of the psychology of interest. Even while stating that "to be in the world means to project to possess the world," Sartre rejects all utilitarian ideas and thinks only of man's quest for being and justification. And although all this looks very much like egoism, Sartre would not admit it. He even suggests the opposite interpretation: that man loses himself so that the absolute may exist.

The main ethical purpose of Existentialist psychoanalysis is to make man renounce the "spirit of seriousness." We already know that the latter means ascribing more reality to the world than to man and considering man as a result of the world, a part

---

[1] *L'Etre et le Néant*, p. 720.

of the tangible world. The main consequence of this spirit of seriousness is that under its domination man will consider values as transcendent data independent of human subjectivity, and will transfer the valuable qualities of things from their ontological structure to their material constitution. But, according to Sartre, the possession of a thing is not desirable because we like or need it, but because ownership of it symbolizes the ideal value of a unification of the being-for-itself with the being-in-itself. The result of the spirit of seriousness, which governs the world, is that the symbolic values of things are sucked up "as if by a blotter." Things themselves, in their opacity, are considered as an irreducible desirability. Thus the spirit of seriousness implies an ethics of bad faith, which helps man to hide from himself his own aims in order to escape anxiety. For the spirit of seriousness objects are "mute exigencies" requiring a passive obedience.

Now Existentialist psychoanalysis will reveal to man the true aim of his search, which is a kind of synthetic merger of the being-for-itself he is, with the being-in-itself he recognizes and wants to possess. Sartre thinks that many men have applied this Existentialist psychoanalysis to themselves. Knowing that the aim of their search is being, they would not appropriate things to themselves for the things' sake, but would try to realize a symbolic appropriation of their being-in-itself.

But even then, as long as men are governed by the spirit of seriousness and believe that "their mission to make exist the in-itself-for-itself is written in the things," they are condemned to despair, for they discover that "all human activities are equivalent. Thus to take to solitary drinking or to lead nations amount to the same thing." [2]

The terrifying practical consequences of such an axiology of equivalence have been painted by Albert Camus, in his tragedy *Caligula.* "This world is without importance," the tyrant says, "and he who recognizes it conquers his freedom." [3] And he uses his freedom in order to humiliate, terrorize, and kill his subjects

[2] *Ibid.,* p. 721.
[3] *Op. cit.,* p. 121.

ad libitum, since "a person is always free at the expense of another person" and "all actions are equivalent." [4]

Sartre thinks that Existentialist psychoanalysis will save us from the despair of nihilism by teaching us that man is the being through whom values exist, that values are not written in things but that we are writing them into things. But with this Sartre is again only expressing Nietzsche's wisdom, and again without mentioning his name. In his *Will to Power,* Nietzsche says:

All beauty, all sublimity which we have lent to real and imaginary things, I want to claim as the property and creation of man: they are his most beautiful apology. Man as a poet, as a thinker, as God, as love, as power: With what royal generosity has he loaded things in order to impoverish himself, in order to feel himself miserable! Up to now his greatest abnegation was that he admired and venerated and hid from himself that it was he who had created what he admired.[5]

In our chapter on "Freedom and Values: Sartre and Nietzsche" we showed that Sartre's "spirit of seriousness" is only a new edition of Nietzsche's "spirit of gravity."

There is a very strange element in Sartre's discussion of the ethical aspects of Existentialist psychoanalysis: he considers it a great merit that it unfolds to man the true aim of his strivings and that this aim is the synthetic merger of the being-for-itself which he is, with the being-in-itself he wants to possess. But had not Sartre stated before that the idea of this merger, the idea of God, is self-contradictory, and that man is a "useless passion"? Thus in revealing to man the true aim of his strivings, Existentialist psychoanalysis only shows him that even ontologically his projects are senseless, contradictory, and unattainable. I do not see how man is more advanced than before by this knowledge.

Here is one of the reasons why the optimistic interpretation Sartre has tried to give to his Existentialism during these last years appears to be an optimism of defiance, an optimism in spite of a desperate situation. To be sure, the ethical implications of Existentialist psychoanalysis have only been sketched by Sartre,

---

[4] *Ibid.,* pp. 142, 179.
[5] *Wille zur Macht,* II, 107.

and he has reserved their development to a new theoretical work which has not yet been published. But Simone de Beauvoir, for years Sartre's closest collaborator, tried, in her book *The Ethics of Ambiguity,* to clarify some of the questions left open in *Being and Nothingness.*

She states that only a person possessed by the "spirit of seriousness" would try to achieve the impossible synthesis of the for-itself and the in-itself called God, and that the "authentic" man would be willing not to "be" in order to "exist." We know that existence is basically man's lack of coincidence with himself and with external being. Madame de Beauvoir thinks that our only salvation is "to accept the lack and to side with a man who exists, against the idea of a God who does not exist." [6]

To be sure, we cannot truly "possess" the snowfield over which we are gliding on our skis, but this does not prevent us from enjoying it with a feeling of triumph. "In his vain attempt to be God, man makes himself exist as man," Simone de Beauvoir says; [7] and she insists that man should not seek a foundation for his existence outside himself, since he alone can provide such a foundation. She demands that the "joy of existence" be affirmed at every moment, and seems to be opposed to Sartre's affirmation that "man is a useless passion," since the concepts "useless" and "useful" have no meaning outside human existence.

Finally, Madame de Beauvoir denies the equivalence of all human activities, affirming the privileged character of some of them: those which serve the freedom of other people. With Sartre she thinks that man's liberty can be achieved only through other people's freedom, so that the struggle for the former becomes one for the liberation of our fellow men. But since liberty is never definite, it must be conquered again and again. In this sense Madame de Beauvoir, like Sartre, adopts explicitly Trotzky's idea of "permanent revolution." [8] But, as we remarked earlier, this idea implies the contradiction that the revolutionary would never be able to enjoy the freedom for which he fought,

[6] *Pour une Morale,* p. 80.
[7] *Ibid.,* p. 19.
[8] *Ibid.,* p. 166.

because he would have to overthrow it by a new revolution, and so on *ad infinitum*.

Since freedom is the source of all values, Sartre says, man cannot want anything but freedom. But this existentialist freedom is very problematic. Let us recall another consequence of the revelation by Existentialist psychoanalysis that values are not offered ready-made to our consciousness but are the product of our active, creative freedom. Since nothing justifies us in adopting this value rather than that, this hierarchy rather than that, and since nothing prevents us from revoking our choice of values and replacing it with another, we are entirely responsible for the values we have chosen. We have already seen that this explains man's "ethical anxiety." Now we see that we owe its revelation to Existentialist psychoanalysis. And through this revelation the new discipline leads us to an " authentic" existence, which is an existence conscious of our freedom and responsibility and, consequently, an existence in permanent anxiety.

In his tragedy *Les Mouches* ("The Flies") Sartre gave us an impressive picture of such an authentic existence in the character of Orestes. Having had the sudden revelation of his freedom, Orestes accepts joyfully all its consequences. He recognizes that he is the source of all values, that there is neither good nor evil unless he invents them, and he accepts the terrifying responsibility and ethical anxiety linked to his free choice of values.

When I asked Sartre if Existentialist psychoanalysis had found any practical application, he answered in a letter, dated October 3, 1948: "I tried to apply it twice: once to the study of an individual (*Baudelaire*), the other time to the study of a collective problem (*Réflexions sur la Question juive*)." The latter of these studies appeared in an English translation under the title *Anti-Semite and Jew*.[9] Both are masterful psychological essays and much more convincing than Sartre's theoretical attempts to link Existentialist psychoanalysis to ontology in *L'Etre et le Néant*.

In his study of Baudelaire, Sartre tries to show in a concrete way that what one calls a man's destiny is always identical with

---

[9] *Anti-Semite and Jew* (New York, 1948).

his free choice of himself. Baudelaire always chose to exist for himself as he appeared to the look of other people." Baudelaire is the man who has chosen to see himself as if he were another self: his life is only the history of his failure." [10]

We are reminded of the passage in *The Reprieve* where Daniel cries out his need of being seen, so that his essence would be congealed and he would be relieved of his responsibility for what he is. "To be a homosexual, just as the oak is an oak. Why can't I be what they see?" [11] So Daniel becomes religious in order to be seen permanently by God.

As Sartre's Existentialist psychoanalysis of Baudelaire tries to show, the great French poet's life was under the spell of a similar passion for coincidence with himself and for being justified by the gaze of other persons.

At first it was through the gaze of his adored mother that Baudelaire sought definition and justification of his essence. Later it had to be other persons, especially beautiful frigid women, whose gaze he needed in order to know what he was and be justified in his being. In his worst debauches with low girls he imagined himself to be under the severe gaze of one of these goddess-like women, who would see him as he was and relieve him of the responsibility for his free acts. In his poems Baudelaire seemed often to identify himself with Satan; and Sartre's Existentialist psychoanalysis finds that this too served the same purpose. "For what is Satan basically if not the symbol of disobedient children who ask to be petrified in their peculiar essence by the paternal gaze?" [12]

Just as Baudelaire's destiny was his free choice, so is that of the anti-Semite in Sartre's application of Existentialist psychoanalysis to a collective problem.

The anti-Semite has chosen to be a criminal, and a criminal pure of heart. . . . Anti-Semitism is only a justification of his existence. His futility is such that he will eagerly abandon this justification for any other, provided that the latter is more distinguished. . . . In espousing anti-Semitism, he does not simply adopt an opinion, he chooses him-

[10] *Baudelaire*, p. 31.
[11] *The Reprieve*, pp. 133-134.
[12] *Baudelaire*, p. 88.

self as a person. He chooses the permanence and impenetrability of a stone, the total irresponsibility of the warrior who obeys his leaders. . . . He is a man who is afraid. Not of the Jews, to be sure, but of himself, of his own consciousness, of his liberty, of his instincts, of his responsibilities, of solitariness, of change, of society, and of the world—of everything except the Jews. . . . The existence of the Jew merely permits the anti-Semite to stifle his anxieties at their inception by persuading himself that his place in the world has been marked out in advance, that it awaits him, and that tradition gives him the right to occupy it. Anti-Semitism, in short, is fear of the human condition. The anti-Semite is a man who wishes to be a pitiless stone, a furious torrent, a devastating thunderbolt—anything except a man.[13]

In his brilliant story "L'Enfance d'un Chef," which he might equally well have called "The Making of an Anti-Semite," Sartre has individualized this type in the person of young Lucien Fleurier, who takes his way into the viscosity of an unauthentic existence, away from freedom and responsibility.

Besides being a fascinating psychological portrait of the poet, Sartre's *Baudelaire* also outlines the general scheme of man's moral evolution as seen by Existentialist psychoanalysis: The child considers his parents as gods. They embody the universal reason, the world of absolute values. When the parents look at the child, he feels justified. Since the parents cannot be mistaken, the child is as his parents see him. As a true essence among true essences, the child has his place in the world. Everything he meets is already classified for him, each object has a kind of label on which the parents have written its value.

However, as the child grows he loses this absolute security in the realm of values. He becomes taller than father and mother, he goes to school and discovers one day that father and mother do not know everything, that they can be mistaken, that they are not infallible, but are just ordinary people. Suddenly the child sees them in their normal size, unjustified and unjustifiable, their majestic ideas degraded to the rank of personal opinions.

Now the adolescent realizes that the whole system of values he has received must be reconstructed, and that the severe look of his parents no longer fixes and justifies his essence. The child

[13] *Anti-Semite and Jew*, pp. 50-54.

loses his truth: "Unjustified, unjustifiable, he suddenly experiences his dreadful freedom. Everything has to be redone; the child emerges suddenly in his solitude, and in nothingness." [14]

In Jean Anouilh's tragedy *Antigone* young Hemon says to King Creon: "Father, it is not true! it is not you. . . . You are still as powerful as you were when I was a child. . . . I am too lonely and the world is too naked if I can no longer admire you." But Creon replies: "People *are* entirely alone, Hemon, the world *is* naked. And you have admired me too long. Look at me! To become a man means to see some day one's father's face as it is!" [15]

In Arthur Miller's *Death of a Salesman* an adolescent's life is broken the day he realizes that his father is not the paragon of perfection he had imagined.

When the adolescent has lost his childhood paradise, two ways are open to him. He can try to find substitute gods for the gods called mama and papa, and thus find a new paradise. Robert Campbell calls them god-society, god-the-other-person, god-people, god-gaze.[16] The young person would then feel himself justified in the eyes of these new gods. They would give him ready-made patterns of values, which he could accept blindly, and he would be relieved of the necessity of choosing his values for himself, under his own responsibility and with all the anxiety which such responsibility entails. This new paradise is obviously one of bad faith, of unauthenticity, a running-away from freedom, a solidification of consciousness into viscosity and thinghood.

The other way open to the adolescent who has lost his childhood paradise is that of authenticity. The authentic man will accept his freedom, will realize that values are not transcendent entities which he can receive ready-made, that he has to invent and to choose them, free, without help, without excuse, condemned to decide without any possible recourse, with the whole responsibility for his choice resting on his shoulders and, in his

[14] *Baudelaire*, p. 61.
[15] *Antigone* (Paris, 1946), p. 109.
[16] *Jean-Paul Sartre ou une Littérature philosophique*, p. 273.

heart, all the terrifying anxiety that it entails. The authentic existence is chosen by Sartre's Orestes, who exclaims:

Suddenly freedom dashed upon me and penetrated me: There was no longer anything in heaven, neither good nor evil, nor anybody to give me orders. . . . I am condemned to have no other law than my own. For I am a man, and each man has to invent his own way.[17]

This portrait of Orestes is that which Existentialist psychoanalysis offers to man as the only moral ideal. It is a great and terrifying image—terrifying, because its basic tonality is anxiety. Trying to convert his beloved sister Electra also to authenticity, Orestes admits this anxiety by saying: "The anxiety which devours you, do you think that it will ever cease to gnaw me? But what does it matter? I am free!"

We may legitimately doubt whether this Sartrean freedom has kept any resemblance to human happiness with which it was always supposed to be closely associated. In Camus' *Caligula* the Roman tyrant is asked by his mistress: "Is this dreadful freedom still happiness?" And the emperor answers: "Be sure, Caesonia, that without it I would have been a satisfied man. Thanks to it, I conquered the divine clear-sightedness of the solitary man." [18]

There is no doubt that in seeking freedom Sartre's heroes do not seek happiness. This is obvious also in Sartre's play *Les Mains sales,* presented in New York under the title of "Red Gloves." Trying to explain why he killed the Communist leader Hoederer, whom he admired deeply, Hugo, a young idealist similar to Orestes, says: "I found myself too young. I wanted to hang a crime around my neck, like a rock. And I was afraid it would be too heavy to carry. What a mistake! It is light, horribly light!" [19]

To understand the strange psychology of Sartre's heroes we have to consider it as what it truly is: a reflex of his axiology. To be sure, Hugo surprised Hoederer kissing his (Hugo's) wife, Jessica, and even though Hugo admits that he is no longer in love with Jessica, he nevertheless shoots Hoederer to death. "For a

[17] *Les Mouches*, pp. 100-101.
[18] *Op. cit.*, p. 209.
[19] *Les Mains sales* (Paris, 1948), p. 247.

long time I had been living in tragedy. I shot, in order to preserve the tragedy." [20] These words of Hugo's show a conception
very close to that of the celebrated Spanish Existentialist, Miguel
de Unamuno, who taught that we should welcome suffering and
anxiety, for through them we become more conscious of the
tragic sense of life.

But to return to Sartre's tragedy *Les Mouches* ("The Flies"):
There it is suggested that the first step toward an authentic life
is to defy God, all gods who want to impose upon man another
law than that which he would give to himself by choosing it, including the god-society. In a powerful scene of *Les Mouches* (influenced by Giraudoux's *Electre*), Sartre's Orestes defies Jupiter
by exclaiming:

You are the king of the gods, Jupiter, the king of the stones and of
the stars, the king of the waves, of the sea. But you are not the king
of men. . . . Men are free, and human life begins on the other side of
despair! [21]

One almost believes that one hears not Orestes but Prometheus, especially the Prometheus of Goethe's wonderful poem,
who exclaims:

> Here I sit, forming mankind
> In my own image,
> A race resembling me
> To sorrow, to weep,
> To taste, to have pleasure
> And to have no need of thee,
> Even as me! [22]

When, in Sartre's tragedy, Orestes leaves Argos, he is bowed
under the "precious burden" of his freedom and responsibility

[20] *Ibid.*, p. 244.
[21] Pp. 99-102.
[22] Goethe, *Gedichte*, in *Werke* (Basel, 1944), I, pp. 256-258.

> Hier sitz ich, forme Menschen,
> Nach meinem Bilde,
> Ein Geschlecht, das mir gleich sei,
> Zu leiden, zu weinen,
> Zu geniessen und zu freuen sich,
> Und Dein nicht zu achten,
> Wie ich!

and followed by the howling crowd of Furies, symbols of his anxiety.

Thus we see that while Freud's empiric psychoanalysis tries to *deliver us from anxiety,* Sartre's Existentialist psychoanalysis tries to *give us anxiety,* the anxiety of an authentic life. Consequently Existentialist psychoanalysis cannot be considered a therapy.

And yet, in one way, not in a medical sense but in a moral sense, we may consider Existentialist psychoanalysis a therapy: for it tries to cure man from the infantile disease of unauthenticity and lead him to the *age of reason* of maturity, where he can stand alone, able to assume his freedom, his autonomy, and the responsibilities it implies.

At the end of World War II Sartre depicted the image of a man who has reached his age of reason in the following words: "War leaves man naked, without illusions, abandoned to his own forces, and having finally understood that he can rely only on himself." [23]

In his play *Le Diable et le bon Dieu* ("The Devil and the Good Lord"), published in 1951, Sartre gave another, even more forceful expression to his ideal of the sovereign man who, having liberated himself from all supra-natural illusions, accepts proudly and joyfully, his human task as the only legislator of good and evil on earth. It is a Nietzschean ideal and also again reminds us of Goethe, for the hero of *The Devil and the Good Lord* is the same Goetz von Berlichingen who had been immortalized by Germany's greatest poet. At the moment of his conversion to atheism, Sartre's Goetz exclaims:

God is silence! God is absence! God is the loneliness of man! There is nobody but me: I alone have decided about evil. I alone have invented the good. I alone am accusing myself today. I alone can absolve myself. I, the man! If God exists, man is nothingness! . . . God does not exist! Joy and tears! No more heaven, no more hell: nothing but the earth.

One almost believes he can hear Nietzsche's admonition to man to be faithful to the earth. Turning toward his beloved

---

[23] "La Fin de la Guerre," *Les Temps Modernes* (October, 1945), p. 167.

Hilda, Sartre's Goetz uses Nietzsche's words to announce to her that "God is dead!" [24]

Unlike Orestes, Sartre's Goetz is not followed by the howling crowd of Furies. But if he is an "authentic" man, he will not escape ethical anxiety, which is the price of liberation.

[24] "Le Diable et le bon Dieu," *Les Temps Modernes* (August 1951), pp. 292, 294; Nietzsche, *Zarathustra,* Vorrede, p. 12.

CHAPTER TWENTY-FOUR

EXISTENTIALISM AND PSYCHIATRY

We just affirmed that, offering man anxiety, Existentialist psychoanalysis cannot be considered a mental therapy—unlike empirical psychoanalysis, which in many cases, deliberately, undertakes and succeeds in freeing man from anxiety. We feel, however, that before coming to our final conclusions we have to consider the opinions of some psychiatrists. The French mathematician Robert Campbell, one of the most penetrating and enthusiastic apologists of Sartre's philosophy, affirmed in an article published in 1950, that some psychiatrists ascribe a certain "therapeutic value" to Existentialist psychoanalysis.[1] Campbell refers especially to the study of Dr. Paul Abély on "Bad Faith in Delirious Persons."[2] We have read this study, but we do not find that this psychiatrist actually ascribes a "therapeutic value" to Existentialist psychoanalysis. What Dr. Abély really did was to reveal that in many cases of hallucinatory psychosis the patient tries to escape into "bad faith," as defined by Sartre, in order to evade his anxiety. Dr. Abély quotes Sartre and comments:

I use the term "bad faith" in a philosophical sense. It is not a question of a cynical lie . . . , but a negation of his own truth; the subject lies to himself, he is more the deceived one than the deceiver, 'his bad faith is faith.' He tries to escape from himself, to flee from himself and also to displace his original responsibility, to project it into the external world. It is a question . . . of . . . escaping at any cost from his own psychic danger, of changing it into an exterior danger . . . , and this is *another way of trying to recover his freedom*: to become able to defend himself against something. By this winding process arises the delirium of persecution, of demoniac possession, the delirium

[1] "L'Existentialisme en France depuis la Libération," *L'Activité philosophique contemporaine en France et aux Etats-Unis* (Paris, 1950), II, pp. 149-163.
[2] "La mauvaise Foi chez les Délirants," *Annales médico-psychologiques* (Paris, 1948), II, 5, pp. 620-624.

of influence the echo and flight of ideas, auditive, coenesthopathic, psychic, olfactic, genital, and other hallucinations . . . *this ensemble of phenomena is nothing but the effective echo of bad faith.*[3]

Dr. Abély believes that this Sartrian concept of bad faith can be applied in the majority of the cases of delirious persons and that it is particularly important in the cases of the so-called chronic delirium. He concludes by saying:

For the moment I tried to introduce the new concept of 'bad faith' in the analysis of these states of delirium, its clinical and physiological modalities. I believe it is able to shed some light on these syndromes, which are still very controversial and badly elucidated.[4]

These opinions of the French psychiatrist are certainly very interesting and may prove that the pictures of certain psychological mechanisms as sketched by Sartre are basically correct. But do they affirm a "therapeutic value" of Existentialist psychoanalysis? I do not think so. In the only concrete case described by Dr. Abély, he found bad faith as a *symptom* of the hallucinatory delirium; but he says that the recovery of his patient was achieved by electric shocks. The same is true in all other cases to which this psychiatrist refers in a summary way. In all of them bad faith appears as a symptom of the mental illness and Existentialist psychoanalysis as a means to *uncover,* but *not to cure,* either this symptom or the whole psycho-pathological condition. We may conclude that the concept of bad faith introduced by Sartre's Existentialist psychoanalysis is part of the psychiatric *symptomatology* but not, as Campbell's remark suggests, of psychiatric *therapy.*

As far as therapy is concerned, Dr. Abély proposes different methods, such as prefrontal lobotomy, electric shock, lowering of the patient's blood pressure, everything but Existentialist psychoanalysis. And this seems very obvious to us, since all the methods mentioned are able to give the patient *freedom from anxiety,* while Existentialist psychoanalysis offers him only *freedom with anxiety.*

---

[3] *Ibid.,* p. 622.
[4] *Ibid.,* p. 624.

In the previous chapter we intimated that if Existentialist psychoanalysis is not a medical therapy, it might be considered a moral therapy, trying to cure man of the infantile disease of un-authenticity and leading him to the age of reason, where he can stand alone, able to assume his freedom, his autonomy and the responsibilities it implies. From the point of view of psychiatry it turns out, however, that this moral therapy of Existentialist psychoanalysis can be very dangerous. This is the opinion expressed in an interesting study by a Swiss psychiatrist, Louisa Duss of Geneva. It was published in the same volume of the *Annales médico-psychologiques* in which Dr. Abély made his report. It cannot have escaped the attention of Robert Campbell, for it covers forty-three pages of the issue mentioned, while Paul Abély's report is only five pages. Nevertheless, Campbell did not mention Madame Duss's study, while insisting on Dr. Abély's. Could it be because the former is less favorable to Sartre? However this may be, Madame Duss's study deserves careful consideration. Its title is *"Critique psychiatrique de l'Existentialisme"* ("Psychiatric Criticism of Existentialism") and its subtitle *Expérience existentialiste chez un Schizophrène"* ("An Existentialist Experience of a Schizophrenic").[5] Madame Duss studied the case of a schizophrenic girl named Renée and found strange relations to Existentialist philosophy. Three years after the publication of Madame Duss's study, Renée's case became known in the United States, but only under its psychiatric and psychoanalytical aspects, without any reference to its philosophical implications. In 1951, an English version of Renée's autobiography was published in this country,[6] and in addition, the girl's analyst, Madame Marguérite Sechehaye, a great Swiss authority, gave the American reader an account of her new method, called "symbolic realization," by which Renée was cured.[7] Neither of these English publications referred to Existentialism, even though Madame Louisa Duss's French article about Renée considers particularly the Existentialist aspects of the girl's schizophrenia. A

[5] "Critique psychiatrique de l'Existentialisme," *Annales médico-psychologiques* (December, 1948), II, 5, pp. 553-595.

[6] M. Sechehaye, *Autobiography of a Schizophrenic Girl* (New York, 1951).

[7] *Symbolic Realization* (New York, 1951).

comparison between Madame Duss's analysis and Madame Sechehaye's American publications shows that Madame Duss must
have had some additional information on the case, which does
not appear in the two books published in America. In part it
came from personal conversations between Mmes Sechehaye and
Duss.

Renée, daughter of a French mother and a Swedish industri-
alist father, was brought up in Geneva. She combined a remarkable intelligence and a keen logical sense with certain mystical
tendencies. A devout Catholic, filled with religious exaltation, she
rose each morning at five to attend mass. She had an unhappy
childhood, suffering from the mental cruelty of her father and a
lack of love from her mother. At the age of thirteen she received
a deep shock when her mother told her that she had been an un-
wanted child. She suffered from mental troubles linked with her
puberty (hebephrenia), and at the age of nineteen developed a
delirium, accompanied by autodestructive tendencies, which
necessitated her confinement in an asylum.

During the years of the development of her schizophrenic
condition Renée retained a strange lucidity which allowed her to
observe and, after her recovery, to describe her mental and emotional experiences in a remarkable autobiography. Freud thought
that such patients, having turned away from outer reality, are
more aware of their inner reality, about which they make astounding revelations. Renée's case proves it. Examining her reports and those of her analyst, Madame Duss found that the
mental experiences of this young schizophrenic were, in many
respects, those reported by the Existentialists, and, especially, by
certain heroes of Sartre's novels. Examining this material myself,
I agree with many of Louisa Duss's interpretations and conclusions, but not with all of them. Madame Duss's study seems to be
based mainly on Foulquié's interpretation of Existentialism [8]
rather than on a close study of Sartre and Heidegger. I have also
the impression that Madame Duss's final conclusions are too
radical, because they neglect the emotional factors in Renée's
mental illness, whose recognition and symbolic realization by her

[8] P. Foulquié, *L'Existentialisme* (Paris, 1947).

analyst, Madame Sechehaye, led to the girl's recovery. For these reasons I shall first present some results of my own examination of Renée's confessions from the point of view of Existentialist philosophy, and then consider them in the light of Madame Duss's interpretations.

According to Renée's autobiography, her mental illness started with feelings of unreality. Describing these feelings, Renée says that suddenly the outer world seemed to be

limitless, unreal, mechanical and without meaning. . . . Pupils and teachers were puppets revolving without cause, without objective. I recognized nothing, nobody. It was as though reality, attenuated, had slipped away from all these things and these people. Profound dread overwhelmed me, . . . I looked around desperately for help. . . .[9]

This slipping away of reality in awed dread is known to the readers of Existentialist literature. It has been described by Heidegger in abstract terms and concretized by the hero of one of Sartre's novels. Heidegger wrote:

In dread . . . all things and we with them sink into a sort of indifference. But not in the sense that everything simply disappears; rather, in the very act of drawing away from us everything turns toward us. This withdrawal of what-is-in-totality, which then crowds round us in dread, this is what oppresses us. There is nothing to hold on to. The only thing that remains and overwhelms us whilst what-is slips away, is the 'nothing.' . . . In dread we are 'in suspense' [*wir schweben*: 'we are floating']. Or, to put it more precisely, dread holds us in suspense because it makes what-is-in-totality slip away from us.[10]

Experiencing Heidegger's "dread" concretely, Roquentin, hero of Sartre's novel *La Nausée,* describes his feelings in terms which strongly recall those of Renée. Sitting in the reading room of a public library, Roquentin says:

I strongly pressed in my hands the volume I was reading. But the most violent sensations were dulled. Nothing looked real. I felt myself surrounded by a scenery of cardboard which, suddenly, could be displaced.[11]

Renée continually speaks of her "dread," "anguish," or "anxiety," which always had the indefiniteness and objectlessness described

[9] *Autobiography,* p. 7.
[10] "What Is Metaphysics?" *Existence and Being,* p. 366.
[11] *La Nausée,* p. 105.

by Kierkegaard, Freud, Heidegger, and Sartre, and which, as we know, is the dominating pathos of Existentialism. It is also, as we see now, the dominating pathos of schizophrenia. Often Renée's anguish—"anguish no resolve could allay" and that "squeezed" her heart—was accompanied by the impression that something terrifying, awful, would occur, a catastrophe which, in fact, never did occur. Walking in a street of Geneva, Renée suddenly felt that

. . . everything seemed to stop, to wait, to hold its breath, in a state of extreme tension. . . . Something seemed about to occur, some extraordinary catastrophe. An overpowering anxiety forced me to stop and wait.[12]

On another occasion Renée "had the impression that some dreadful thing was about to occur . . . something horrible, overwhelming. I waited, holding my breath . . . but nothing happened."[13]

These experiences are familiar to Sartre's Roquentin who, while walking through the streets of Bouville, again and again says to himself:

Everything may occur, everything may happen. . . . I ran along the docks . . . the houses with their gloomy eyes watched me fleeing. I repeated to myself in anxiety: Where shall I go, where shall I go? Everything may happen.[14]

In her book *Symbolic Realization,* Madame Sechehaye reports that, as a child, Renée "sucked the rust of fences in order to 'become stiff like iron' and sucked stones to 'become cold and hard' like them."[15] I do not know whether Madame Sechehaye ever read Sartre's novels. If she did, she must have noticed the strange analogy between her patient's wish to become hard like stone and similar wishes of some of Sartre's heroes. The most typical example is Daniel in *The Reprieve,* who exclaims: "If I had been an insensible stone figure, incapable of sound and move-

---

[12]*Autobiography,* p. 11.

[13] *Ibid.,* p. 25.

[14] *La Nausée,* pp. 105-106.

[15] *Symbolic Realization,* p. 25.

ment, blind and deaf. . . ." [16] Also Mathieu Delarue, in the same novel, longs "to melt" into a stone, "to fill himself with its opaqueness and repose." [17]

The common motive of these strange longings of Sartre's heroes is the hidden wish to escape the responsibilities of human existence. There is no doubt that this is also Renée's dominating motive. Her analyst describes her retreat into autism as "a refusal of life's responsibilities." [18]

Renée's discovery of the "existence" of things was just as awe-inspiring to her as it was to Roquentin in Sartre's *La Nausée*. Renée writes:

When, for example, I looked at a chair or a jug, I thought not of their use or function . . . but as having lost their names, their functions and meanings; they became "things" and began . . . to exist. This existence accounted for my great fear. In the unreal scene, in the murky quiet of my perception, suddenly 'the thing' sprang up. The stone jar . . . was there facing me, defying me with its presence, with its existence. . . .[19]

We remember similar experiences described by Sartre's Roquentin:

Existence revealed itself suddenly. It had lost its inoffensive aspect of an abstract category. . . . The diversity of things, their individuality, was nothing but an appearance, a varnish. This varnish had melted. What was left were monstrous soft masses in disorder, naked in frightening nudity.[20]

Roquentin's discovery of his existence and its gratuitousness is so terrifying to him that it gives him nausea.

To exist is simply to be there; the existing beings appear but can never be deduced. . . . Everything is gratuitous, this garden, this town, I, myself. When we realize this, then it turns our hearts, everything begins to float . . . that is nausea.[21]

[16] *Le Sursis*, p. 133.
[17] *Ibid.*, p. 362.
[18] Sechehaye, *Symbolic Realization*, p. 73.
[19] *Autobiography*, pp. 34-35.
[20] *La Nausée*, p. 166.
[21] *Ibid.*, p. 171.

Renée too felt this nausea when she discovered her own existence in its complete gratuitousness.

I think that I could be not I: I am appalled at the thought that I could have been in another person's place. . . . Then things would not exist for me as they exist.[22]

Madame Duss, who did not make such a detailed comparison as I am trying to present here, spoke of an "Existentialist experience of a schizophrenic." My inclination, however, is to see in the analogies mentioned also some *schizophrenic experiences of Existentialists*. Conditions like those described in Heidegger's "suspense" or in Sartre's "nausea" can hardly be encountered in normal individuals; they have a definite pathological tinge, and the fact that they are also the most striking symptoms of Renée's schizophrenia can be considered a proof of this contention. Some of Renée's symptoms could be designated as manifestations of a "Heidegger-complex" (the anguished sliding away of reality); some as those of a "Sartre-complex" (the awe-inspiring discovery of existence); and also a definite "Kafka-complex" can be found in her. By a Kafka-complex I mean guilt obsession, without the subject knowing wherein his sin lies. Franz Kafka, who twenty years after his death in 1924 was proclaimed a great Existentialist writer, described this unreal guilt in different stories, and especially in *The Trial* (*Der Prozess*). The hero of this gloomy novel, Josef K. (read, "Kafka") is accused and found guilty of a crime of which he knows nothing and which nobody would define for him. But his ignorance of the evil of which he is accused does not prevent a profound feeling of guilt from dominating him. He writes letters of entreaty to the unknown prosecutor, but in vain. His feeling of guilt and his ignorance of its cause remain unchanged to the end of this nightmarish-novel. Although some of Kafka's enthusiastic partisans have called *The Trial* a "supra-human work," [23] one has the impression that the unreal world in which Josef K. moves—a world of unmotivated events, of strangest confusions of places and persons—is that of a

[22] Duss, *op. cit.*, p. 561.
[23] See M. Brod, *Franz Kafka's Glauben und Lehre* (Munich, 1948), p. 70.

schizophrenic. I think also that in this respect Renée's *Auto-biography of a Schizophrenic Girl* is extremely revealing. Her "Kafka-complex" is as clear as noonday. For example:

I was guilty, abominably, intolerably guilty, without cause and without motive. . . . Indeed, I knew not wherein lay my sin, but the ignorance did not prevent a profound feeling of guilt. . . . One day I wrote a letter of entreaty to the unknown author of my suffering, to the Prosecutor, asking him to tell me what evil I had done, that I might finally know. But because I did not know where to send my letter, I tore it up.[24]

With the development of her schizophrenia Renée became, step by step, aware of all the basic principles of Existentialism and tried to live up to their rigorous requirements: she realized the problems of choice, freedom, commitment, total responsibility, ethical anxiety, existence as conflict, subjectivity of values, the gaze of other people, etc. For example, she wrote: "People wish me to behave like a poor person, because I am poor. . . . But I decide, I wish, *I choose* to behave like a rich person. . . . Who has the right to judge me?"[25] Evidently nobody; for according to the Existentialist doctrine, there are no standards of good and evil as long as each of us has not set them up in his own way. In the English edition of her memoirs Renée writes that at the psychiatric hospital a doctor asked her how she liked the hangings in her room. "Awful," she replied, and she adds:

In saying this, I didn't have the least intention of being disagreeable. But at that time, according to my concept of the world, things did not exist in and of themselves, but each person created a world after his own fashion. Therefore it seemed natural that the doctor should find the hangings pretty, the nurse find them interesting, and I find them awful.[26]

The "concept of the world" of which Renée speaks here is exactly that of Existentialism, which teaches that things become realities only by the fact that man takes interest in them and in-

[24] *Autobiography*, pp. 28-29, 54.
[25] Duss, *op. cit.*, p. 563.
[26] *Autobiography*, pp. 54-55.

cludes them in his projects. Each man sets up certain relationships among things, and as soon as he loses his interest in them
they fall back into the condition of brute existents. The last quo-
tation from Renée's autobiography also expresses the doctrine of
the subjectivity of values, the negation of all universal essences
and general norms, which, as we know, is likewise an integral
part of Sartre's Existentialism.

The same is true of the necessity for committing oneself, for
choosing and assuming a total responsibility for one's choice,
which is not sanctioned by any general norm or objective essence.
And also Sartre's doctrine that each individual act engages the
whole of mankind [27] is incorporated in Renée's pathological philosophy, and the responsibility springing from this principle was
taken by her most seriously. It became "obsessional" to her, recounts her analyst, Mme Sechehaye: The girl "did not dare buy
herself a roll or a piece of bread when hungry. The two pennies
it cost might have satisfied the hunger of some poor man who
might otherwise kill someone because of hunger." [28] Explaining
the theoretical suppositions of this idea, Renée writes: "Since
every man was responsible for all other men, each of his acts had
a repercussion on other things." [29] It is almost as if she had read
Sartre's sentence: "If we say that man is responsible for himself,
we do not want to say that he is responsible for his strict individuality, but that he is responsible for all men." [30] And yet we
cannot believe that Renée had read Sartre when she had the obsession of total responsibility for all men, for the mental conditions she describes in her autobiography refer to a period of years
which ended in January, 1938. At this time none of Sartre's basic
theoretical works had been published. Is it not strange that
many of his philosophical positions should appear to have been
anticipated by a schizophrenic girl? This we have to admit, however, when we read the following passage of Renée's memoirs, reported by Dr. Duss:

[27] *L'Existentialisme*, pp. 24-27.
[28] *Symbolic Realization*, p. 26.
[29] *Autobiography*, p. 28.
[30] *L'Existentialisme*, p. 24.

Everything I do has an incredible importance, because it has unforeseeable consequences, which follow every action. I feel myself already committed by the mere fact that I am in the world. . . . Also, to do nothing involves my integral responsibility, which I cannot escape. For if I do not do anything, *I choose* to do nothing, and everything which will result from my decision. What can I do in order to do well? [31]

All this is also taught by Sartre, who, as the reader will remember, said that "freedom is freedom to choose, but not freedom not to choose. For not to choose is to choose not to choose." [32]

Also the Existentialist theme of the existence of "the other" self and his tendency to "enslave" me by his "gaze" occurs again and again as an obsession in the schizophrenic mental experiences of Renée. Mme Sechehaye told Mme Duss that Renée suffered terribly from the fact of being "looked at" by other persons, that she felt that by this gaze the other person took possession of her subjectivity, degrading her to the condition of an object, trying to "enslave" her, and that in order to defend herself against this tendency she tried to enslave the other person's freedom through her gaze, trying to change him into an object. All this is well known to the reader, from our analysis of Sartre's theories and the experiences of certain persons in his novels, especially of Daniel in *The Reprieve*.[33]

We also remember the Existentialist thesis of guilt and conflict by the mere fact of our existence. "Conflict is the original sense of the being-for-others," Sartre says, for each of our projects limits the other person's freedom. From this springs the concept of guilt. By my mere existence in a world where other persons exist,

I am guilty toward the other person. . . . The original sin is my springing up in a world where the other self exists, and whatever my later relations toward him may be, they will be nothing but variations of the original theme of guilt.[34]

[31] Duss, *op. cit.*, p. 562.
[32] *L'Etre et le Néant*, p. 561.
[33] See earlier chapters: Ch. 13, "Our 'Being-for-Others' and Their 'Gaze'"; Ch. 19, "Sex and Love in Existentialist Psychoanalysis."
[34] *L'Etre et le Néant*, pp. 431, 481.

It is like a paraphrase of these Sartrean theses when Renée writes:

Every moment and without intentions we enter into conflicts with other persons. It is a struggle, silent and terrible, in order to resist their "grasp" and to stay in the authenticity of one's being. . . . And I do the same with my neighbors. I am committed by the mere fact of being in the world, etc.[35]

According to Dr. Duss, it was the Existentialist thesis of total responsibility and guilt of everybody for everything and toward everybody which finally drove Renée to complete insanity. Sartre wrote: "With each of my acts the meaning of the world is at stake and the place of man in the universe. . . . And one wishes that we be not seized with awe before such total responsibility?" [36] Renée makes exactly the same inference with her pitiless logic, when she writes: "Each of my actions leaves a commotion behind it, which will indefinitely change by the repercussion of my initial act, so that future individuals will have to suffer the consequences of my acts. . . . To think of this is appalling!" [37]

Renée's analyst reports that once, on the bank of a river, Renée threw a few stones into the water, but suddenly stopped and exclaimed:

The least gesture involves the whole universe. This stone I am throwing now ricochets and leaves behind it a wake of waves; it may contribute to cause a shipwreck in the ocean. Consequently I shall be the cause of the shipwreck, and I will have to assume the total responsibility. . . . I am guilty of everything, of absolutely everything! . . . . By my mere existence I am guilty and I involve the whole world in my disgrace. . . . How terrible this eternal load on our human shoulders! To be sure of nothing, to be unable to rely on anything, and, nevertheless, to be obliged to commit oneself always totally. . . .[38]

These terrifying requirements of Existentialist philosophy went beyond Renée's strength. "How much would I have wished to be relieved from my responsibility, only for a second!" she exclaimed.

[35] Duss, *op. cit.*, pp. 562, 565, *passim.*
[36] Quoted by Duss, *op. cit.*, p. 563, from *Action* (Paris, 1947).
[37] Duss, *op. cit.*, p. 563.
[38] *Ibid.*, pp. 563-571.

In her despair Renée sometimes uttered these unconscious and shocking words: "I should prefer to escape into madness to avoid this consuming fear." [39] She finally did escape into madness, and although she declared later that her hope of finding there relief from her sufferings was vain, Mme Duss thinks that Renée found a pseudo-equilibrium in her delirious construction which she called "the system" and that it helped to reduce her anxiety. The "system" imagined in Renée's delirium was a kind of mechanical organization responsible for the world, thus relieving her from responsibility.

To be sure, in the system we are equally guilty, but not in the same way as in life. Everything is mechanical in it. . . . If one raises his arm, one is guilty; if one puts it down, one is guilty. . . . But if I am guilty, abominably guilty, I am, at least, no longer responsible, either for myself or for the world. For the true chief of the world is the system, the mechanical organization.[40]

However, this pseudo-equilibrium of Renée's delirium did not last long. It was followed by a violent crisis of hebephrenic, catatonic restlessness and a crisis of accentuated stupor. "Except for moments of agitation or intense crises of guilt, I fell . . . into complete apathy. The world was a moving picture, taking place without my participation." [41] Renée's delirium became incoherent, she fell into infantilism, into automatism, echolalia, caducity, interrupted by aggressive and auto-destructive impulsions, until Madame Sechehaye saved her from definitive insanity by applying her new method, called "symbolic realization."

The conclusions that Mme Duss draws from this case are crushing and, it may be, even too radical. She thinks of Renée as a person who truly and sincerely tried to live up to the rigorous principles of Existentialism and who became insane. In order to escape the terrifying responsibility of the individual in a world deprived of universal norms for good and evil and general categories or logical essences, she returned, in a pathological form, to a world of essences, classes, norms, universal categories: the

[39] *Autobiography,* p. 23.
[40] Duss, *op. cit.,* p. 572.
[41] *Autobiography,* p. 68.

world of her delirium, which she called "the system." The Existentialists would say that she exchanged her freedom for security, and would despise her. From all this Mme Duss infers that the principles of Existentialism are not consonant with life. Man is unable always to use his free will and judgment without being able to rest upon any universal principle and without being directed by any general norm. For a person who wishes to carry out this principle of freedom to the utmost in his individual choice, without being guided by general norms and with the total individual responsibility required by Existentialism, there is only one alternative left, according to Mme Duss: suicide or insanity. Renée avoided suicide only because she escaped into insanity. This was the only way to evade the terrifying responsibility which her Existentialist philosophy tried to load upon her shoulders. By her psychotic construction of a universal "system" into which she could discharge her responsibility for the world, Renée was able to reduce her anxiety so that it did not totally crush her.

Trying to apply the Freudian psychoanalytic technique to Existentialist psychoanalysis itself, Mme Duss thinks that the latter constitutes a return to the sadistic-masochistic state of our psychism. This fixation, she thinks, explains the apparent need of the Existentialist philosophers to crush their disciples under a terrifying responsibility; it also explains the kind of morbid pleasure the masters of Existentialism seem to feel in developing the irrational, almost inhuman consequences of this responsibility, which, after all, is exaggerated.

Does this mean that Existentialism is a philosophy of lunatics? From reading the confessions of Sartre's Roquentin or of Kafka's Joseph K., one truly has this impression. But such a conclusion would go too far. Mme Duss thinks that the difference between a normal Existentialist philosopher and a pathological Existentialist, like Renée, is that the former dissociates himself emotionally from his intellectual thesis and does not truly apply it to his own life. This "bad faith" of the Existentialist philosopher is in a certain way his self-defense against his mental self-destruction by this philosophy of despair and nothingness. But the pathological Existentialist, like Renée, is deprived of this kind of self-defense through bad faith. She is sincere, and follows the requirements of Existentialist philosophy to the end, trying to test to the utmost the thesis of total responsibility in a normless world. The result is total madness.

There might be a good portion of truth in Mme Duss's conclusions, but it seems to me that they do not follow cogently from Renée's case. Mme Duss presents the case of this schizophrenic girl as if her main unsatisfied mental need had been of an intellectual, gnosiological character: the need of a system of categories and norms of universal validity. But from reading Mme Sechehaye's extremely interesting work on *Symbolic Realization* and her "Analytic Interpretation" of Renée's autobiography, one understands clearly that the girl's psychic needs were mainly *emotional*. The crux of her mental illness was that as an infant she had been deprived of maternal love. Mme Sechehaye explains:

Renée could not love herself, since her mother had refused to nourish, hence, to love her. When the ego is no longer charged with libidinal energy produced by the introjection of maternal love, destructive forces soon invade it. As Freud has shown, there is a complication of drives. When the libidinal drives are frustrated, the drives to self-preservation lose their defensive energy and abandon the ego to self-destruction. He sees in the latter one aspect of the death-instinct linked to primary masochism.[42]

We understand now the true purpose of Renée's delirious construction called the "system." Renée's mother had seemed to condemn her desire for nourishment and had created in the child the idea that it was bad to want to eat. Consequently the desire to live was also blameworthy. Therefore Renée refused food and had often to be nourished artificially. Yet her irrepressible desire for food created in her terrifying feelings of guilt. "These guilt feelings," explains Mme Sechehaye, "were alleviated by *self-punishment which attended the System*." [43] Here is the true purpose of Renée's delirious "system," which is very far from Mme

[42] *Symbolic Realization*, p. 118.
[43] *Ibid.*, p. 135.

Duss's supposition that it provided for the universal categories and norms which Renée had lost by her Existentialist philosophy. Having not been loved by her mother, having, symbolically, been condemned to death by her mother, Renée felt guilty about her wish to live. "These guilt feelings demanded punishment and punishment consisted in having guilt feelings." [44] The "system" which forbade her to eat and gave her feelings of guilt for whatever she did or omitted doing was, then, well adapted to Renée's condition.

As we saw, Renée's basic need was love, maternal love. Among her delirious constructions was one in which she believed herself to be the Queen of Tibet, "a country where one finds all the necessities of life, especially heat [!] and where one no longer suffers from not being loved." [45]

Mme Sechehaye's brilliant idea was to offer her patient a *symbolic realization* of her frustrated emotional demands. Once she gave her apples, but Renée refused them, pointed to her analyst's breasts and said: "I want apples from Mummy like that." Realizing that the apples meant maternal breasts, maternal milk, maternal love, Mme Sechehaye took an apple, cut it in two, offered the halves to Renée and said: "It is time to drink the good milk from Mummy's apples." [46] Renée, who at this period was 21 years old but had regressed to the infantile stage of magic participation, leaned toward Mme Sechehaye's shoulder, pressed the apple upon her analyst's breast, and began to eat.

The girl describes the almost miraculous effects of this symbolic realization of her frustrated emotional need of maternal love by writing:

I ate, or rather, I drank, my milk. A nameless felicity flowed into my heart. . . . I was fully content, with a . . . contentment of a tiny baby, quite unconscious. . . . I left with the nurse . . . and when we were outside I realized that my perception of things had completely changed. Instead of infinite space, unreal, where everything was cut off, naked, and isolated, I saw Reality, marvelous Reality, for the first time. . . ! [47]

44 *Ibid.*, p. 136.
45 *Ibid.*, p. 45.
46 *Ibid.*, p. 51.
47 *Autobiography*, pp. 79-80.

The complete success of Mme Sechehaye's symbolic realization of maternal love shows that Renée's true need was emotional and not intellectual. Were Mme Duss's supposition correct—that what Renée needed was a new belief in universal essences, which she had lost through her Existentialist philosophy—then Madame Sechehaye would have been compelled to offer her patient a symbolic realization of Plato's world of ideas. Of course, one may be of the opinion that there is no love and security without essences. However this may be, Mme Duss's judgment may contain a certain portion of truth, for there is little doubt that Renée's Existentialist concept of total responsibility of the individual in a normless world had very bad effects on her mental condition; it certainly increased her pathological anxiety.

The analysis of the psychiatric aspects of Existentialism has not shaken, but rather strengthened, our conviction that Existentialist psychoanalysis cannot be regarded as a *mental therapy* since it gives *freedom with anxiety,* while a true mental therapy would give *freedom from anxiety.* And if Existentialism is to be used as a *moral therapy,* it cannot be in the form of a metaphysical thesis, as in Sartre, but only in that of a moral fiction, an ethical "as if." We shall try to explain this in the last chapter.

Before closing the present analysis, still one more fact must be taken into consideration: that Renée's case seems to give some confirmation to Sartre's psychoanalysis of foods. As explained in a previous chapter,[48] Sartre thinks that each kind of food has a symbolic significance, that each represents being in a different symbolic way. To a certain extent this idea seems to be substantiated by Mme Sechehaye's method of "symbolic realization." We have seen already that apples truly symbolized maternal love. "On the mantelpiece were always two beautiful apples representing maternal breasts, given me by Mama to protect me. At the least anxiety I ran to them and at once was reassured," Renée recounts.[49] On another occasion she describes how her

[48] Ch. 22, "The Psychoanalysis of Qualities and Foods: Viscosity and Nausea."

[49] *Autobiography,* p. 82.

analyst—in whom she had found a new mother—tried to assuage
the girl's terrible feeling of guilt by bringing her whipped cream
and placing a spoonful of it in her (the girl's) mouth. "Take
some white snow," Mme Sechehaye said to her patient, "it will
purify Renée. When Mama gives Renée snow, the crime will
disappear; Renée will be pure again." [50] And the girl describes
how, while she was swallowing the whipped cream, symbol of
moral purity, her penetrating feeling of guilt and unworthiness
was at once tempered.

Thus a definitive symbolic character of whipped cream was
revealed by its positive therapeutic effects, just as, in the other
case, the symbolic meaning of the apples had become obvious. I
think that these interesting experiences may be considered a confirmation of Sartre's ideas on the psychoanalysis of foods.

But, again, certain restrictions are necessary: Sartre's Existentialist psychoanalysis considers the symbolic significance of
foods as their "metaphysical coefficient," [51] which, therefore, is
permanent and unchangeable. This rigid, metaphysical concept
of the symbolic significance of foods has not been confirmed by
Mme Sechehaye's experiments in symbolic realization. Without
referring to Sartre's psychoanalysis of foods (which she seems
not to know) Mme Sechehaye recounts how she tried to satisfy,
symbolically, Renée's wish to retreat into her analyst-mother's
body. Freud had already spoken of man's nostalgia for his prenatal life, the life of the foetus, passive and free from responsibilities. In order to give symbolic realization to this emotional
demand of Renée, her analyst had her lie down in a room whose
green shades had been pulled down so that it was filled with
green light. Mme Sechehaye gave her patient a sedative, hot
compresses, and herb infusions, which represented symbols of
maternal refuge. Renée says that she felt wonderfully relieved,
and her moral pain was assuaged in that state of perfect passiv-
ity. But one difficulty arose when this experiment was repeated:
Renée suffered from nausea (not only from Existentialist, but

50 *Ibid.*, p. 90.
51 *L'Etre et le Néant*, p. 695.

also from physiological nausea), which increased with the hot drinks she was taking in her mother-analyst's symbolic body. To counteract this nausea the doctor ordered ice cream. Now, ice cream is cold, and the contrary of the symbol of the maternal warmth. Madame Sechehaye says that Renée was completely bewildered to see that the heat which she had desired so much made her suffer and that she had to eat cold ice cream to relieve her nausea when resting in her mother's body. The analyst got around this difficulty by saying to the girl that she was going to take away her nausea with a liquid that was "a mother's liquid." She was then able to give Renée the ice cream, which relieved her.

This example shows that the symbolic character is not a permanent "metaphysical coefficient" of a given food, but is psychologically variable and dependent on the ideas with which one associates it. Although Mme Sechehaye's experiments do not substantiate Sartre's metaphysical conceptions of symbolism, they seem to confirm his general psychoanalytical theory of the symbolic character of food.

CHAPTER TWENTY-FIVE

FINAL CRITICAL CONSIDERATION
AND CONCLUSION

Existentialist psychoanalysis tries to investigate certain mental data which empirical psychoanalysis and individual psychology considered as irreducible. To push back the limits of apparently irreducible data means to expand the field of scientific investigation, and in this sense Existentialist psychoanalysis may have some scientific merit, which only the future can confirm. For the time being, it is only a rough draft. Sartre himself says that Existentialist psychoanalysis has not yet found its Freud, but there is little doubt that he will be that Freud.

What seems to me defective, is his method of psychoanalytical investigation; for it is the method of Husserl's phenomenology. Sartre considers qualities like viscosity, fluidity, solidity, etc., "objective natures," or essences in Husserl's sense, and tries to discover their meaning through Husserl's phenomenological "intuition." However, intuition is always subjective, in spite of the phenomenologists' protestations. Basing philosophy on intuition, Husserl, nevertheless, pretended to give it the character of a *"strenge Wissenschaft,"* a rigorous science. And so does Sartre with his Existentialist psychoanalysis, when he says, for instance: "The sweet . . . *expresses* viscosity, when we eat a spoonful of honey or molasses, just as an analytical function expresses a geometric curve." [1] But is this relation between sweetness and viscosity, to which he wants to give the objective character of a mathematical function, not merely subjective? Is there more than a personal, subjective "intuition" in the following statement? "If I am eating a pink cake, the taste is pink; the slight

[1] *L'Etre et le Néant,* p. 707.

sweet perfume and the unctuousness of the butter cream *are* pink." [2]

In order to become a true science, Existentialist psychoanalysis must become independent of the phenomenological method, which, according to its creator, Husserl, wants to make decisive discoveries "without the apparatus of syllogisms and proofs." [3] But there *is* no science without proofs.

The difference between Freud's and Sartre's psychoanalysis in their attitudes toward therapy has already been mentioned. While Freud's empirical psychoanalysis belongs to the realm of *mental* hygiene, Sartre's Existentialist psychoanalysis belongs rather to that of *moral* hygiene, which, as we have seen, sometimes lives at the expense of mental health. Philosophically speaking, Freud's psychoanalysis is a rationalism, directly in the line of Spinoza's. In Spinoza's rationalism suffering is revealed as an error, arising from the limited understanding of individual existence; but in recognizing things *sub specie aeternitatis* we are relieved from our suffering. Thus Spinoza's ethics is tantamount to a liberation of man from his sufferings through knowledge. I think Freud's psychoanalysis also can be considered a liberation of man from his sufferings through knowledge, for in recognizing our repressed tendencies under the guidance of the psychoanalyst, we are delivered from the sufferings they once caused us. In this sense Spinoza's and Freud's teachings are rationalistic. Reason appears as the great liberator.

Sartre's Existentialist psychoanalysis, on the contrary, gives us not liberation from suffering, but more suffering. It does not give us *liberation,* at all. It gives us *liberty.* And that is different. For liberty is a gift of Danaë. We cannot embrace the beautiful goddess of freedom without accepting her Siamese-twin sister, anxiety. They are joined to each other by an unbreakable bond, as we have seen in Sartre's philosophy, in his novels, and, most impressively, in his tragedy *Les Mouches.* Clearing the way to the recognition of our freedom, Existentialist psychoanalysis thus does not free us from our suffering but brings us the suffer-

---

[2] *Ibid.,* p. 707.
[3] "Philosophie als strenge Wissenschaft," *Logos* I (1910), p. 341.

ing of an existence in *authenticity*. Ascribing to this authenticity an absolute positive value, considering it an absolute ideal which would justify the sufferings of our anxiety, Sartre's Existentialism can be interpreted as an absolute "ethical idealism" and, at the same time, an "irrationalism"; for the acceptance of the sufferings of an authentic existence cannot be justified by reason. On the contrary, reason shows us that all those persons who lead an unauthentic life do not suffer at all. They live in bad faith, running away from the admission of their freedom and thus escape responsibility for their choice of values. Trying to evade anxiety, they live comfortably in bad faith, accepting values as ready-made things and considering themselves as justified by their little functions within a society for whose values they are not responsible.

A life in authenticity, as preached by Sartre, gives us only *one* reward for the sufferings it imposes upon us: the moral satisfaction of living no longer in bad faith, of being sincere, of being no longer "*salauds*" (stinkers). But only an irrationalistic approach to existence can consider this moral satisfaction an adequate reward for the sufferings of anxiety; only an irrationalistic idealist like Sartre's Orestes can praise "the freedom of the prisoner loaded with chains on the floor of his dungeon, and of the crucified slave." [4]

Thus our first conclusion will be that Sartre's Existentialism *is not a nihilism,* as it seemed to us earlier, but a kind of absolute ethical idealism. With this term we designate the attitude of affirming an idea merely for the sake of the values bound up with it, without any regard to the advantages or disadvantages flowing to the agent from the realization of that idea. While Sartre's unconditional affirmation of an "authentic existence" merely for the sake of the values bound up with it, without regard to subsequent sufferings, is a typical example of absolute ethical idealism, it is obvious that the absolute value he ascribes to authenticity and sincerity cannot be justified by his own philosophy; for we know that the latter does not admit any value of supraindividual validity, given before an individual choice, since Sar-

[4] *Les Mouches,* p. 94.

tre thinks that each individual has to choose his values freely and may even revoke his choice and replace it with another. According to this philosophy, the acceptance of the absolute value of authenticity could even be characterized as a manifestation of unauthenticity, that is of the spirit of seriousness, which considers values as transcendent data, independent of human subjectivity. Yet it is in this way that Sartre accepts the absolute value of authenticity and sincerity; so it would seem that only through a fortunate inconsequence of his philosophy does the latter escape nihilism and become an irrationalistic absolute idealism.

Like Nietzsche's philosophy, that of Sartre passes through nihilism in order to overcome it.

It seems to us that Sartre's striving against the comfort of an unauthentic life in bad faith, and his preaching of an authentic life in sincerity, with all the sufferings linked to it, is only a new form of the message brought to us in the second half of the nineteenth century by Hendrik Ibsen. There is no doubt that the great Norwegian, too, preached against the ease of an unauthentic existence in bad faith and summoned us to accept an authentic existence in sincerity, at the price of moral sufferings. We find this message in most of Ibsen's dramas. Beginning with *The Wild Duck*, it is Hjalmar Ekdal who lives in bad faith, entirely satisfied with his unauthentic existence built on a lie, the lie which Ibsen calls "life-lie" (*Livslögnen*). We remember that Sartre has defined bad faith as a lie, a lie to oneself, and Ibsen's life-lie, or life-illusion, is also a lie to oneself. Ibsen calls it "the stimulating principle" of life; [5] and Sartre's "bad faith" has exactly such a strong stimulating function.

Now comes Gregers Werle, the idealist, who tries to pull Hjalmar out of "the poisonous marsh" of an unauthentic life. In the name of the "claim of the ideal" he wants Hjalmar to accept an authentic life built on sincerity, with all the suffering it involves. These sufferings soon appear: Hjalmar's family life is destroyed and his daughter commits suicide.

In *An Enemy of the People* we find a similar message from Ibsen. There is Dr. Stockmann who wants to free a whole town

[5] *The Wild Duck* (New York, [1911]), p. 432.

from bad faith and lead it to authenticity. Finally, he stands alone, consoling himself by saying that "the strongest man in the world is he who stands alone." [6] Sartre's Orestes also stands alone in his authenticity, suffering alone the attack of the Furies.

But Ibsen's Peer Gynt, whose existence is entirely unauthentic, lives happily in bad faith and does not stand alone. By means of fancy lies he helps his mother to a mild death, and spares her an awakening to the authenticity of Heidegger's mortal anxiety. Peer Gynt is the embodiment of unauthenticity, which is also symbolized in Ibsen's fabulous trolls.

In Ibsen's *Brand* we see the pastor of this name fighting the ease of bad faith in a Christian community and trying to convert it to an authentic Christendom. He accepts all the sufferings of an authentic life, sacrificing his happiness, his wife and child, and, finally, his own life in order to uproot the dominance of bad faith, the comfortable lies in the traditional way of practicing religion. "All or naught!" is Brand's battle cry in his fight against bad faith and for authenticity. It was also the battle cry of his model, Sören Kierkegaard, the founder of Existentialism, whose whole life was a striving for authenticity in the realm of Christian faith, a struggle against the bad faith of those who lie to themselves by pretending to be Christians without trying to live up to the severe and austere requirements of an authentic Christianity.

Miguel de Unamuno, the great Spanish writer and Christian Existentialist, calls Ibsen's *Brand* "*el reflejo de Kierkegaard en el arte dramatico*" ("Kierkegaard's reflection in dramatic art"); and he adds: "*Cuanto dure Brand durará Kierkegaard*" ("Kierkegaard will last as long as *Brand*").[7]

And yet it seems to us that Kierkegaard was of bad faith. He was engaged to a lovely girl, Regine Olsen, who adored him. But suddenly he broke with her, brutally accusing her of being on a lower religious level, accusing the Church of being of bad faith in making terms with marriage, although it is "sinful." For woman is the supreme enemy of the spirit; she is the devil who

---

[6] *An Enemy of the People* (New York, [1911]), p. 216.

[7] *Mi religión, y otros ensayos* (Buenos Aires-Mexico, 1942), p. 55.

draws young men to her snare. In some of his writings Kierkegaard turned sentimental, declaring, in an obvious allusion to his
behavior toward Regine, that "each man must offer up his Isaac,
his best."

The matter of Kierkegaard's erotic life is still controversial,
and our expression here is but a personal opinion. But it seems
to us that the above-mentioned reasons which Kierkegaard gave
for his breach with Regine were lies, lies to the world and to himself. And it also seems to us that the Copenhagen magazine
Korsar was not wrong when it accused Kierkegaard of odious
behavior toward Regine and an indelicate exploitation of this behavior in his books. From Kierkegaard's conversations with Emil
Boesen during his last illness, we are left thinking that the "authentic" reason for his rupture with Regine Olsen might have
been his physical disability, against which he had sought medical
advice but which was incurable. In his interesting book on
Kierkegaard, E. L. Allan writes:

One cannot but think in this whole connection of some form of sexual
impotence, so that it would finally be of a lack of virility that he accused himself. May this be a case in which Adler's analysis applies,
and a life-long mental conflict can be traced back to some organ inferiority? [8]

We entirely agree with Allan's assumption and are inclined to
think that the striving for authenticity of the pope of modern
Existentialism was a manifestation of bad faith. In Kierkegaard's
case Sartre's Existentialist psychoanalysis seems to be outwitted
by Adler's individual psychology.

All these considerations show us that to the names of the Stoics,
Pascal, Descartes, Kant, Schelling, Fichte, Hegel, Schopenhauer,
Kierkegaard, Nietzsche, Marx, Bergson, Husserl, Marcel, Valéry,
Heidegger, Jaspers, Bachelard, Freud, Adler, Croce, Schnitzler,
Malraux, and Salacrou, we must add that of Ibsen, as one of
Sartre's spiritual forefathers. As far as literary form is concerned,
Sartre also adopted Schnitzler's "interior monologue," in which
the principle character sets down his thoughts as they are actu-
ally formulated in his mind, with all of the seemingly irrelevant

---

[8] *Kierkegaard, His Life and Thought* (London, 1935), p. 30.

associations of ideas. Those who read Schnitzler's *Leutnant Gustl* and *Fräulein Else* will not be astonished by the form in which Sartre's Mathieu and Boris express their thoughts.

(To be sure, in his essays on literature Sartre criticized Schnitzler's interior monologue, but this did not prevent him from exploiting it thoroughly.)

Many people have been surprised at the literary form of Sartre's *The Reprieve,* where he describes facts not in the usual chronological order, but simultaneously. We are told what happens at the same time in Paris, Prague, Godesberg, Morocco, etc., often in the same sentence and with the same personal pronouns. When, in this novel, Sartre says "he," we never know immediately which one of his persons is meant, whether it is one in Paris or another thinking and acting at the same time in Sudetenland or Africa. Many readers find this bewildering. Yet it only carries out one of the ideas André Gide has expressed but, fortunately, not developed in his novel *Les Faux-Monnayeurs* ("The Counterfeiters"). Speaking of the reform of the novel, Gide criticizes the naturalistic school, which wanted to give "a slice of life" (*une tranche de vie*), but would always cut it longitudinally, in time. Why not cut it transversally, in width, that is to say, make a cross section through simultaneous events? Gide asked. Sartre tried it out, violating Lessing's sensible laws, and not with the best results.

Yet it would be wrong to consider Sartre an eclectic writer. For the foreign elements he uses are deeply enriched by the synthesis in which he unites them. Sartre's is a syncretic talent, a genius of synthesis. When, in his short story *La Chambre,* he describes a woman who tries to enter the world of insane ideas and feelings of her beloved but lunatic husband and thus to pierce "the wall" between reason and madness, Sartre certainly carries out an idea hinted at in Balzac's novel *Louis Lambert.* But what in Balzac was only a light sketch of amazing inspiration became in Sartre's story a master painting, carried out with the deepest, gloomiest, and most powerful colors of human passion.

And so it is also with Sartre's philosophy and Existentialist psychoanalysis. Everywhere the ideas or germs of ideas of his predecessors are developed, seen from new angles, brought to interesting conclusions. Sartre's power of synthesis, his imposing dialectic, the penetrating subtlety of his novels, and his forceful dramatic genius all proclaim him one of the most fascinating personalities of our time.

What is the final result of Sartre's philosophy? He has examined all human projects: love, desire, hate, indifference, the enslavement of other persons, the appropriation of inanimate objects; and all these projects turned out to be failures. To be sure, one may not be of Sartre's opinion that love is nothing but the wish to be loved, so that it amounts to an endless fooling mirror game. I am of the opinion—and I have developed this idea in two of my books—that of all human projects love comes closest to overcoming the opposition between subject and object.[9] Love, consequently, may to a certain extent free the individual from his cosmic loneliness. And in another of my books I tried to show that love is the only human attitude which ties man to the present and thus redeems him for moments from his everlasting projection toward the future.[10]

However, in Sartre's philosophy love is a failure, and so is man's fundamental project to be God by possessing the world. "For the idea of God is contradictory and we lose ourselves in vain; man is a useless passion." [11]

Closing his big philosophical treatise on this gloomy note, Sartre seems to have achieved what Camus and Juin reproach him for: rationalizing the absurdity of existence.[12] L'Etre et le Néant really demonstrates the necessity of the absurdity and contingency of our existence, which Roquentin, the hero of the novel La Nausée, had only felt irrationally. L'Etre et le Néant is a logical demonstration that man's existence cannot be demonstrated logically; it gives an ontological foundation to the fact that man's existence has no ontological foundation. It is a justi-

---

[9] See A. Stern, *Die philosophischen Grundlagen von Wahrheit, Wirklichkeit, Wert*, pp. 404-21; *La Filosofía de los Valores*, pp. 207-210.

[10] See A. Stern, "Eros et le Rire," *Philosophie du Rire et des Pleurs* (Paris, 1949), pp. 186-93.

[11] *L'Etre et le Néant*, p. 708.   [12] See above pp. 31-32.

fication of man's not being justified. It is a most intelligent demonstration of absurdity.

And yet, in spite of proclaiming the failure of man's project to become God and thus to find a foundation of his existence, Sartre's philosophy finally gives man the attributes of divinity and a foundation—in the form of freedom. In commenting on Descartes, Sartre describes the concept of freedom as defined by the father of modern philosophy. But in Descartes, absolute freedom, which invents reason and values and has no limits other than itself, is a divine prerogative, while Sartre pretends that absolute freedom is human freedom. He concludes by writing:

We do not reproach Descartes for having given to God what belongs to us (man); we admire him rather for having . . . developed to the end the requirements of the idea of autonomy and for having understood, a long time before the Heidegger of *Vom Wesen des Grundes*, that the unique foundation of being is freedom.[13]

To be sure, in looking more closely we realize that this divine freedom, which Sartre so proudly proclaims as our human patrimony, is reduced to miserable remnants. What is left of this boundless human freedom, "not limited by any order of truths nor values which would be offered to our consent as eternal things" [14] when Sartre later restricts it, by our facticity, our situation, and finally admits that it is only a freedom of choosing and not of obtaining? I do not think a God would be satisfied with that type of freedom. Sartre says that a slave in his chains is as free as his master, adding: "The life of the slave who revolts and dies in the course of the uprising is a *free life*." [15] In many cases Sartre's freedom is reduced to the choice between bearing chains or dying. We find it already in Schiller's *Wilhelm Tell*, when Gertrud Stauffacher exclaims:

> None are so weak but one last choice is left.
> A leap from yonder bridge—and I am free.[16]

[13] "La liberté cartésienne," *Situations I* (Paris, 1947), pp. 334-335.
[14] *Ibid.*, p. 335.
[15] *L'Etre et le Néant*, p. 635.
[16] *Wilhelm Tell*, in *Schillers Werke* (Stuttgart, 1885), III, Sc. 2, p. 9:
> Die letzte Wahl steht auch dem Schwächsten offen,
> Ein Sprung von dieser Brücke macht mich frei.

Nothing shows better the extreme impoverishment of Sartre's proud, godlike human freedom than his words "We were never more free than during the German occupation." [17]

Sometimes Sartre's insistence on man's sovereignty and god-like freedom, in spite of the most oppressing situation, sounds, willy-nilly, almost as ironical as Voltaire's comments on Leibniz's idea of freedom. As a soldier in the Bulgarian (read Prussian) army, Voltaire's hero Candide is asked whether he would rather be thrashed thirty-six times by the whole regiment or receive a dozen lead bullets at once in his brain.

Although he protested that man's will is free and that he wanted neither one nor the other, he had to make a choice; by virtue of that gift of God which is called liberty, he determined to run the gauntlet thirty-six times. . . .[18]

Voltaire's Candide, having to choose between being thrashed to death or shot to death has about the same freedom of choice as Sartre's slave, who must choose between dying in his chains in prison, or dying in a jail-break. Voltaire, however, recognized that a choice between two destructive necessities is no freedom at all, but its bloody caricature, while Sartre stubbornly maintains that it is godlike freedom. The inconsistency of this attitude is reflected in the fact that, as far as freedom of will is concerned, the skeptic atheist Sartre is much closer to the optimistic creator of the *Theodicy*, Leibnitz, than to the skeptic deist Voltaire.

It is on this concept of freedom that Sartre bases the final optimism of his Existentialism. For if people are vile, feeble, wicked, cowardly, it is not because of their biological inheritance, or the influence of their environment, or any other organic or social determinism, but because they freely choose themselves as vile, feeble, wicked, cowardly. Thus they are responsible for their vices. But this implies also that "it is always possible for the coward not to be a coward." [19] His becoming a hero only depends finally on his free choice to become heroic.

---

[17] *Republic of Silence*, p. 498.
[18] *Candide*, in *Oeuvres choisies* (Paris: [1878]), II, p. 49.
[19] *L'Existentialisme*, p. 62.

We may reply that genetics and psychology have established the fact of inheritance and that sociology has proved the influence of environment. To this Sartre would answer that science is only one among many projects of existence, which presupposes existence and freedom, and that "human freedom is not limited by any order of truths," for "reason comes into being by freedom." [20] Finally, he probably would retort that the biologists and sociologists, who insist on the factors of inheritance and environment in order to explain man's moral character, are themselves of bad faith in trying to escape their moral responsibilities under the pretext of a scientific determinism.

Thus Sartre's strategic position in his defense of freedom appears to be impregnable. And yet the foundations of his concept of freedom are not of the solidest. He has told us that "freedom coincides . . . with the nothingness which is in the heart of man." [21] But he is not able to tell us what nothingness is, because it is undefinable. Any definition of it would have to say "nothingness is . . . this or that," but this would be a *contradictio in adjecto,* by which the verb affirms what the noun denies. Sartre's nothingness, which he inherited from Heidegger, is almost a mystical entity, and yet it is the basis of his concept of freedom.

Perhaps Sartre himself feels the logical weakness of his demonstration of freedom, for he relies now more on Descartes' aphorism: "We know our freedom without any proof, by the sole experience we have of it."

But even if we granted Sartre that, thanks to freedom, there is always a chance for the cowardly to become courageous and the vile to be noble, would this be a sufficient reason for optimism? Not for Existentialism; because for it the world even then would continue to wander aimlessly, still devoid of purpose. And —what is even more important—Existentialism cannot recognize the superior value of courage and nobleness, for, according to its own presuppositions, there are no values of universal validity. Each individual has to invent his own system of values and can

[20] "La liberté cartésienne," *Situations I,* p. 333; *L'Etre et le Néant,* p. 567.
[21] *Ibid.,* p. 516.

revoke and replace it with another as soon as he wants to make another choice. Values, we have been told by Sartre, are valid only within a definite, individual *project*.

Consequently, if by his free choice the coward has a chance to become courageous and the vile man to become noble, it would not indicate the world's progress toward a higher degree of moral perfection, for only the "rotten spirit of seriousness" can ascribe to the values of courage and nobleness a superior rank of universal and everlasting validity. Thus if Sartre's Existentialism wants to be optimistic *in spite* of having dried up all sources of optimism, its optimism seems to be an *optimism of defiance*.

But the strange thing is that Sartre really believes in the superior value of courage and nobleness independent of any definite project, although his system excludes this belief. As a result of the ruthless German behavior in occupied France, we saw Sartre even affirm the absolute character of good and evil,[22] in open violation of his axiological relativism. If that is so, then Sartre's philosophy is both more moral and more dogmatic than he is either theoretically able or emotionally willing to admit.

In spite of the vague nature of Sartre's nothingness as the basis of human freedom, this freedom seems to have certain citizen-rights within human consciousness, although no such absolute rights as Sartre's grants it. For there is no doubt that the subject feels himself free and responsible. But as soon as he tries to *think* of himself, he has to think of himself as determined. For to think means to determine. As soon as the subject determines himself, he becomes a determined object. And as a determined object he is determined and no longer free.[23]

Thus, I should say that subjectively man's existence is felt and lived as free, but objectively he must be thought of as determined. This position, although more restricted than Sartre's, would nevertheless enable philosophy to draw most of the ethical benefit from his theory of freedom. Since the subject feels and lives himself as free, although he cannot think himself as

---

[22] *What Is Literature?* p. 219.

[23] See A. Stern, *Pensée transcendantale-logique et Pensée anthropologique-psychologique-cérébrale* (Paris, 1937), pp. 45-51.

free, I believe that he may adopt the thesis of moral freedom at least in the sense of an "as if," a fiction in Vaihinger's sense. Fiction is a legitimate error, whose reason of being has to be justified by its success.[24] In this sense I should say that the individual should act "as if" he were free, for he feels that he is free and responsible, although this freedom theoretically cannot be thought with the categories of the mind.

Considered not as a metaphysical reality but as an ethical "as if," Sartre's concept of freedom certainly could fulfill its whole moral mission by helping to prevent biological and sociological determinism from becoming a pretext for moral laziness and fatalism. The drunkard has to act "as if" he were free to become a sober man, although alcoholism runs in his family. The coward has to act "as if" he were free to choose to be courageous, although his education and environment may not have given him much chance to develop heroic feelings and attitudes.

The same is true of responsibility. The subject feels that he is responsible for his choices, although when thinking of himself he appears as an object determined by so many outside factors that almost no place is left for responsibility.

In considering responsibility as an absolute postulate, Sartre certainly goes much too far. The tragic experience of young Renée, brought into a desperate psycho-pathological condition by the obsession of her total individual responsibility for all the illnesses of the world, has clearly shown that the idea of an unlimited responsibility cannot be upheld as an absolute imperative.[25] With persons of weak mental equilibrium it will lead to a psychosis, and with sane people it simply will not work because of its extreme character. "If I am mobilized in a war," Sartre writes, "this war is my war. . . . I deserve it, because I could have evaded it by suicide or desertion. Not having evaded this war, I chose it." Thus I am "as responsible for the war as if I myself had declared it." [26] I think that this thesis of Sartre's perverts the moral meaning of the idea of responsibility. *Summum jus,*

[24] H. Vaihinger, *Die Philosophie des Als-Ob* (Berlin, 1911), pp. 1-13.
[25] See Ch. 24, "Existentialism and Psychiatry."
[26] *L'Etre et le Néant,* pp. 639-641.

summa injuria ("The highest justice is the greatest injustice"), the Romans said. Likewise, we may say that when driven to this extreme, the idea of responsibility refutes itself. No patriotic man will try to evade his military obligations if his country is implicated in a war for its survival. Are we therefore entitled to say that any man who complies with his civic duty has "chosen" the war and is "responsible" for it? By taking this position we mock the ideas of choice and responsibility.

But as soon as we consider the Sartre-Dostoevski idea— everybody is responsible for everything to everybody—not as a metaphysical principle but as an ethical fiction, as a moral "as if," we can realize all its benefits for ethics. If we had said to a French citizen during the German occupation that he "is" responsible for the war Hitler had started, he would have rejected this accusation as false. But if we had said to him that he ought to act "as if" he were responsible for the war, our suggestion might have enhanced his sense of responsibility.

There is still another element of great ethical importance in Sartre's philosophy. His Existentialist psychoanalysis has called our attention to the fact that many persons—among them even a genius like Baudelaire—have a tendency to see themselves as they are seen by other people. To be sure, sometimes we need another person to see through his eyes how we are, who we are. But we already know that, according to Sartre, under the gaze of other people the self changes from a subject, which is in the making, into an object, which *is* what it is, which coincides with itself and is petrified. And in this Sartre certainly is right. As long as he lives, every coward is a coward *en sursis,* on reprieve, who can become a hero. But under the gaze of other people the coward is no longer on reprieve, he is definitely a coward, his essence has been fixed and pinned down by the other person's gaze as though he were dead.

Now if a person always sees himself through the eyes of other people, he sees himself as petrified in his essence, as definitely a coward, a drunkard, a miser, who is no longer in the making, who is not on reprieve and therefore cannot change. And if he cannot change, why should he make any moral effort to try? A person

who sees himself through the eyes of other people exists no longer
for—himself, but only for—others. He transposes the center of
gravity of his existence from himself into the consciousness of
other people, he ceases to a certain extent to be an ego. And seeing himself through the eyes of other people as a drunkard or a
homosexual, in the same way that an oak is an oak, he will say
to himself that he can cease being a drunkard or a homosexual
as little as an oak can cease being an oak. And this would kill in
him all moral effort to change, to make himself into something
more worth while.

I think that from this deep insight of Sartre's Existentialist
psychoanalysis a bridge leads across to Adler's individual psychology with its superiority goal. In the latter we can discern a
lack of being-for-itself. An individual possessed by the goal of
superiority always looks at himself in the mirror of other people's
consciousness, where he appears as a petrified thing. When Lucien Fleurier, a Fascist in the making, in Sartre's story *"L'Enfance d'un Chef"* (in *Le Mur*), is introduced to a young Jew,
during a party in a friend's home, he, at first, wants to shake the
hand the Jew extends to him. But suddenly Fleurier remembers
that his Fascist friends consider him as somebody who mortally
hates Jews and would kill them all if he could. Thus he suddenly
sees himself through the eyes of other people; and immediately
he gives up his first gentle impulse, refuses the young Jew's hand,
puts his own hands in his pockets, and leaves the party. And
when, the next day, his friend, toward whom he feels guilty, tells
him that he respects his "conviction" without sharing it, Lucien
Fleurier again sees himself proudly through the eyes of other
people, who see in him somebody who "has a conviction" which
has to be respected. Seeing himself through the eyes of other people, he feels himself justified by their gaze and from now on is
lost as a being-for-itself, as a consciousness in the making. He
feels himself "full of respect for himself." Through the gaze of
other people he has acquired the unchangeable, impenetrable
character of a rock, and in this respect he resembles Mauriac's
Bernard Desqueyroux. Finally, seeing himself through the eyes

of these other people, Lucien is a rock for himself, a dead thing from which noble initiatives can never be expected.

On the other hand we have Herostratus in Sartre's short story "Erostrate," whose basic project is not, as Robert Campbell believes, only hatred but that of being exclusively for-others and not for-himself. He wants to have a permanent place in other people's consciousness; and because he sees himself only through the eyes of others he lives entirely under the gazes of other people. Therefore his only obsession is to amaze them, be it by a crime. *"Voilà ce que je voudrais, les étonner tous,"* he says to himself.[27] He, too, is lost as a being-for-itself, as a man, for he has become entirely a being-for-others.

Now it seems to me that Adler's "vanity" or "will to superiority" is closely related to the tendency of certain of Sartre's individuals to exist only for others, to see themselves only through the eyes of other people. We designate a person as conceited when he is concerned only with the image he offers to the gaze of other people. He has his center of gravity outside himself and is half a man and half a thing, the half which is looked on. Only weak personalities need to exist in the consciousness of other people in order to exist for themselves. Vanity, certainly, is a form of Adler's inferiority complex.

There is a very valuable imperative we can draw from Sartre's analysis of those persons who exist only through the gaze of other people and therefore exist according to these gazes. We may formulate it in this way: Let us be for-ourselves and not for-others, let us not be petrified things, existing through the judgment of other people, but selves! Let us be not viscous substances, but action, with the fluidity of water! I think that these ethical principles which we can draw from Sartre's Existentialism, even without sharing his ontological presuppositions, are valuable enough to justify it.

We saw that Sartre created a place for "conscience," "guilt," and even "sin," in spite of his atheism. "We are cast in the world, already face to face with the other person; our springing up is a

---

[27] "Erostrate", *Le Mur* (Paris, 1939), p. 77.

free limitation of his freedom. . . . It is from this strange situation that the concept of guilt and sin originates. It is vis-à-vis the other person that I am guilty." [28]

All this explains that, in spite of the fact that Sartre's books have been put on the *Index librorum prohibitorum* of the Vatican, some Catholic thinkers have adopted a favorable attitude toward his philosophy. Even Maritain is not entirely negative, and in Marcel and Mounier we find more preparedness to understand Sartre and to agree with certain of his theses. Although rejecting the conclusions of the author of *Being and Nothingness*, Gabriel Marcel admits "fully the validity and power of some of Sartre's premises" and calls his anthropology "irrefutable." [29] And the late Emmanuel Mounier even accepted certain Sartrean conclusions, as can be seen from the following comments by this liberal Catholic thinker:

What is important for an existing being is . . . the authentic life, the perpetual liberation of my freedom, the perpetual breaking away from the inertia of things. . . . That transcendence of human existence with relation to life and matter, that rebellious character of spiritual affirmation . . . that sovereign empire of creative freedom which turns man into a kind of god, this intimate link between man and matter, and this threatening which, nevertheless, he finds in it—with all this we are, as it seems, wholly in a *Christian universe*.[30]

And Mounier adds that Sartre cannot be unaware of the fact that, in certain respects, he is a Christian in spite of his atheism.[31] It seems to us that these affirmations are correct. Sartre's philosophy expresses man's eternal struggle to free life from the chains of matter and mechanism, from natural and social pressure, and to come to an individual, self-dependent, free ethical existence. Sartre has these tendencies in common with Bergson and Lecomte du Noüy, both of whom were theistic thinkers. There is in the whole of Sartre's Existentialism, in the persons of

---

[28] *L'Etre et le Néant,* pp. 480-481.

[29] *The Philosophy of Existence* (New York: Philosophical Library, 1949), pp. 32, 33.

[30] "Perspectives existentialistes et perspectives chrétiennes," *Pour et contre l'Existentialisme* (Paris, 1948), p. 135.

[31] *Ibid.,* p. 138.

his novels and dramas, the theme of the gnawing conscience, which is a Christian theme. In all of his writings, his heroes perpetually scrutinize their consciences, and this is a typical Christian attitude. It is perhaps not a pure coincidence that Renée, the girl who tried to live up to all the moral requirements of Sartrean Extentialism, had been a devout Catholic, trained by a rigorous education in the art of pitilessly scrutinizing her conscience. Many of Sartre's heroes are concerned with only one thing: that at the moment of their death their essence may enter eternity in nobleness, courage, purity—although Sartre's type of Existentialism does not provide such eternal values and even definitely excludes them. Why are the heroes of Sartre's great tragedy *Morts sans Sépulture* concerned only with their eternal essence, since, being atheists, they do not believe in a Last Judgment? A true iconoclast, like the late Communist philosopher Politzer, once said to Sartre: "I do not give a penny for your eternal essences!" [32] Yet one has the impression that Sartre would give his life for them.

In spite of his atheism and the pornographic character of a part of his work, we may apply to Sartre the words by which Nietzsche characterized his Zarathustra, and say: Sartre is the most pious of all those who believe not in God.

[32] R. Campbell, *Jean-Paul Sartre ou une Littérature philosophique* (Paris, 1947), p. 296.